"DEMETRIOS IS NOW JIMMY:"

GREEK IMMIGRANTS IN THE SOUTHERN UNITED STATES, 1895 -1965

With best wishes,
to my DoP sister Anna,

By

LAZAR "LARRY" ODZAK

[signature: Lazar Larry Odzak]

MONOGRAPH PUBLISHERS

Durham, North Carolina

August 2018

First Edition in the United States in 2006, by
Monograph Publishers
Suite 1816, 1800 Country Lane, Durham, NC 27713

Library of Congress Control Number: 2006923181

Odzak, Lazar "Larry," 1933-
"Demetrios Is Now Jimmy," Greek Immigrants
in the Southern United States, 1895-1965

Hardcover ISBN: 09778024-1-8
Paperback ISBN: 09778024-0-X

CONTENTS

Acknowledgements

My sincerest appreciation goes to my professors, without whose guidance, patience, suggestions, and constructive criticism I could not have undertaken this work. Drs. George Pozzetta, Gary Mormino, Bertram Wyatt-Brown, Jeffrey Adler, Thomas Gallant, Daniel Schafer, and James Button, all faculty members of the Universities of Florida System, gave me all the help and encouragement I needed. I also acknowledge the genial assistance given me by the staff of the University of Minnesota Immigration History Research Center, directed by Dr. Rudolph Vecoli, who provided me with innumerable resources. I especially extend my gratitude for the courtesies, assistance, and hospitality extended me by numerous Americans of Hellenic descent, on whose knowledge, advice, and hospitality I relied as I gathered historical information throughout the Greek Orthodox communities in the South. Mistakes and omissions are entirely mine. A special thank you goes to the University of North Carolina at Chapel Hill, specifically its Center for Slavic, Eurasian, and East European Studies, which accepted me as a Visiting Scholar, granted me the use of UNC facilities and libraries, and enabled me to complete this book. I am particularly indebted to my wife Hope, whose endless love and support ultimately carried the day.

Foreword

This work explores the arrival of Greek immigrants in southern urban areas, from about 1895 to 1924, and their remarkably rapid adjustment to life in the New South. Research reveals that these immigrants adapted at an unusually swift rate to the common cultural, social, commercial, and even political life of their white neighbors. Simultaneously, they strove to preserve selected features of their own traditions. Their undertaking contrasted with the large immigrant communities in the industrially developed northeastern and midwestern urban areas, where the Old World cultures of Greeks and other groups survived longer, changed more slowly, and adjustments to American ways encountered more resistance. In this respect, the experiences of immigrants to the southern states both reconcile with and differ from those described in recent literature in the field of American immigration and ethnicity.

This work covers new ground by examining the issues of newcomers' accommodation to existing cultural and structural forces in cases where the immigrant group was just large enough to create its own viable community yet lacked the "critical mass" to retard the process of acculturation. By the second generation, many ethnic traditions changed and even new ones emerged, to advance the local interests of Greek Americans. Using a comparative approach, this work traces the paradigmatic process of selective adaptation, which took place whenever small groups of immigrants chose to settle in diverse urban areas where few others of their ethnic and cultural background had established themselves.

Lazar "Larry" Odzak
January 2006

CHAPTER 1

IMMIGRANTS:

AN INTRODUCTION TO ADAPTATION AND ACCULTURATION, BUT NOT ASSIMILATION

Few historians explored the experiences of Greek immigrants to the South.[1] Apparently, most scholars shared the opinion of author Peter W. Dickson, who observed that "Greeks tended to avoid the Deep South as a place to begin a new life."[2] Sociologist Charles Moskos reasoned that the South played a minor role in Hellenic immigration because the region had "little industrial employment or commercial opportunity and [it was] one in which antiforeign sentiment was most pronounced."[3] Such accounts suggest that hardly any of the nearly 400,000 Greeks who arrived in the United States between 1890 and 1921 ever settled in the South. These assumptions, however, do not withstand close historical scrutiny. By 1910, small but vigorous Hellenic communities existed in a number of southern cities, formed by Greeks who had migrated South from large northern urban and industrial centers.

Table 1 (at the end of this chapter) represents a rounded count of Greeks in various cities where they had established communities during the first decade of the 1900s.[4] Recently, Moskos reexamined his earlier assessment of the Greek immigrant experience in the South and concluded that of all the Greeks who came to the United States before 1920, one in ten had settled in the states of the old Confederacy.[5] Moreover, Moskos found that most Greeks in the South were self-employed and relatively prosperous. They "ran their own small businesses, restaurants and lunchrooms, confectioneries, fruit stores, and shoeshine parlors."[6] Continued needs of an expanding population in southern cities and towns provided the incipient businessmen with opportunities to achieve relative prosperity. Adjustment in social, economic, and cultural areas of their lives to distinct southern ways went hand in hand with their economic upward mobility. Moreover, this adjustment and adaptation to life and society in the South proceeded in diverse ways and at an accelerated rate, faster than that experienced by their compatriots and other immigrant groups who settled in larger numbers in other areas. Historian Theodore Saloutos maintained that these small commercial activities thrust Greek entrepreneurs into "closer contact with the American public [and] accelerated the process of Americanization."[7] Moskos went even further than Saloutos and argued that Greeks in the South realized "earlier than [their] compatriots in other parts of the United States" that America would become their permanent home. Based on this observation, he asserted that Greeks who settled in the South first made the transformation from immigrants to Greek Americans. Moskos confirmed that Greeks in the South achieved economic and residential upward mobility faster and in greater proportion than Greeks elsewhere in the United States and identified this process as the "southern variant" of Greek immigrant experience in America.[8] As they became small entrepreneurs, first generation Greeks who settled in the South adapted well to their new environment. They Americanized their polysyllabic names, joined American fraternal and political organizations, formed families, and even began to intermarry. Around the turn of the century, they participated in and contributed to the development of the "New South."

At the same time, these Greek entrepreneurs endeavored to preserve selected features of their traditions and culture, particularly the religion and language. For that purpose they established fraternal or communal organizations, with periodically elected officers, regulated in a similar way as societies or parish congregations. Such an organized community, known in Greek as the kinotis, usually embraced the majority of Greeks in the area, who organized chiefly to establish a Greek Orthodox Church and to hire a priest, so they and their families could again partake in the traditional religious life. Such communal organizations appeared not only in the north-eastern and mid-western cities, inhabited by thousands of Greeks, but also in the South, in places where as few as eighty Greek migrants had settled. In southern cities and towns, where immigrants ventured in relatively scant numbers, one can trace the establishment of Greek Orthodox communal organizations to the earliest days of this century.[9] For the most part, this dissertation will explore this process of accelerated adjustment and simultaneous preservation of selected traditions, and consider reasons that might have caused this unique variation of immigrant adaptation to the host society.

Moreover, as provocative as Moskos' conceptualization of the southern variant may be, until now it remained untested and unproven. His sources were both general in scope and scarce in number. Except for a few articles, no detailed studies of southern Greek communities exist. As a result Moskos was not able to explore in depth the dynamics taking place in any specific settlement or trace them over time. Concurrently, this paper will test Moskos' hypothesis of the southern variant. By exploring in some detail the experiences of Greeks in Atlanta and Savannah, in Birmingham and Mobile, in Jacksonville and Tarpon Springs, and in other southern cities, a more rounded understanding of the Greek immigrant experience can be gained. From this better informed perspective, a keener appreciation is possible of the process of adaptation of ethnic groups and their adjustment and development into ethnic Americans. We now know that the opposites of assimilation and ethnic preservation were never as far apart as they were portrayed in the 1970s and 1980s. Indeed, individual families who formed the Hellenic immigrant communities in the South managed to do both, to meld into the southern environment and to retain coherent ethnic identities.

This process has long been an issue among historians. Oscar Handlin maintained in his immigrant study *The Uprooted* that migration from Europe worked terrible hardships on the immigrants.[10] Like so much seaweed, they washed up on American shores, they worked, had children, and died. According to Handlin, however, they remained uprooted, because they had left the security of known surroundings and lost the families and traditions they had cherished back home. Exploited in factories like commodities, he contended, the immigrants grew disillusioned with this experiment in American life and remained alienated. Handlin found that "the history of immigration is a history of alienation and its consequences."[11] As late as the 1970s, Thomas Wheeler saw immigrants in much the same light. "The America of freedom has been an America of sacrifice, and the cost of becoming American has been high. For every freedom won, a tradition lost. For every second generation assimilated, a first generation in one way or another spurned. For the gains of goods and services, an identity lost, an uncertainty found."[12] Clearly, for Handlin, Wheeler, and those historians who agreed with their analysis, the immigrants' plight could in no way mitigate the powerful assimilative forces at work in America. In their opinion, second and subsequent generations would continue to assimilate, almost in a straight-line fashion, into the American mainstream, a "vital center" that encouraged the overcoming of alienation by incorporating the foreigners into the civic, economic, and cultural life of the nation.

Until the publication in 1963 of Nathan Glazer's and Daniel Moynihan's Beyond the Melting Pot, scholars studying immigrants generally shared the expectation that assimilation would remain the chief means to understand the immigrant experience. Beyond the Melting Pot, however, proposed an alternative interpretation.[13] The authors described how various ethnic groups in New York City demonstrated a persistence of ethnicity that belied the historical paradigm. Although the nationalistic aspects of ethnicity faded in two or three generations, the concept of common ethnicity in the cultural sense continued to serve the group as a means of mobilizing behind issues relating to its socioeconomic position in the larger society. As ethnic groups used their ethnicity to advance common interests, their special sense of identity persisted. One year later, in 1964, Rudolph Vecoli further developed the new approach. In his classic critique of Handlin's The Uprooted, Vecoli persuasively maintained that the old-world culture survived the ocean crossings and significantly influenced the ensuing adaptation in America.[14] Vecoli argued for more scholarly sensitivity to the distinctiveness of each ethnic group in the broader pattern of the American experience. He asserted that southern Italian immigrants were far from uprooted; they brought with them a vital culture and many traditions and institutions which they used to meet their needs in the new land. Vecoli's emphasis on distinctiveness of each ethnic group and the tenacious vitality of its European cultural values, with its anti-assimilationist thrust, soon set the tone for a remarkable outpouring of immigration scholarship in the 1960s and 1970s, an outpouring which was produced by numerous scholars both within and without the historical profession. These studies demonstrated that ordinary people had taken an active role in shaping their own lives, whether in the workplace, the marketplace, the church pew, or the home.

In the turbulent 1960s, with history considered from the bottom up, and in the three short decades since then, an increasing number of studies, monographs, and articles by new social historians such as Vecoli, Kathleen Neils Conzen, John Bodnar, Ewa Morawska, George E. Pozzetta, and others substantially widened the field of immigration and ethnicity.[15] Many works dealt with the first generation of "new" immigrants, men and women who arrived during the mass immigration period and with their offspring, the second generation. Social historians displayed a variety of approaches to the subject, and immigrant diversity, as suggested by Vecoli, served to identify the general direction of this more recent work. Writers articulated the experiences of neglected people who were earlier perceived as having no voice.[16]

Pluralism in immigration history reached its zenith with Michael Novak's work *Rise of the Unmeltable Ethnics*.[17] Taking up the case of Poles, Italians, Greeks, and Slavs—PIGS—Novak argued that not only had the melting pot failed to occur, but also that it will never do so. He suggested the time had come for America to understand and appreciate the diversity of her ethnic elements, and to recognize a new cultural pluralism. The ideology that everyone must conform to "American" traditions, in Novak's opinion, may have been devised simply as a means of reducing the political and economic power of the latter-day immigrant groups.[18]

In an attempt to synthesize all this diversity, John Bodnar's *The Transplanted: A History of Immigrants in Urban America* provided an explanation of the immigrant experience in the framework of people adapting to the new capitalistic order.[19] The entire immigrant saga revealed that far from taking a leap into the unknown, immigration represented an intelligent, well-planned family strategy. Opportunities in America as well as the family networks here acted as a pull, while deteriorating social and economic situations in specific places of origin worked as a push for immigrants. Kinship constituted the best employment agency; family found jobs for members and friends; kin was the "stable core" of the ethnic clusters in American cities.[20] By being actors, by making their own rational decisions, Bodnar's "transplanted" stood very much in contrast to Handlin's "uprooted." Bodnar emphasized the continuity of social forms from the pre-migration experience and highlighted the immigrants' attempts to recreate, within the new American context, the culture and institutions they left behind. Immigrants sought to gain a measure of control over their lives by effectively using the institutions they brought with them, particularly the core institution of the family-household, and by developing institutions such as churches, synagogues, and schools that responded to their needs as ethnic Germans, Italians, Greeks, or Jews.

In contrast to the earlier depiction of immigrants as victims, Bodnar was intent on showing the relative autonomy of immigrants in the process of constructing their lives. Moreover, instead of seeing culture as a determinative, all-powerful force over the immigrants, he found culture to be a flexible tool, a resource that could be used in a multiplicity of ways towards multiple ends. The diverse immigrant cultures were similar in only one respect, they provided a pragmatic world-view capable of responding in subtle and ingenious ways to daily realities in the New World. The *mentalité* they created was "an amalgam of the past and present, acceptance and resistance" and clearly dependent on a variety of pre-migration experiences.[21]

Scholars have recently begun to consider the timing of migration, state policies, patterns of chain migration, levels of prejudice, and the receiving locations and economies to better understand the immigrant experience. The resulting surge of American immigration history added new dimensions to the knowledge about ethnic groups in America. Social historians found ethnicity to be an enduring dimension of American society, rather than a transitory phenomenon.[22] Although urban and rural environments and markets dictated fairly rapid economic adaptation, at the same time immigrants remained committed to a varying degree of cultural and linguistic maintenance.[23] In addition, Vecoli noted, American culture has not remained a static entity, but rather a dynamic force, expressive of the pluralistic, polyglot population. As it sought to control and shape immigrants into consumers, compliant workers, and responsible citizens, it was also affected and changed by immigrants and their children. Vecoli concludes that the term "syncretism" best expresses the process by which both immigrants and the host society took what they most valued from the past, what they most liked about America, what they learned from their neighbors, and what they had to do to survive, to fashion a new identity and behavior. Children of immigrants from southern and eastern Europe "did not become just Americans; rather they became ethnic

Americans."[24] Ethnicity thus became a key concept in the analysis of this process of immigrant adaptation.

Just as in the 1970s scholars rejected the assimilation theory and endorsed pluralism, so over the past few years and into the 1990s several writers took the experience of eastern and southern European immigrants beyond pluralism to a new perception, asserting that, in time, the immigrants adopted and accepted some common values, even as they retained certain cultural differences. Juxtaposing assimilation and ethnicity, sociologist Charles Hirschman went as far as to suggest that "the assimilation theory may have been dismissed prematurely." [25] Reviewing several new books on ethnic identities, Hirschman saw persuasive evidence that very little ethnicity survived in the third and fourth generation descendants of European immigrants who arrived about 1900. A high degree of assimilation must have occurred, he found, when in one case seventy percent of the respondents denied that ethnic identity of their spouses had *any* impact on their marriages, and only twelve percent of parents attached *great* importance to their children's ethnic identity.

Without ethnic families and primary groups that sustain shared experiences, ethnic cultures cannot survive. His review included a work which maintained that the "meaning" of ethnic identity, to most respondents, whether of Polish, Italian, or any other ancestry, offered an opportunity to celebrate a particular ethnic holiday, or to enjoy ethnic foods. However, ethnicity certainly did not determine one's career, marriage partner, friends, or neighborhood. Hirschman then concluded that only "symbolic" ethnicity prevailed over assimilative tendencies. His conclusion is disputed by historians Kathleen Neils Conzen, David Gerber, Ewa Morawska, George Pozzetta, and others who find ethnicity to be enduring from one generation to the next, even though it may be adapted or "reinvented in response to changing realities both within the group and the host society.[26] These historians persuasively argue that ethnicity is not a collective fiction, but a process of construction which incorporates, adapts, and amplifies "preexisting communal solidarities, cultural attributes, and historical memories."[27] It is grounded in real life and social experience. Examples of such ethnicities abound; some of these constructed historical memories are the ubiquitous celebrations of Irish St. Patrick's Day, Greek Festivals, German Oktoberfests, Italian Columbus Day parades, Kwanzaa pan-African culture holidays, and others.

One might agree with Philip Gleason that a simple resolution cannot do justice to such a complex situation. Years ago he found it unfortunate that assimilation and pluralism tend to be taken as absolute opposites that rule out each other. In Gleason's view, both terms are "rich and complex in implication" and rather than being mutually exclusive, "they overlap and merge into each other."[28] They overlap because each was intended by its originators to comprehend the full spectrum of tendencies in American society, the impulse to unity and the tendency toward multiplicity, the elements shared universally as well as the features that set people apart. Whereas assimilation laid greater stress on *unum* than on *pluribus*, pluralism reversed the emphasis, but both terms comprehended all facets of the immigrant experience. The following chapters describe a variety of ways newcomers to the South used to reconcile the thrust to assimilation with the compelling need to preserve cultural autonomy.

When they decided to go into business in one or another of the New South cities, Greek immigrants manifested vacillating and some-times contradictory adjustments to the unique new environment. Their approaches to adaptation will test current studies of ethnicity in American life, which hold that immigrants followed diverse paths leading in the general direction of integration with the host society, but stress that no matter how "American" the newcomers became, a distinct ethnic component always remained, even if it was an invented construct. For a majority of the men who came to America to work, the journey across the ocean was just an extension of the work-seeking migration patterns they had practiced in Europe.[29] Initially, Greek immigrants, like their counterparts from other parts of Europe, answered the call for more labor; they intended to work hard, make money, and, with a few exceptions, they desired to return to their country of origin. But within a short few years after they arrived in the South, many decided to remain permanently in the United States and declared their intention to become citizens. They found that advantages in America, a chance to own one's own business, to progress economically, socially, and even politically, and to raise their children here, outweighed what the old country had to offer. On the other hand, as evidenced by the churches, social halls, and other institutions established by the newcomers, religious and social traditions—albeit adapted to fit the

New World—well survived the initial "transplanting" and buttressed the ancestral culture. These events demonstrate that Greek migrants who came south experienced a process of selective adaptation, which included willing accommodation as well as calculated resistance to the ways of their new environment.

Historian George Pozzetta suggested that the end result was "a syncretic outcome, in which both immigrants and mainstream society have been changed."[30] Rather than confusing the ambivalent pattern of adjustment with labels such as "assimilation" or "pluralism" one prefers to use the term "selective adaptation," because it elucidates much better the complex process of change which started as soon as immigrants arrived and which has no discernible ending. Assimilation implies that the immigrants, in time, give up their old traditions, culture, and ways of life and accept those of the dominant society.[31] In fact, immigrants did accept the economic ways of life, and even selected to conform to many social practices in their new habitat, yet they retained some cultural and religious customs, albeit adapted to the Southern ambience. Such characteristic customs and cultural traditions transcended even class differences. Immigrants described here adopted the evolving yet singularly American *economic* and *political* tenets, even as they retained and adjusted some of their own *cultural* traditions, rooted in the ethnic core. Enterprising changes and further adjustments occurred from one generation to the next, as each one reconstructed important pillars supporting the structure of their ethnicity, to present an improved image to their fellow Americans.[32] This dynamic process of selective adaptation over time may be different from one individual to the next, and from one group to the next, but it best fits the immigrants encountered in the following pages.

One must also ask the question, what drew the Greeks to the turn-of-the-century-segregated South? What kind of work and benefits awaited them in the area where industries were reported to be few and far between, where urbanization lagged behind that in the North, where wages were low, and labor unskilled? Indeed, a different South drew newcomers to growing urban areas. Greeks and other migrants were attracted to the "New South" envisioned and promoted by a more modern generation of southerners such as prominent newspapermen William Mahone of the Richmond *Whig*, Henry Watterson of the Louisville *Courier-Journal*, and Henry Grady of the *Atlanta Constitution*.[33]

This New South, especially specific cities and industries, did experience substantial growth and development. Led by Atlanta and
Birmingham, urban population doubled and in some cases tripled, so
that by 1900 fully 15 percent of the population dwelt in cities. Interior
towns attracted merchants and bankers who eventually took over the
credit and supply functions formerly provided only by port factors.[34]
New railroads added momentum to the growth of inland towns as well
as coastal port cities. In Florida alone, Henry Flagler's railroad initiated
growth that quadrupled the population of Jacksonville and led to the
founding of Miami, while Hamilton Disston's rail-line helped Tampa
grow from a population of about 5,500 in 1890 to nearly 38,000 people
in 1910.[35] This was the South that excited the imaginations of Greeks
and other migrants, the South they perceived to be opening itself to
new ventures, the South which at times encouraged immigration.[36]
Inhabitants of growing cities needed services: groceries, fruits, quick
lunches, shoe-shines, pool-rooms, cafeterias, bars, cafés, and a myriad
of other provisions, which the well-traveled Greek, Jewish, Syrian, and
other newcomers were eager to furnish. Moreover, white newcomers
did not encounter intuitive problems of racial segregation, nor were
they instinctively confined to low-paying, unskilled jobs solely because
of the color of their skin.

C. Vann Woodward complained that the vast majority of newcomers
remained in the northeastern states, providing American industries and
manufactories with workers as well as consumers, and that only a scat-
tering came south.[37] It is true that in comparison to the northern urban
areas, especially those with a heavy concentration of industries, fewer
immigrants chose to move south. Nevertheless, thousands did migrate
there to look for economic niches where their services were needed
and welcomed. They helped build Birmingham, Miami, and other new
places. Cubans, Italians, and Spaniards developed the cigar manufac-
ture in Ybor City; Greeks expanded sponge fishing and merchandising
in Tarpon Springs. In the final analysis, New South advocates may have
failed to achieve their complete goal of a diversified economy with a
strong manufacturing base, but the South of 1900 was certainly distin-
guished by expanded rails, larger factories, major mines, and above all,
growing cities.[38]

Of course, in any exploratory passage through the South one is
bound to encounter dissimilarities between particular urban areas as

well as between the specific Greek communities examined here. Chapter
two deals with places and situations which may be considered typical:
the growing New South cities which had room for budding Greek entrepreneurs, who generally did well in their sandwich shops, lunch rooms,
restaurants, flower shops, shoeshine parlors, fruit stores, confectioneries,
and sundry other small businesses. Henry Fairchild, Theodore Saloutos,
Charles Moskos and others thought these hard-working and commercially astute people to be representative of Greek immigrants to the
southern states. The chapter investigates the combination of conditions, features, and motives that made these small entrepreneurs so
successful in a region considered unfriendly to foreigners.

Even as they adapted to life in the New World, Greek immigrants
established fraternal organizations for a variety of purposes: to organize
mutual aid in the New World and to extend help to the villages back
home, to fulfill the immigrants' own social needs, to organize parishes
and build churches. Chapter three deals in part with the usual old-
country oriented fellowships, fraternities, and associations, and in part
focuses on an unusual organization, formed by astute and pragmatic
Hellenes especially to sidetrack discrimination and prejudice encountered in the southern states. The chapter follows the activities of the
American Hellenic Educational and Progressive Association (AHEPA),
as its members prospered and the fraternal order grew to reflect the
brothers' established place and increasingly conservative position in
southern, as well as national society and politics. In a similar vein
chapter four describes the uneasy establishment and complex growth
of the Greek Orthodox religious institution on this continent. The
Greek Orthodox Archdiocese in America grew and developed from a
parochial, old-country controlled immigrant church into a modern,
outreach-oriented American religious denomination, counting among
its adherents thousands of converts. In 1997, both the American
Hellenic Educational and Progressive Association (AHEPA) and the
Greek Orthodox Archdiocese in America celebrated the 75th anniversary of their creation.

Although most Hellenic communities throughout the South have
shared features, several southern cities and their Greek parishes display
unique aspects of Greek immigrant experiences, worthy of separate
scrutiny. Chapters five, six, and seven round out such an examination
of dissimilar southern municipalities and the diverse growth and devel-

opment of their Hellenic populace. Chapters five and six respectively portray New Orleans, Louisiana and Birmingham, Alabama, with their individual Greek communities, and demonstrate that in real life perfect synthesis is seldom possible. Chapter seven of this work considers another unconventional Greek community in the South, which came into existence for the sole purpose of gathering and processing natural sponges in the shallow, warm waters of the Gulf of Mexico. Greek sponge fishermen from the Aegean modernized the process by introducing the diving suit and caused the growth to national repute of this once insignificant Florida industry. Within a decade of 1904, when the first Greek sponge diver saw a rich crop of sponges spread in profusion on the shallow ocean floor off Florida's Gulf coast, Greek sponge fishermen and their families, numbering several thousand people, immigrated directly to Florida and settled in Tarpon Springs, a Floridian village on the Gulf of Mexico, to make their living off the rich sponge harvest. They recreated in Florida a sister village to the seaside villages they left on the sun-drenched Aegean. Hundreds of Greek sponge-boats lined the docks of Tarpon Springs, serviced on shore by Greek and American entrepreneurs, financiers, boat-builders, buyers, packers, and sponge exchange auctioneers. Tarpon Springs replaced Key West as the new center of Florida's sponge industry. Dominated by Greek spongers and businessmen, the industry brought millions of dollars annually into Florida's economy. At a time when immigrants from southern and eastern Europe easily evoked scorn and disdain in other parts of America, transplanted spongers earned the respect and acceptance on part of the American populace in and around Tarpon Springs.

Economic prosperity, then, achieved by a majority of Greek entrepreneurs, was at the root of their successful adaptation and settlement in the southern cities. This adaptation included not only the newcomers' continuous effort to fit into the distinct, southern environment, but also the southerners' acceptance of the newcomers as neighbors, as fellow-businessmen, as frequent co-members of local fraternal and business associations, and—in case of intermarriages—as in-laws. Just as one perceived the economic growth and development of the New South as a condition which enabled the commercial success of Greek immigrants, so also must one look to the immigrants themselves for the attitudes they brought with them which were an essential part of their accomplishment and progress. The degree of pressure to succeed and the speed with which the Greek migrants adapted to the new and distinctly southern ambience were both influenced by the Greeks' innate cultural values. The pressure to succeed was particularly exerted on the men by the deeply felt concept of honor and driven on by the inordinate fear of failure and the attendant shame. A number of scholars have examined this typically Mediterranean phenomenon.[39] Most Greeks, although imbued with a strong sense of independence, were intensely concerned with how they appeared to others in the conduct of their daily life. One's worth as a person was "determined in the public forum—the *deme* or larger "family" of peers and superiors called community."[40] A man's peers measured his success or failure and their perception alone determined whether one was accorded respect or relegated to ridicule and shame. Another dominant element of Greek culture, a fierce competitiveness, was closely connected to the pressure to succeed, to achieve what Greeks love most—to be regarded as an honorable man. This love of honor, denoted by the Greek word *filotimo*, was the essence of self-esteem, and demanded fulfillment of one's obligations, an ability to adequately participate in the daily give-and-take with other men, and a pride in one's purposes, appearance, and demeanor.[41]

Men who managed to get to America, often on family money or on borrowed funds, were almost trapped into succeeding. To come to America, to be given such a great opportunity for success, and to return to Greece as a failure was unthinkable. The pent-up envy of those left behind would inevitably turn into ridicule and dishonor. Initially, most Greeks in America eked out a frugal living, but sent hard-earned dollars to provide for their daughters' or sisters' dowries, to clear debts, or to buy for the family back home the extra field or beast of burden. There was evidence that per immigrant, Greeks sent more money back home than other nationalities.[42] A majority of Greek immigrants intended to return home after several years, when they achieved the immediate financial goals and realized some savings. One would expect that those who succeeded should have been returning home to high regard among their peers.[43]

They had discharged their obligations as their self-esteem and their love of honor—*filotimo*—demanded. They had avoided the shame of failure for themselves and their families; they could now enjoy their secure social and economic status. In fact, although a vast majority of

Greek immigrants sooner or later met their economic objectives, only a minority actually repatriated.[44] Sociologist Dimitrios Monos points to an ironic twist, which explains why the successful immigrants stayed here. He asserts a general agreement that an immigrant's progress in America was contingent "upon speedy and successful acculturation, adjustment and assimilation, which, in essence, implies forgetting or forsaking old ways, if not values, and adopting new ones."[45] The writer then concludes that it is unlikely that immigrants who have adapted to and adopted the American way of life, who have been accepted by their fellow Americans, and who have attained a measure of success in business, would want to undergo another fundamental process of readjustment by returning to the old country. Thus, the greater the adjustment and success in the states, the smaller the desire to repatriate. However, historian Theodore Saloutos's statistics of successful migrants who returned to the old country for good belie the appealing logic of Monos's theory.[46]

Nevertheless, tracing the experiences of Greek migrants to the southern states, one can see their tendency to seek economic independence through self-employment, to adapt, and to set roots where they found the best economic success. Both, the migrants with their cultural "baggage" of honor and the resulting pressure to make good on the one hand, as well as the ambience of growth in the places to which they migrated on the other hand, contributed to an early decision to remain in America permanently. A sure sign of the desire to settle in any particular location was the newcomers' willingness to spend money to purchase or build a church. A great number of the new "Americans," however, returned home to visit the family, perhaps even to get a bride. Again, the innate norms of Mediterranean society came into play; appearances were essential to note the visitors' success. The sojourner felt compelled to be very generous with his hard-earned money, to bring gifts to all family members and friends, to treat everyone at the local coffee house and tell endless tales of hard work and good earnings and good prospects for the future. Even if all of one's savings were spent on the visit, the munificent exhibition presented to all proof positive of success in America and insured high regard among one's family and peers.

TABLE 1
(rounded) counts of Greek immigrants in different regions of the USA in 1910:

City	No. of Greeks
Northeastern United States	
Boston, Massachusetts	1,500
Lowell	7,000
Haverhill	700
Lynn	1,500
New Bedford	450
Springfield	300
New York, New York	20,000
Newark, New Jersey	500
Manchester, New Hampshire	3,000
Nashua	1,500
Providence, Rhode Island	500
Philadelphia, Pennsylvania	1,800
Pittsburgh	3,500
Southern United States	
Charlotte, North Carolina	100
Atlanta, Georgia	500
Augusta	80
Savannah	500
Jacksonville, Florida	175
Tarpon Springs	2,000
Pensacola	250
Mobile, Alabama	350
Birmingham	500
Elsey	300
New Orleans, Louisiana	550
Reading	350
Western United States	
St. Louis, Missouri	2,000
Omaha, Nebraska	1,500
Pueblo, Colorado	900

Denver	600
Garfield, Utah	400
Salt Lake City	2,000
Ely, Nevada	400
Galveston, Texas	300
Los Angeles, California	600
Oakland	450
San Francisco	3,000

Midwestern United States

Cincinnati, Ohio	500
Detroit, Michigan	400
Milwaukee, Wisconsin	600
Sheboygan	450
Chicago, Illinois	15,000

Notes

1   There are many definitions of "the South;" however, for the purpose of this work, the term will apply to the Carolinas, Georgia, Florida, Alabama, Mississippi, and Louisiana. A majority of Greeks who arrived in the years of mass immigration labored in the factories and mines in the Northeast, namely Massachusetts, New York, Pennsylvania, and Ohio, as well as in the Midwestern states such as Indiana, Illinois, Iowa, and Missouri, with more joining the railroad labor-gangs across the West and all the way to California. See Table 1.

2   Peter W. Dickson, "The Greek Pilgrims: Tsakonas and Tsintzinians," in Dan Georgakas and Charles Moskos, eds., *New Directions in Greek American Studies* (New York, Pella Publishing, 1991), 40. For additional opinions see Theodore Saloutos, *The Greeks in the United States* (Cambridge, Harvard University Press, 1964), and Charles S. Moskos, *Greek Americans: Struggle and Success* (New Brunswick, N.J., Transaction Publishers, 1980).

3   Moskos, *Greek Americans*, 25. Also see the *Thirteenth Census of the United States, 1910* (Government Printing Office, Washington, 1914), the Abstract, 85, where a graphic depiction of the South as defined here showed, in 1910, "less than 5 per cent" of "foreign-born whites and native whites of foreign or mixed parentage combined in the total population," with the exception only of Florida and Louisiana, whose population had a low "5 to 10 per cent" of such foreign-born. At the same time, most northern states had "50 per cent and over" and the population of most western

states contained "35 to 50 per cent" of foreign-born.

4   Quantification is important to this work, not only to show numbers of immigrants one is dealing with, but also to make clearer comparisons between large Greek immigrant communities in the northern states and their small but vibrant counterparts in the southern cities. One also needs an accurate record of Greeks in any specific location where they formed fraternal, social, or religious organizations, so one can see the "critical mass" necessary to consolidate a number of individuals into a successful association. A variety of sources provided the enumeration of individual immigrants and manifested the growth of various communities or parishes. These were primarily the decennial censuses of 1890, 1900, 1910, and 1920; city directories; written histories and church records of specific communities; contemporary Greek businessmen's directories; and, finally, historical works where one finds counts gathered and collated by historians such as Henry Pratt Fairchild, *Greek Immigration to the United States* (New Haven, Yale University Press, 1911), Babis Malafouris *Greeks in America* (New York, Isaac Goldman Co., 1948), and Theodore Saloutos, *The Greeks in the United States*. Comparing census schedules with all other sources, one cannot escape the conclusion that the decennial censuses invariably exhibited a remarkable undercount. Accordingly, some figures and tables in this work reflect a reasonable and sensible conciliation of this variety of sources. Table 1 consists of rounded numbers obtained from *the Thirteenth Census of the United States, 1910*; appropriate city directories; Dio Adallis, *Adallis' Greek Merchants' Reference Book and Business Guide* for various cities; and church records, year-books, and commemorative albums.

5   Charles Moskos, "Ethnic Life - The Greeks," in Charles R. Wilson and William Ferris, eds., *Encyclopedia of Southern Culture* (Chapel Hill, University of North Carolina Press, 1989), 431.

6   Moskos, *Greek Americans*, 25.

7   Saloutos, *The Greeks in the United States, 280*; concepts such as "adaptation," "adjustment," "assimilation," and "Americanization" are discussed in this chapter.

8   Moskos, "Ethnic Life - The Greeks," in Wilson and Ferris, eds., *Encyclopedia of Southern Culture*, 431-432.

9   Research and church-records kindly provided by His Grace Bishop John of Atlanta, historian and Bishop of the Greek Orthodox Church in the Americas, show when early Greek communities organized church activities:

1864	New Orleans, Louisiana	1911	Augusta, Georgia
1902	Birmingham, Alabama	1912	Mobile, Alabama
1905	Atlanta, Georgia	1916	Jacksonville, Florida
1907	Tarpon Springs, Florida	1917	Charlotte, North Carolina
1907	Savannah, Georgia	1924	Raleigh, North Carolina
1909	Pensacola, Florida	1925	Miami, Florida

1910   Charleston, South Carolina
        See Chapter 4, Table 9.

10   Oscar Handlin, *The Uprooted* (New York, Grosset & Dunlap, 1951), 6, "The
        immigrants lived in crisis because they were uprooted. In transplantation,
        while the old roots were sundered, before the new were established, the
        immigrants existed in an extreme situation. The shock, and the effects of
        the shock, persisted for many years; and their influence reached down to
        generations which themselves never paid the cost of crossing." Also see
        Oscar Handlin, "Immigration in American Life: A Reappraisal," in
        Immigration and American History, Henry Steel Commager, ed.
        (Minneapolis, University of Minnesota Press, 1961), at 15: "No group
        could restore the old community or preserve the traditional values against
        the corrosive forces that transformed these people."

11   Oscar Handlin, *The Uprooted*, 4.

12   Thomas Wheeler, ed., *The Immigrant Experience: The Anguish of Becoming
        American* (New York, Dial Press, 1971) 1-2.

13   Nathan Glazer and Daniel Patrick Moynihan, *Beyond the Melting Pot: the
        Negroes, Puerto Ricans, Jews, Italians, and Irish of New York City* (Cambridge,
        the MIT Press, 1963), at 22, "the point about the melting pot [was] that
        it did not happen." The terms "Americanization" and "acculturation" are
        considered to be essentially equivalents to "assimilation."

14   Rudolph J. Vecoli, "The Contadini in Chicago: A Critique of the
        Uprooted," *Journal of American History* 51 (1964-1965), 404-417.

15   Virginia Yans-McLaughlin, *Family and Community: Italian Immigrants in
        Buffalo, 1880-1930* (Ithaca, Cornell University Press, 1977); Kathleen Neils
        Conzen, "Immigrants, Immigrant Neighborhoods, and Ethnic Identity:
        Historical Issues," *Journal of American History* 66 (December 1979), 603-
        615; Olivier Zunz, *The Changing Face of Inequality: Urbanization, Industrial
        Development, and Immigrants in Detroit, 1880-1920* (Chicago, University
        of Chicago Press, 1982); Rudolph J. Vecoli, "The Formation of Chicago's
        'Little Italies,' " *Journal of American Ethnic History* 2 (Spring 1983), 5-20; John
        Bodnar, *The Transplanted: A History of Immigrants in Urban America*
        (Bloomington, Indiana University Press, 1985); Ewa Morawska, *For Bread
        With Butter: the Life-Worlds of East Central Europeans in Johnstown,
        Pennsylvania, 1890-1940* (Cambridge, Cambridge University Press, 1985);
        George E. Pozzetta and Gary R. Mormino, *The Immigrant World of Ybor
        City: Italians and Their Latin Neighbors in Tampa, Florida, 1885-1985*
        (Chicago, University of Illinois Press, 1987); Rudolph Vecoli, "From *The
        Uprooted* to *The Transplanted*: The Writing of American Immigration History
        1951-1989," in Valeria Lerda, ed., *From Melting Pot to Multiculturalism*
        (Rome, Bulzoni Editore, 1991), 53; George E. Pozzetta ed., *American
        Immigration and Ethnicity* (New York, Garland Publishing, Inc., 1991).

16   Peter Kivisto, "The transplanted then and now: the reorientation of
        immigration studies from the Chicago School to the new social history,

" *Ethnic and Racial Studies* 13 (October 1990), 455-481, at 469.

17   Michael Novak, *The Rise of the Unmeltable Ethnics* (New York, the Macmillan Company, 1971-1972).

18   Ibid., 257, 72, 138, 229.

19   John Bodnar, *The Transplanted: A History of Immigrants in Urban America* (Bloomington, Indiana University Press, 1985).

20   Ibid., xvii.

21   Ibid., 210.

22   Rudolph Vecoli, "Return to the Melting Pot: Ethnicity in the United States in the Eighties," *Journal of American Ethnic History* 5 (Fall 1985), 17.

23   Rudolph Vecoli, "From *The Uprooted* to *The Transplanted*: the Writing of American Immigration History, 1951-1989, in Valeria Lerda ed., *From 'Melting Pot' to Multiculturalism* (Rome, Bulzoni Editore, 1990), 25-53.

24   Vecoli, "From *The Uprooted* to *The Transplanted*," 53.

25   Charles Hirschman, "What Happened to the White Ethnics?" *Contemporary Sociology* 20 (March 1991), 183; also see Hirschman's "America's Melting Pot Reconsidered," *Annual Review of Sociology* 9 (1983), 397-423, for a pro-assimilation viewpoint.

26   Kathleen Neils Conzen, David A. Gerber, Ewa Morawska, George E. Pozzetta, and Rudolph J. Vecoli, "The Invention of Ethnicity: A Perspective From the USA," *Journal of American Ethnic History*, 12, (Fall 1992), 3-41.

27   Ibid., "The Invention of Ethnicity: A Perspective From the USA," 4-5.

28   Philip Gleason, "Confusion Compounded: The Melting Pot in the 1960s and 1970s," *Ethnicity* 6 (1979), 10-20, at 18.

29   Bernard Bailyn, *The Peopling of British North America: An Introduction* (New York, Vintage Books, 1988), especially see *Proposition Three*, on 60, that after the initial phase of colonization, "the major stimuli to population recruitment and settlement were, first, the continuing need for labor, and, second, land speculation;" Roger Daniels, *Coming to America* (New York, Harper Collins, 1990), 185-237; Frank Thistlethwaite, "Migration from Europe Overseas in the 19th and 20th Centuries," in Herbert Moller ed., *Population Movements in Modern European History* (New York, Macmillan, 1964), 73-92, is a pathbreaking essay setting US immigration into the wider European perspective.

30   George E. Pozzetta, ed., *American Immigration and Ethnicity*, volume 13, *Assimilation, Acculturation, and Social Mobility* (New York, Garland Publishing, 1991), vi-vii.

31   Social Science research seminar on Acculturation, *American Anthropologist* 57, (1955), 1240-1252; also see Kimball Young, *Sociology: A Study of Society and Culture* (New York, American Book Company, 1949), for a similar explication. Assimilation denotes a blending of the folkways, mores, and ways of life of two or more groups or societies of people. Acculturation is defined as a "culture change that is initiated by the conjunction of two or more autonomous systems," a process during which the dominant or

host culture's values, traits, and patterns of behavior are learned.

32   Kathleen Conzen, et al., "The Invention of Ethnicity: A Perspective From the USA;" Werner Sollors ed., *The Invention of Ethnicity* (New York, Oxford University Press, 1989), especially the discussion on pp. ix-xx.

33   Rabinowitz, *The First New South 1865-1920* (Arlington Heights, Illinois, Harlan Davidson, 1992), 30.

34   Ibid., 52-68; also see David Goldfield, *Cottonfields and Skyscrapers* (Baton Rouge, Louisiana, State University Press, 1982) for remarkable growth in the South, even though it never could match the astonishing urban, commercial, and industrial growth in some northern states

35   *Thirteenth Census of the United States, 1910*, Population of Cities Abstract, 63.

36   George E. Pozzetta, "Foreigners in Florida: A Study of Immigration Promotion, 1865-1910," *Florida Historical Quarterly*, 53 (2), (October 1974), 164-180; at 172, by 1910, the major immigrant groups in Florida were Cubans, Germans, English, and Italians, with "appreciable numbers" of Finns, Turks [or ethnic Greeks from the Mediterranean regions of the Ottoman Empire], Chinese, Russians [mostly Russian Jews], and Greeks; but also see 175: one government report warned "the doors [should] not [be] opened too wide, that those people of undesireable classes of nationalities [sic] are not thrust upon us..."

37   C. Vann Woodward, *Origins of the New South 1877-1913* (Baton Rouge, Louisiana, State University Press, 1951), 299: "the flood tide of European immigration...swept past the South leaving it almost untouched and further isolating it in its peculiarities from the rest of the country."

38   William J. Cooper Jr. and Thomas E. Terrill, *The American South* (New York, McGraw Hill, 1996), 2nd ed., 481-485.

39   Stanley Brandes, "Reflections on Honor and Shame in the Mediterranean," in David D. Gilmore ed., *Honor and Shame and Unity of the Mediterranean* (Washington, D.C., American Anthropological Association, 1987), 121-134; David Gilmore, "The Shame of Dishonor," in ibid., 2-21; J. G. Peristiany and Julian Pitt-Rivers eds.,*Honor and Grace in Anthropology* (Cambridge, Cambridge University Press, 1989), passim; J. G. Peristiany ed., *Contributions to Mediterranean Sociology* (The Hague, Mouton, 1968), passim.

40   Bertram Wyatt-Brown, *Southern Honor: Ethics and Behavior in the Old South* (New York, Oxford University Press, 1982), xii.

41   Dimitrios Monos pointed out that the cultivation of "honorable" behavior is reinforced by a most effective form of social control—ridicule. As self-esteem is of utmost importance, to avoid ridicule, the culture has devised appropriate mechanisms for its protection, even in cases of personal failure. The mechanisms always attribute failure to conditions beyond the individual's control, not to personal inadequacy. Excuses are conjured up: there was the unexpected illness, government established unexpected regulations; people one trusted were dishonest, etc. Dimitrios Ioannis Monos,

"Upward Mobility, Assimilation, and the Achievements of Greeks in the United States, With Special Emphasis on Boston and Philadelphia," Ph.D. dissertation, University of Pennsylvania, 1976, 70-74.

42   Fairchild, *Greek Immigration to the United States*, 191-193 wrote that no matter what the income was of Greek laborers and small entrepreneurs, they always managed to save a part and send a part home. There was evidence that the Greeks sent the "highest average remittance of any of the [European immigrant] nationalities."

43   Theodore Saloutos, *They Remember America: the Story of the Repatriated Greek-Americans* (Berkeley, University of California Press, 1956); Saloutos makes the case that upwards of 30 percent of Greek immigrants to the whole US repatriated and disproportionately influenced issues in Greece; however, one could argue that few of the repatriated came from the southern states.

44   Monos, "Upward Mobility, Assimilation, and the Achievements of the Greeks in the US," 73-74.

45   Theodore Saloutos, *They Remember America: the Story of the Repatriated Greek-Americans*.

46   See Table 9 (Chapter 4) for an enumeration of the southern cities where Greeks settled in sufficient numbers (by 1925) to organize a *kinotis* and found a Greek Orthodox church.

CHAPTER 2

"DEMETRIOS IS NOW JIMMY:"

A HISTORICAL OVERVIEW OF THE FORMATION AND DEVELOPMENT OF GREEK IMMIGRANT COMMUNITIES IN THE SOUTHERN UNITED STATES

Greek immigrants to the turn-of-the-century "New South" tended to exploit significant increases of population and notable commercial expansion to start their own small businesses.[1] As proprietors of shoe-shine parlors, restaurants, fruit stores, sandwich shops, cigar stands and similar enterprises, Greek newcomers were in daily contact with American customers and rapidly adapted to ways that improved both their economic and social position. As a result of their adaptation and economic success, they experienced upward mobility decades earlier and in greater proportions than their immigrant compatriots in the Northeast and the Midwest. This striking mobility, mixed marriages, applications for citizenship, use of English at home, Americanization of names, and other changes indicate the early transformation of these immigrants into ethnic Americans and confirm the existence of the "southern variant" mentioned by sociologist Charles Moskos.[2] Moskos characterized this process as the prototype of Greek ethnic development in the United States. He asserted that Greeks in the South realized earlier than their compatriots in other parts of the United States that America would become their permanent home. Based on this observation, he concluded that Greeks who settled in the South first made the transformation from immigrants to ethnic Americans.[3] An examination of the experiences of Greek migrants to southern cities, and of the Greek immigrant communities formed there during the early 1900s, confirm his assertion and show that the Greeks' adaptation and development in the South were essentially different than immigrant experiences elsewhere in the United States.

In the 1890s, Greek migrants began filtering into the South, lured by the rapid urban growth of some southern cities. New Orleans, Birmingham, and Atlanta led the way, but a collection of other cities, both inland and along the coasts, were swiftly expanding. Although common to all these local and regional trading centers, economic advance took place in different ways and at diverse rates; in turn, the dissimilarities could not help but influence the seasoning of Greek immigrants. Beyond question, Atlanta grew into the most typical of the New South cities. Smaller towns and commercial centers, both inland and along the coasts, strove to match the hustle of the Gate City.

In the 1880s, Atlanta emerged as a booming metropolis, a transportation hub, and the trading center of the Southeast. The Gate City attracted many events of national and worldwide interest, such as the 1881 World's Fair and Great International Cotton Exposition, and the 1887 Piedmont Exposition.[4] By the end of the 1880s Atlanta's population passed the 65,000 mark.[5] Although the depression of the 1890s caused some decline in growth and progress, during the same decade Atlanta's streetcar lines acquired electric cars, the city managed to pave streets, build brick sidewalks, and construct underpasses, viaducts, and eight bridges. Atlanta's growth expanded into what had formerly been farm land and woods on its outskirts.[6]

In 1890, after spending two years in Chicago and probably drawn by glowing reports about its growth, Greek immigrant Alexander Carolee decided to migrate to the Gate City of the South. He worked as a bartender and supported his wife Mary and daughter Alice.[7] Nicholas Matrangos, Chris Matrangos, and Nicholas Tountas, all originally from Carolee's Greek mainland district of Argos, and lately of Chicago, followed Carolee to Atlanta, and engaged in fruit vending, grocery sales, and quick lunch preparation. Other Greek migrants who had spent a few years in Chicago, New York, and other northern cities, and who originally came from the islands near Asia Minor, also arrived in Atlanta. The 1900 Census recorded thirty-two single Greek immigrants and six families there. Fully 74 percent, or twenty-nine men out of thirty-nine, were self-employed in twelve fruit stalls or shops, ten grocery stores, and several restaurants and candy stores.[8] Needs of the city's nearly 90,000 inhabitants provided the demand for a variety of goods and services. By 1910, Atlanta's population soared to 154,839, accompanied by a fourfold increase of Greek immigrants.[9]

TABLE 2
Greeks in Atlanta according to the Thirteenth US Census, 1910:

	Male adults	Female adults	Children
single men	288		
6 Greek-American families	6	6	6
27 Greek families	27	27	67
married men, families back home	19		
total	340	33	73

Sometime during this decade, Alexander Carolee, the bartender, had become the owner of a bar and poolroom. A Greek businessmen's directory, published in Atlanta about 1912, identified him as a pioneer of the Greek community as well as "one of the wealthiest, too, owning extensive real estate property in the city."[10] By now, restaurant owners represented the largest number of self-employed Greek businessmen in Atlanta. The 1910 Census revealed no fewer than forty restaurateurs, in addition to thirty grocery and fruit store owners, and forty-four other entrepreneurs in a variety of occupations.[11] Atlanta's wholesale dealers, operating in the largest transshipment depot in the Southeast, supplied all of the meats, fruits, vegetables, and numerous other wholesale staples to the Greek retailers.

The oldest Matrangos brother, Nicholas, had achieved fame as "the first one to start a lunchroom in Atlanta."[12] In 1911, Nick Matrangos and two partners owned and managed the Peachtree Café, a first-class table service restaurant in downtown Atlanta. In the same year, at age 41, Nick Matrangos had become a member of the Odd Fellows and, like Carolee, invested in real estate. Nick's partner Charles Keramidas also owned his large house and other "valuable real estate property." Charles had married "an accomplished American lady" and had one child.[13] Characteristic of a number of Greeks in Atlanta, the third partner, Angel Mitchell had Americanized his last name, as did his cousins Jim, Pete, and Victor Mitchell, and the proprietor of Mitchell's Cafe, George Mitchell.

TABLE 3
Self-employed Greeks in Atlanta, in 1910

owners of restaurants, quick-lunches, cafés	40
owners of fruit stores and stands, grocers	38
candy makers, confectioners, ice cream factory	23
shoe-shine parlor operators, hat cleaners	6
barbershop owners	3
owners of saloons, poolrooms	8
peddler of notions (1), house-painter (1)	2
merchants (cotton 2), (wholesale (1), retail (2)	5
total	125

Employed Greeks in Atlanta, in 1910

work at restaurants, quick lunches, cafés	121
work at fruit stores and stands, grocers	23
work at candy makers, confectioners	27
shoe-shine boys, hat cleaners	3
barbers or apprentices	8
saloon and poolroom waiters and bartenders	7
salesmen (souvenirs 1), (coffee 1), (retail 1)	3
various other and unknown jobs	23
total	215

Another early immigrant to Atlanta, Georgios Papageorgakopoulos, first made his living by peddling fruit after he arrived in the Gate City about 1892. The 1900 Census recorded him under his new American name "George Moore" and listed his occupation as a grocer.[14] Representative of so many Greek entrepreneurs who migrated south and prospered, by 1910, George Moore had established the Moore Ice Cream Company and employed dozens of Greeks and African Americans both in the plant and on delivery operations.[15]

MOORE, GEORGE, 72 Central Avenue. (Phones as above)......AXXVM-C1
Soda Fountain, Candies, Cigars, etc., Magazines, Newspapers.

GEORGE MOORE enjoys the greatest popularity of any business man of his nationality—in fact, he is known, we may say, to every man, woman and child. He is one of the wealthiest as well as progressive and influential Greeks. His name and business are before the Atlanta public every day in large letters.

In 1893 he left his native land, the beautiful county of Amaliada, the sporting center of the Greeks, the Olympia, directing his course straight to the most prosperous city of the South—Atlanta. After a number of business ventures, after a number of successes and failures, after working for a time at two dollars a week, his great tenacity and business ability came to the surface and set him high above the many of his countrymen in business. He has not only helped himself, but helped a great number of other Greeks. If praise is due, certainly George Moore deserves all the credit. He owns a confectionery, an ice cream and candy factory, valuable real estate property and five large houses in town. His reputation is high, and his Greek as well as American friends like him very much and respect his wishes and are proud of him. We wish him all success.

A page from the *Adallis' Greek Merchants' Reference Book and Business Guide – Atlanta*. (Ca. 1912) Depicted on this page is young businessman George Moore (Papageorgakopoulos), in Atlanta since 1893. Courtesy of Mrs. Mary Farmakis, Atlanta, Georgia.

A few Greek businessmen with some savings looked to invest in new and still speculative ventures. For example, Angelos Soteropoulos immigrated to New York in June, 1903 and after four years of hustling moved to Atlanta in 1907 with enough money to buy an interest in the Majestic Theater, although he hedged his risks by also acquiring a partnership in the Eagle Café, then located at Marietta and Peachtree streets. During the next decade, he built and managed more theaters in Atlanta, branched out to Macon, and altered his name to Angel Sparks.[16]

As their economic position became stronger during these first few years of the new century, Moore, Carolee, the Matrangos family, the Mitchell clan, and other Greek immigrants, numbering about 150 people, formed an organized Greek community and established a Greek Orthodox Church congregation. Whenever enough Greeks settled in a city, they formed a *kinotis* - a community, usually formalized by the election of a council at an open meeting of interested Greeks.[17] It is not easy to determine exactly how many potential congregants needed to know each other and when several of them might decide to call a meeting of all those compatriots who could be interested in forming a new parish. Chapter four of this work deals in more detail with religious life in developing Greek communities and the establishment of church parishes in the South. Invariably, however, the early activities of any Greek immigrant *kinotis* centered primarily, though not exclusively, on the procurement of a building for church services and the hiring of a suitable priest.[18] Accordingly, the elected council actively sought new members and donations. At times, the congregation was incorporated in accordance with local laws. Members met periodically and usually had an annual general meeting when councilmen were elected or re-elected to administer the communal accounts and any community-owned buildings.

In Atlanta, probably no more than thirty Greek businessmen organized the *kinotis* on November 1, 1902. The men decided to adopt the name the Greek Orthodox Society "Evangelismos," dedicating the society and the future place of worship to the Annunciation of the Mother of God. Members present elected their Board of Officers, consisting of seven men, led by businessman Gerasimos Avgerinos, who had adopted the Americanized name G. Algers.[19]

TABLE 4
Greek-owned businesses in Atlanta, ca. 1911, according to
Adallis' Greek Merchants' Reference Book and Business Guide

Fruit and grocery stores	23
restaurants, cafés, quick lunches	42
Hotels	2
shoe-shine parlors	3
confectioners, candy makers, ice cream products	34
cigar/cigarette makers, coffee importers	3
Barbershops	2
poolrooms, saloons	14
moving picture theaters	2
bakery, retail stores, linen supply	6
total businesses advertising with Adallis' Guide	131

Most of Atlanta's Greek families and single men agreed with the need for a priest and church premises, placed their names on the membership roster, and pledged to support the financial needs of the new *kinotis*. By 1905, members of the Society decided to rent a hall on the second floor of a building at 111? Whitehall Street and to convert it into a chapel suitable for church services. The location was most convenient for a good number of Greeks who had businesses and residences in that area. Although not all Atlanta Greeks belonged to the Society, all were free to worship and attend services at the chapel. A traveling priest, father Constantine Bakalarios, conducted the first service on September 5, 1905. For the elections of April, 1906, seventy-two notices were sent out to dues-paying members. The Society's next undertaking, the building or purchase of a church, materialized the same summer, when the Presbyterian church building on the corner of Garnett Street and Central Avenue came on the market for $9,000. In May 1906, members voted to purchase the building, located in a lower middle class area where many immigrants resided.[20] For the next twenty-two years, when a larger house of worship replaced it, the Greek Orthodox Church of the Annunciation on Garnett and Central became a center for both religious and social activities and a gathering place where entire families could meet, perpetuate cultural traditions, exchange information, and learn from one another how to adapt to their new habitat.[21]

Atlanta's Greek Orthodox Church of the Annunciation, established in 1905, resided in this building, at Pryor and Richardson Streets, from 1928 to 1967. Photo courtesy of Father Homer P. Goumenis, Dean, Greek Orthodox Cathedral of the Annunciation, and Dr. Evangeline Papageorge, Atlanta.

Rapid growth similar to Atlanta's but on a somewhat smaller scale occurred in Florida's Jacksonville, the River City, that sprouted where the navigable St. Johns River enters the Atlantic Ocean. Publicist James Esgate noted as early as 1885 that commerce played an increasing part in that urban economy, with coastal shipping, railroads, wholesale houses, and retail shops proliferating.[22] In the mid-1890s, S. Paul Brown described Jacksonville as a center "of finance, commerce and transportation" and a world-renowned orange market.[23] Lumber mills, wharves, warehouses, and railroad tracks multiplied along the water-front. Jacksonville's population growth matched the surging commercial expansion.[24] The 28,429 residents counted in the 1900 Census were nearly twice the population of 1890, and the number doubled again to 57,700 people in 1910.[25] With its railroads and the port open to inland, coastal, and transoceanic shipping, Jacksonville became a regional entrepot, a transportation hub for transshipment of goods, and Florida's largest city. Such growth probably induced the first Greek immigrant to Jacksonville, Andreas Coroneos, to settle there in 1889 and be the *proto-poros* (pathfinder) for other Greeks. A sense of the early economic and social adjustments experienced by Jacksonville Greeks can be gained from an examination of the careers of Coroneos and other Greek pioneers who led their Greek compatriots to the River City.

In the late 1870s Andreas Coroneos came to New York from the Aegean island of Santorini. In just over a decade he had shifted south to Jacksonville and established himself as owner of a store selling fruit, cigars, and groceries.[26] Coroneos had apparently found an economic niche in the River City that he could successfully exploit. He obtained all the tobacco products from well established local cigar factories, while wholesale fruit and grocery companies supplied perishable stock.[27] He strove to display his fruit tastefully and to sell it out daily, since he operated on a very thin profit margin. As Jacksonville's population grew, more Greeks arrived and opened more fruit stores as well as restaurants and other businesses.[28] Newcomers were lured to such enterprises by the advice and practical help supplied by compatriots already in these occupations. In addition, arriving family members were used as reliable, willing, and available help. After learning the business, they often struck out on their own.

Within a few years, Coroneos' economic status improved. The 1910 *Jacksonville City Directory* listed him as one of the partners of "Boulas and Coroneas Fruits" with stores at three locations. In addition, he owned a house in a comfortable middle class area within a few blocks of the stores. Social mobility, demonstrated by membership in fraternal organizations, followed improved economic status. The *Greek Merchants' Reference Book* of 1911 confirmed Coroneos as "Jacksonville's oldest Greek pioneer," listed his large cigar and fruit store in downtown Jacksonville, and indicated that he was not only "a full citizen," but also a member of "the Odd Fellows, W.O.W. [Woodmen of the World],

Fraternal Union, and the Beavers."[29] Although the 1910 Census missed Coroneos, it included his partner James Boulos. Boulos had arrived in the United States from Sparta before the turn of the century and settled in Jacksonville about 1905. By 1914 he too had become an American citizen and was "one of the wealthiest Greeks in the city," the owner of "more than ten houses," and the president of the Greek Mutual Benefit Society.[30] Boulos had evidently used income from his fruit stores to maximize opportunities in a growing realty market.

A.

ATLANTA QUICK LUNCH, Geo. Brown, Proprietor..............................C2
405 West Bay Street. Phone 3263-J.

Geo Brown is a slight modification of Geo. Bracatzas. He is an Argive, the land of the Golden Fleece, during the Heroic Ages of Greece. In 1896, the spirit for invading distant lands possessed him, and he forthwith headed for the shores of these United States, settling in Atlanta, but two years after selecting Jacksonville as his future field of progress. No doubt he is well known in the city, as his picture here does him no justice whatever. Mr. Brown is the proprietor of two hotels, The New Travelers and the New Central, besides the above eating place. He is a member of the Odd Fellows, married to an American lady, and the proud father of three children. He is one of the most well-liked Hellenes in the South.

George Brown (Bracatzas), shown in *Adallis' Greek Merchants' Reference Book and Business Guide - Jacksonville* (ca. 1912). Courtesy of Mr. Jerry Felos, Jacksonville, Florida.

George Bracatzas was another early Greek immigrant attracted to Jacksonville, but he made his start by selling sandwiches and coffee. A Greek mainlander, Bracatzas migrated to Jacksonville about 1898, two years after he first arrived in the United States. He had married a Scottish-born wife, Ellen, and the 1910 Census indicated they had seven children, ranging in age from 2 to 20. His first investment was an eating place, the Atlanta Quick Lunch. Bracatzas soon Americanized his name to "Brown." Within two decades after migrating to the River City, he became "the proprietor of two hotels, The New Travelers and the New Central," both situated at the western end of Jacksonville's business district.[31] In 1910, his oldest son, twenty-year-old Emmanuel, was a fruit merchant; son Henry, who was eighteen, worked as a clerk in his father's restaurant, while Constantine, only fourteen, held a job as a real estate office clerk. Brown's union with a Scots woman was only one of several mixed marriages among Jacksonville's Greeks at the time.

By 1910, Greek immigrants to Jacksonville numbered well over one hundred people. There were sixty-nine single Greek men and one woman, in addition to seventeen families. Five of the families consisted of Greek husbands and Anglo wives and twelve were all Greek.[32]

TABLE 5
Greeks in Jacksonville in 1910

	Male adults	Female adults	Children
single people	69	1	
5 Greek-American families	5	5	6
12 Greek families	12	12	3
Total	86	18	9

Although clustered in the same general area of the city, in Jacksonville's western part of downtown and bordering on black parts of the La Villa district or in economically and socially advanced Riverside, Greek residences were dispersed throughout the neighborhood and never formed an immigrant ghetto.[33] Self-employment by Jacksonville's Greeks in that year stood at a remarkable 65.5 percent. Fully two-thirds of the working adults were self-employed merchants. Of the remainder, all but four people worked for their relatives and compatriots.[34] Greek businessmen operated eighteen eating establishments, thirty grocery and fruit stores, and sundry confectioneries, hotels, and other enterprises. Greek-owned enterprises were scattered throughout Jacksonville's downtown area, along Bay and Main Streets, just as they dotted Atlanta's Whitehall (later Peachtree) Street, Edgewood Avenue, and South Broad Street.[35] By 1910, some of the early migrants had prospered, penetrated into the white, mainstream society, and moved into residential areas that reflected their improved incomes.[36]

TABLE 6
Greek-owned businesses in Jacksonville, Florida, in 1910

Fruit and grocery stores	30
restaurants, cafés, and quick lunches	18
hotels	2
tailors	3
shoe-shine parlors	2
huxters	3
confectioners, candy makers	3
pool parlor	1
fish retail store	1
total Greek-owned businesses	63

By 1915 the Greek community in Jacksonville had grown to about 160 people. Some twenty-five Greek and Greek-American families resided there, in addition to about seventy-five single Greek men who lived throughout downtown, some in rooms at the back of their stores and restaurants.[37] As in Atlanta, this number constituted the "critical mass" necessary for the next step in community building. Jacksonville's Greeks formed their *kinotis* in 1916. On November 2 of that year, several community members elected to the council filed a charter for "The Oriental Greek Orthodox Church - The Revelation of St. John the Theologou" with the Clerk of the Duval County Circuit Court.[38] By 1921, a second charter, widened to authorize operation of an educational institution, incorporated "The Greek Community of Jacksonville, Florida."

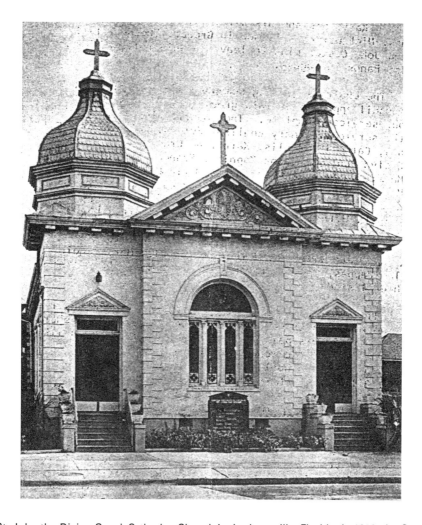

St. John the Divine Greek Orthodox Church in Jacksonville, Florida. In 1919, the Greek community purchased the building, a former synagogue, located at the corner of Laura and Union Streets. The refurbished church building served nearly fifty years, until 1968, when the community built a modern church, on Atlantic Boulevard, designed by parishioner and award winning architect Ted Pappas. Photo from a 1960s church bulletin, courtesy of Mr. Jerry Felos, Jacksonville, Florida.

Among the petitioners were some early pioneers, such as fruit store owners James Boulos, Constantine Maglaris, and Peter Pappas, restaurateurs James Stathis and Nick Paleologos, confectioner Victor J. George, and fishmonger Jim Kalogerakos.[39] Members of the community voted to purchase a house located at the fringe of downtown, just north of the railway station, and to refurbish the building to serve as a church, school, and meeting place. By 1919, the *kinotis* decided to sell this property and relocate all activities to the spacious church downtown at 46 West Union Street, rebuilt by architect Henry Klutho after the Great Fire of 1901. The Greek Orthodox community purchased the handsome structure for $20,000, installed an *iconostasis*, and worshiped there until 1968.[40]

To the north and east of the Atlanta - Jacksonville axis, in the port-cities of Savannah and Charleston, as well as in entrepots such as Augusta, Charlotte, and Raleigh, Greek migrants followed a similar pattern of settlement, self-employment, and socio-economic betterment. In a like manner, to the south and west of the axis, in the Gulf coast cities of Pensacola, Mobile, Montgomery, and New Orleans, Greek immigrants arrived and much like members of other immigrant groups, specifically Syrians and East-European Jews, sought to exploit economic niches opening in the New South. They sold fruit, operated sandwich shops and shoe-shine stands, tried their hand at a variety of other businesses, and saved.[41] Then they brought more family from Greece, Asia Minor, or the Aegean islands, expanded the business, prospered, and reached for acceptance by the larger community. Rather than reduce all immigrants' activities to a pale common facsimile, in this examination of Greeks who were settling in the southern states, it is best to follow the mandate of historians George Pozzetta and Gary Mormino, that "Inquiries of this sort are best guided by the specific experiences...in identifiable locations over precise periods of time, not by framing of generalized models."[42]

The Greek community of Savannah, Georgia, served as one example for the rapid but not always smooth adaptation of a first generation group of newcomers into the southern environment. The first Greek migrants arrived in Savannah towards the end of the Gilded Age, in the 1880s and 1890s. Although the 1900 Federal Census reported a total of 191 Greeks in the whole of Georgia, Greek-American sources believe that this number represented a substantial undercount.[43] *Sholes' Savannah Directory* of 1900 alone listed eighty-six businesses held by Greeks. Of a total of 111 retail fruit stores, Greeks owned fifty-four, close to one-half of all such fruit vending establishments in Savannah. Restaurants were a close second: seventeen of the total number of thirty-seven eating businesses were in Greek hands.[44] When one adds to the owners of these businesses the family members and compatriots who worked in these enterprises, one can see that in 1900, Savannah alone probably had more Greeks than the whole Georgia Census had enumerated.

Purchased in 1907, St. Paul's Greek Orthodox Church in Savannah, at the corner of Barnard and Duffy Streets, served the community for thirty-four years. Photo by author, guided by Charles Masterpolis.

Among the earliest settlers in Savannah were Eli Veruki, proprietor of Veruki's Café and later vice-president of the Savannah Distributing Company, in which another Greek, Johnny Peters, was president and Veruki's partner. Johnny's father, George Peters, came from Crete in 1886 and made a living in Savannah operating Peter's Restaurant at 424 West Broad Street. "Denny" Andeppa joined him in 1889 and operated a saloon nearby; George and Thomas Pesimisses and James Regopoulos followed and formed the American-Grecian Turpentine Corporation of Savannah.[45] Just about every Greek migrant who decided to stay in Savannah started his own small business. In 1905 the Greek newcomers formed and chartered "The Greek-Orthodox Community of Savannah, Ga." In 1907 this *kinotis* purchased St. Paul's Episcopal Church building on the corner of Barnard and Duffy Streets, decided to keep the name of the Saint who brought Christianity to Greece, and hired father Thomas Pappageorge to tend to the spiritual life of the newly established Greek Orthodox Parish of St. Paul.[46] Athan Vainas, who had arrived in Savannah in 1901 and owned the Union Station Fruit Stand, hand-carved the *iconostasis* for the new church. When the community's growth coincided with an unprecedented opportunity to move St. Paul's to a unique classical building in Savannah's historic district, Vainas's carved masterpiece was transferred and installed in the new church.[47]

ST. PAUL'S GREEK ORTHODOX CHURCH
Bull and Anderson Streets

In 1941, the parishioners bought the impressive Lawton Memorial Building from the City of Savannah and remodeled it into the striking church building it is today. Photo courtesy of Father Aris P. Metrakos, 1992, Savannah, Georgia.

According to the *60th Anniversary Album of St. Paul's Greek Orthodox Church in Savannah*, when the Selective Service Act of 1917 became law, many Savannah Greeks joined the American armed forces "as proof of their loyalty and love for the United States." Another more practical reason might have caused their missing to claim an exemption as aliens. By serving in the armed forces "they gained their citizenship." After the war, the Greek community managed to avert any problems with the Klan, and in January of 1924, a number of men formed a chapter of the American Hellenic Educational and Progressive Association, the AHEPA, which then promoted the acquisition of citizenship and "Americanization"[48] The American-born youth presented theatrical performances in Greek and English, and in 1927, the American-born young women formed Sigma Tau Delta, an organization that engaged in activities of a social and charitable nature. During this decade Savannah's Greeks also organized the first Greek-American Boy Scout troop, Troop 20. The community had become acculturated to the extent that on the surface it could hardly be seen as different from the many Protestant parishes in Savannah. As the 60th anniversary album proudly though not quite accurately announced, "The Greek had become fully integrated into the American community."[49]

A parallel pattern of development took place among the Greeks who settled in Charleston, South Carolina. Charleston's Greek Americans trace their Hellenic roots to the 1780s, when Maria Gracia Dura Bin, the daughter of a Greek merchant from Smyrna, in Asia Minor, married to English colonizer Dr. Andrew Turnbull, settled in Charleston after the failure of Turnbull's colony at New Smyrna, near St. Augustine, Florida.[50] Maria Gracia Turnbull's grave still lies in the historic St. Philip's Churchyard in Charleston, but she really could not be considered an immigrant of the same order as her plebeian compatriots who arrived over one hundred years later. The first handful of Greek migrants appeared here after 1900, only after masses of immigrants from south-eastern Europe made their overseas trek to America. Typically, the Greek Charlestonians were self-employed in small businesses, invariably putting members of their family and other compatriots to work. Cousins, brothers, and compatriots trained and learned the business thoroughly and as soon as they could, in turn, went into business for themselves. Again, in addition to the Census and the City Directory, *Adallis' Greek-American Directory* provides extraordinary detail.[51] The publication identified with "those who have recently arrived here," the "new element of rugged, peasant Greeks," who began to immigrate into America from the 1890s on. In the best filiopietistic style of the day, Dio [Dionysos] Adallis, publisher of the directory, explained how "a race so exceedingly different in language and manners, succeeded in carving for themselves an enviable corner." The writer praised his Greek countrymen for their diligence and industry, lauded those who were proficient in English, admired their ability to learn

American ways, indicated that they were commercially successful beyond expectation, and tied their material success to the fact that they "became proprietors of different lines of business." Adallis envisioned in their attitudes "the desirable materials" that "will become inculcated into the character of this glorious young nation" and thus "enhance [America's] strength and growth." As early as 1912 he depicted the Greeks in Charleston as a group whose members were assimilating by joining different American fraternal orders and organizations, bringing over families, intermarrying here, and becoming full-fledged citizens.[52]

Tom Schiadaressi and his brother Spyro were reputed to be the first "new" Greek immigrants to settle in Charleston.[53] They were from the island of Cephalonia, which had a Greek population but was for centuries under English and then Italian rule. The Schiadaressi brothers attracted a significant number of Greeks from Cephalonia to settle in Charleston. According to Adallis, Spyro and Tom developed a thriving business as importers of fruits, foreign delicacies, fancy groceries, olive oils, chocolates and candies. During the decade of the 1890s, the family owned and operated some eleven stores throughout Charleston. Short biographies written about twenty-three Greek Charlestonian businessmen revealed the birthplace of eight of them to be Cephalonia, there were three families from Asia Minor, two islanders—one each from Rhodes and Chios, and ten men whose origins were on the Greek mainland, eight of them Spartans. Adallis confirmed that the Greek settlers in Charleston mainly engaged in fruit sales, restaurants, and saloons, in addition to other businesses. He also indicated that "a great number of them are members of the Order of Eagles," an American fraternal organization.

Perhaps eight of every ten Greeks in Charleston chose to retain their Greek surnames, although they often altered them to a simplified and shortened form. However, as in every other city throughout the South, there were those who "Americanized" the surnames so one could not perceive the Greek origin. Stamates Strilakos became Tom Crofead; other examples of such Americanized surnames were Altine, Bart, Davis, Milton, Mitchell, Peters, and Young. The 1910 census identified 134 people born in Greece who resided in Charleston. That same year, a group of them gathered at the Carpenters' Hall, on Vanderhorst Street, and formed the "Grecian Society of Charleston." The society's main order of business was to find or build a church for the Greek Orthodox communicants in the city.[54] According to Adallis, forty-two men formed the "Greek Society," whereas the community's 75th Anniversary journal sets the number of those present at the initial meeting of the "Grecian Society" at seventy.[55] Whatever was the actual number of those attending, their work proved successful, because the following year the *kinotis* purchased a site and managed to build a church on the corner of Calhoun and St. Phillip Streets, named after the Holy Trinity.[56] Charleston's daily, *The News and Courier*, carried a photograph of the earliest church building, located near the segregated black area, in a working-class Irish neighborhood.[57]

Mr. Nicholas Latto, a retired businessman of Greek origin, together with Mrs. Latto, nee Demos, both residents of the city all their lives, remember the Greek immigrants' commercial success and acceptance into the "white" part of Charleston.[58] Mr. Latto's father had jumped a Greek ship docked in Charleston in the early 1900s and joined the small Greek community there. Sofianos Apostolatos engaged in the typical small fruit and grocery business and learned to speak English.[59] He changed the ancestral family name "Apostolatos" to easier-pronounced "Latto," married, and started a family. He soon opened a big general store in North Charleston, then seen as deep countryside, and in the 1920s moved into bottling soft drinks. With franchises from Hires to bottle root beer in a dozen cities from Florida to Virginia, the Lattos lived well.

Although Greek businessmen employed many blacks, they and their families learned to observe strict segregation. Until well into the 1930s, orderly life proceeded in a divided society where everyone knew one's place. A black maid, Susie, stayed in the Latto house for years and brought up two generations of children. To Nicholas and his siblings Susie was another member of the family who had extraordinary privileges and who could spank the Latto children at her discretion. Despite Susie's status, the children were given strict instructions not to play with black children or Roman Catholic children, and not to venture near any Roman Catholic church. The prohibition to play with black children seemed to be part of the Greeks' prudent observance of the American southern custom of segregation; the parents explained that they did not want to trouble the existing "good" relations between themselves, their white neighbors, and the colored folks.

In contrast, Nicholas Latto remembers constant troubles with the

Irish, especially in connection with church services. The Greeks in Charleston lived in many neighborhoods, determined by economic status. To attend services in the first Greek Orthodox church in Charleston, however, meant that Greeks had to walk through the Irish neighborhood where the church was located. Nicholas recalled how Irish children, and even grown-ups, openly ridiculed any priest who had not trimmed his beard or who donned the tall black monastic hat. Whenever the chant of the cantor drifted outside the building, Irish boys would gather around a window and howl. The same boys frequently threw stones, while their elders exchanged friendly remarks with policemen specifically called to prevent any such trouble during the Easter procession, when the Orthodox faithful walked around the church holding lighted candles.[60]

After a decade in Charleston, pioneer Tom Schiadaressi and his brothers Spyro, Dionisios and Demetrios moved to Augusta, Georgia. *Adallis' Greek Merchants' Reference Book and Guide* told how Tom established a market for fruits "not so much relished at the time," or even "considered as luxuries," when "with an unconquering zeal [Tom] applied himself to create a popular demand for them."[61] The early Madison Avenue concept of creating a market for one's products evidently met with success. The brothers' huge wholesale and retail fruit and vegetables emporium, the California Fruit Store, on Augusta's Broad Street employed "American help."[62] The same merchants' reference book informed its readers that Tom Schiadaressi was well liked by his American friends, that he had become a citizen, and joined the Knights of Pythias. By 1910 there were eighty-eight Greek men in town, operating no fewer than thirty-three businesses, at least four of these dealing strictly with "colored" customers. Like the Schiadaressi brothers, other Greek migrants to Augusta were self-employed in eleven fruit-stores, sixteen coffee shops and restaurants, four candy and ice cream parlors, and diverse other enterprises. Like restaurateur Demetrios Scarmoutzos who became James Smith, a number of others, such as George Carl; Charles, George, and Nick Cocklin; and Peter George adapted their names to sound less foreign and more American and acceptable to their local Augusta neighbors and customers. Nine Augusta businessmen—10 percent—were married. Their families, with a combined total of seventeen children, significantly enhanced the sense of belonging and permanence within the small Greek community.[63] By

1911, just a decade since other merchants followed the Schiadaressi pathfinders to Augusta, the group established a *kinotis*, purchased a church building, and dedicated it to the Holy Trinity.

From Adallis' Greek Merchants' Reference Book and Business Guide – Augusta (ca. 1912), the New York Quick Lunch, owned by James Smith (Demetrios Scarmoutzos), who arrived from Athens, Greece, seven years earlier. Courtesy of Mr. Jerry Felos, Jacksonville, Florida.

Charlotte's Greek colony also came to life around the turn of the century, with its members engaged in operating a number of small businesses, such as the Central Hat Shop, owned by George Pappas. If they did not own a small business, Greek newcomers worked for a relative or a compatriot who did, mainly selling "fruit, produce and food."[64] By 1912, the community had grown to about thirty people. More relatives arrived before World War I stopped the transoceanic migration. In 1914, Arthur Lambros, owner of the New York Restaurant on West Trade Street, brought over his fourteen-year-old nephew Tom Cavalaris, to bus tables and help out in the kitchen. Cavalaris lived with several other men employed by uncle Lambros; all slept in rooms on the floor above the restaurant and even shared beds. Expenses were low and

Cavalaris saved a good part of his salary, at that time $10 a month. In 1918, he opened his own Atlanta Hot Dog Stand, with hot dogs going at five cents each. Three years later, he opened the Busy Bee Restaurant and Pool Room.[65] During the great war, the army established a large military training base, Camp Nathaniel Greene, in Charlotte's west end, that brought to the town an economic boomlet, as well as several dozen young Greek Americans, who were among the soldiers stationed there. In 1919, after mustering out, many of the ex-servicemen, such as Chris Pappas and Angelo Rufos, decided to stay in Charlotte and inaugurated their own businesses, adding these to the number of existing Greek enterprises. Pappas opened an eatery, the Sanitary Lunch, while Rufos established the Southern Fruit Company.

In September 1922, Charlotte's Greek businessmen followed their compatriots in Atlanta and formed another branch of the AHEPA, called Marathon Chapter 2, the second chapter of the fraternal organization whose early goals included the "Americanization" of Greek immigrants. Within months, in 1923, AHEPA members helped organize this city's *kinotis*. Formation of families as well as the numerical growth of the group had reached the "critical mass." Already since 1917, visiting priests had held Liturgies in rented premises. In fact, the Chamber of Commerce frequently rented space to the Greeks on Sundays, and other days, while it also rented the third floor of the building to the local branch of the Ku Klux Klan. The building had only one rest-room, and there is little doubt that Klansmen and Greeks met going in and out of it. There is no evidence, oral or written, indicating that any unpleasant incidents occurred in the building, even though both groups shared the facilities in the days when the Johnson Act quotas were closing the immigration gates at Ellis Island and when Edward Clarke and Elizabeth Tyler sold thousands of memberships in the Ku Klux Klan, devoted to 100 percent Americanism.[66] The Charlotte Greeks bought their own church building in 1929 and dedicated it to the Holy Trinity. In many respects, the Greek community in Raleigh developed very much along the same lines. The critical mass was reached in 1924, when the local Hellenes organized another congregation dedicated to the Holy Trinity.[67]

In 1924 early families such as Costa, Davis, Thevis, and Masouras established Raleigh's Holy Trinity Greek Orthodox Church parish. Church services were held in rented buildings from Salisbury Street to Blount Street until 1937, when the congregation purchased land at 211 S. Pearson Street and completed the building by 1938. From the Commemorative Album 1937-1987 Holy Trinity Greek Orthodox Church, Raleigh, NC, courtesy of Mr. James C. Sarayiotes, Raleigh, North Carolina.

To the south and west of the Atlanta - Jacksonville axis, Pensacola on the Gulf of Mexico also attracted Greek migrants in the early part of the century. Greek fishermen, catching mainly shrimp and snapper, settled here in addition to the entrepreneurs who operated fruit stands, sandwich shops, candy stores, grocery businesses, and restaurant enterprises.[68] Not surprisingly, the earliest Greeks in Pensacola came from seafaring families from the Aegean island of Skopelos and chain-migration brought a disproportionate number of Skopeliotes to this port on the Gulf Coast. Snapper fishing reached a peak in the 1890s, when ice-making plants were established in Pensacola, thus allowing the snapper fleet to range far out into the Gulf of Mexico, as far as the Campeche Banks 400 miles southwest of Pensacola, and bring in the catch preserved in ice. By 1916 some thirty-eight Greek-owned fishing vessels plied the Gulf Coast and their hard-working crews delivered fish to large packers based in Pensacola, such as E. E. Saunders, Pensacola Fish Company, Warren Fish Company, and the Gulf Fish Company. Overfishing depleted the great schools of snapper in the Gulf, especially off Campeche, and by the 1920s the fishermen left for Apalachicola, where fishing was more profitable, or for Tarpon Springs, where the sponge industry flourished.[69]

Fruit stands, small grocery stores, and sandwich shops came to life with even less capital than it took to acquire a small vessel to make a living netting shrimp or dredging for oysters in Escambia Bay. In 1910 Pensacola was a growing Gulf Coast city with a busy harbor and a population of nearly 40,000 people. The port was full of ships and hard-working stevedores unloading cotton, lumber, resin, turpentine, tobacco, and naval stores.[70] Moreover, the city was connected by railways to New Orleans, Montgomery, Birmingham, and other places further north. As in other busy and growing cities in the South, commercial niches opened up in the food and fruit sales, food preparation, and other small service businesses, which the Greek migrants learned to exploit. This economic opening, coupled with their tendency to work hard, use the family in the operation of the small business, and re-invest the earnings, provided these newcomers with financial independence. Success in business depended on their rapid adaptation to the local habits, and in turn, eased their entry into the local community. During the Gilded Age, in the late 1870s and 1880s, the first Greek migrants to the area, Constantine Apostolou Panagiotou, his brother Nicholas, and their nephew Paul Liollio, all from the Aegean island of Skopelos, operated a successful restaurant on Pensacola's South Palafox Street. The two brothers Americanized their surname to "Apostle." In 1887, Constantine Apostle was elected mayor of Pensacola for a one-year term.[71]

By 1910 the Greek immigrant community in Pensacola numbered some 120 people, including members of eight families, five resulting from mixed marriages. Leading members of this community incorporated an association for the purpose of buying a lot and building a church.[72] Names of the founding officers in the charter of the *Anagennisis* - Annunciation Greek Association included those prominent since the earliest days of Hellenic presence on the Gulf Coast, such as

Apostle, Cassimus, Gekas, and Stamatiou.[73] By August of 1910 the trustees completed the church building, dedicated to the Annunciation of the Theotokos, and in summer of 1911 they found and hired a permanent priest, Father Joakim Georges.[74] Unlike in most other Greek parishes, once the church was built, the congregants showed less than enthusiastic support for it. Annual dues amounted to six dollars, and the young treasurer, Victor Bokas, had to visit stores and homes three and four times a month, to collect the fifty cents membership fee.[75]

In two other respects the Pensacola Greeks had a different experience in adapting to their new environment than Greeks in other southern cities. One exception to the good relations Greek merchants had with the local folks in general was their poor standing with the Pensacola police. The officers were notorious for going into stores and helping themselves to cigars, cigarettes, and other items. On the other hand, the police received numerous complaints about the two Greek coffee shops on Baylen Street. There, Greek fishermen and their compatriots who sold fruit and operated small businesses drank cups of sweet, thick black coffee, vigorously discussed politics, and often gambled. Gambling was not only illegal, but the Greeks engaged in it were often very vocal. Residents complained to the police about noise, and in one raid thirty-five Greeks were arrested for gambling and fined five dollars each.[76] Only an increase in the fine, from five to fifty dollars, discouraged the gamblers; the noisy coffee houses converted to common eating establishments which kept regular hours. Pensacola was also the only place where the Ku Klux Klan ran a Greek restaurant owner out of town. The next chapter deals with the Greeks' response to a revived Klan, but the following incident demonstrates how far its tentacles reached. According to the Pensacola Journal of July 9, 1921, on the previous day three cars with hooded figures stopped at Chris Lochas' Riverside Café on Tarragona Street; the robed men entered the Café, handed him a note, and drove off. The note read:

> You are an undesirable alien. You violate the federal prohibition laws, the laws of decency, and you are a running sore on society. Several trains are leaving Pensacola daily. Take your choice, but don't take too much time. Sincerely, in earnest, K.K.K.

Lochas took the incident seriously, after all, the captain of the Pensacola police was a good customer at Riverside Café, but when told of the incident, he made no attempt to intervene. Chris Lochas prudently closed his restaurant and took a holiday with friends in Mobile, Alabama. The Pensacola Klan may have had a specific reason for picking on Chris Lochas or perhaps some of the Pensacola Greeks were not able or skillful enough to show that they were "white" and "100 percent American" as other compatriots did. Ted Carageorge thought that Greeks in Pensacola indeed adapted slower than elsewhere in the South, because there were many Skopelitans here, who maintained very strong ties with their home island. Many returned there to retire, after a lifetime in Pensacola, thus retaining a divided loyalty for most of their adult lives. For example, Nicholas Geeker, very active in the community in the 1930s, returned to Skopelos to retire, taking one of his four sons back with him. Geeker's wife and three sons, however, chose to stay in Pensacola.[77] Carageorge's assertion that not many Greek immigrants from Skopelos chose to settle permanently in the United States was not reflected in fewer applications for citizenship; however, the Daphne chapter #296 of the Order of AHEPA, the fraternal organization formed in Atlanta in 1922 and devoted to "Americanizing" Greek newcomers, did not form in Pensacola until April 1934.[78]

Mobile, Alabama represents another "New South" city where Greek migrants typically both exploited and aided contemporary growth and development. A small number of Greek immigrants settled in Mobile in the last decades of the nineteenth century. They were joined by Greek sailors, who simply jumped ship in the harbor and stayed in the city. Typically, they started their own businesses and attracted others. The Mobile parish produced a well designed and most informative *75th Anniversary [Album] of the Annunciation Greek Orthodox Church*, with a comprehensive history not only of the parish but of a number of Mobile's Greek-American families. Invariably, the family histories confirm the tendency for self-employment and the resulting economic and social upward mobility.[79] Constantine Gus Santis immigrated to America in 1890, when he was nineteen, saved money from his tips working as a boot black in New Orleans, and in 1900 moved to Mobile. There he opened the "Post Office Café" near the First National Bank, close to the corner of North Royal and Dauphin Streets. Evidently the café became well known during the early part of the century, when many Greek newcomers to Mobile worked there as waiters and cooks before opening their own businesses. In 1911 Santis married and in 1912 he became the first president of the newly formed Greek Orthodox *kinotis*.[80] In the same year, Louis Demetropoulos, one of the Post Office Café "graduates," married Lenora Dale Smith, daughter of the American timber man and sawmill owner Thomas Washington Smith. Louis purchased and added more land to thirteen acres inherited by Leonora, and built up "Ferndell Dairy and Farm" into a fleet of milk delivery trucks backed up by a herd of some 250 cattle.[81] Pete Semon, formerly Panayiotis Xirohimonas, owned a grocery store at the corner of South Washington Avenue and Charleston Streets. His brother John joined him as a clerk and also adopted Semon as his new surname. The store yielded a good living and even after Pete and a third brother, Mike retired to their native island of Skopelos, under John's ownership, it became one of the largest independently owned grocery stores in Mobile. Anastasios - Anthony Tattis came to Mobile in 1894; his bride Ellen joined him there in 1906; they owned and operated the very successful "Riverside Café" on South Royal Street until his untimely death in 1929, when his son Anthony and Mrs. Tattis continued the restaurant business. Both Mr. and Mrs. Tattis hailed from the island of Kastellorizo, where in 1906 their families entered into the customary marriage contract, outlining in detail the dower Ellen would bring into her marriage with Anastasios.[82] James George Andreades from the island of Chios arrived in Mobile in 1908, and became a successful restaurateur, as did Nick Costarides, Paul Costarides, Sotiris Griffin, and William Pappas.[83] Manuel and Argero Clikas raised their clan of eight children with moneys derived from a confectionery business.[84]

One can reasonably estimate Mobile's Greek migrant population in 1910 at about 250 people.[85] In the summer of 1912, the candy shop owners, soda fountain and fruit store operators and sundry lunch counter, restaurant, and small business proprietors formed a *kinotis*, the "Greek Orthodox Brotherhood of the Annunciation." The *Mobile Register* of July 12, 1912, reported that "much enthusiasm was displayed" at a meeting "of over 150 representatives of the Mobile colony of Greeks" who formed the "Greek Orthodox Society" whose "object is to be the establishment of a Greek Orthodox church in Mobile as soon as sufficient funds can be secured."[86]

Mobile's Greeks had formed the "Greek Orthodox Community of the Annunciation" as early as 1912. In 1927 the parishioners purchased this building on Government and Dearborn Streets from the First Christian Church. Services of the Annunciation Greek Orthodox Church were held there until 1962. Photo from USA Archives, reproduced in the 1912-1987 Anniversary Album of the Church. Courtesy of Father Dean Gigicos, Sophie Clikas, and Nick Costarides, Mobile, 1992.

In fact, it took another fourteen years to secure enough funds to rent space on the second floor of the Merchants' Bank, on St. Francis and Water Streets, and to organize regular church services by hiring a permanent priest. By carefully reading the abstract of the "official minute book of the community," one can detect strong conflicts that must have plagued the community from 1915 on and well into the 1930s.[87] The disagreements arose from the divided loyalties caused by an emotional and wrenching political power struggle in Greece, waged between King Constantine and his supporters against prime minister Eleftherios Venizelos and his republican adherents.[88] More details of the conflict and its effects on the Greek churches in America will be discussed elsewhere in this dissertation. Only in Mobile did one see a community growth pattern different, and slower, than in the other southern cities. Available sources indicate there may have been just the right mix within the Greek community to form two rather evenly divided sides. As the community split along the Venizelist - royalist line, only a few votes caused sometimes one and sometimes the other side to take the decision-making positions in the *kinotis*. Despite the unquestionable interest Greeks in other southern communities must have had for the situation back home, they managed to keep tuned into the American environment, rather than into the Old World strife and animosities. "Over-attachment" and "absorption" with affairs back in Greece may have been one of the causes for acute differences within the Mobile community, but in part the conflict could have radiated from the stubborn independent personalities of leading members, who refused to submerge their personal opinions into the common cause of the *kinotis*.[89] In time, common interests prevailed and in 1961 Mobile's Greek Orthodox community built its large new church on South Anne Street.

Annunciation Greek Orthodox Church in Mobile, Alabama, drawn by Elaine Clikas of Mobile, for the 25th Clergy Laity Congress Commemorative Year Book. Congress held in 1980 in Atlanta. Courtesy of Father Homer P. Goumenis, Dean, Greek Orthodox Cathedral of the Annunciation, Atlanta.

A closer look at the early Greek immigrants to the South reveals that they were mostly men, individuals who had first spent some time in northern or midwestern urban and industrial areas.[90] After a year or two, perhaps with a modest stake put away, they opted for a fresh start, aware of the ongoing expansion and optimistic future outlook in numerous southern cities. A combination of interconnected circumstances worked to their advantage and made their efforts by and large successful beyond expectations. Both the migrants and the places they migrated to contributed to the aggregate conditions for success. Atlanta, Jacksonville, Mobile, and other New South cities offered exceptional urban growth. Greek newcomers took advantage of the burgeoning population to find economic niches for themselves, particularly in businesses that required little money to start. As evidenced by the 1900 and 1910 federal censuses, the *Greek-American Directory*, annual city directories, and various community year-books, Greek migrants started businesses that required minimal financing and permitted them to earn a living initially even with sparse knowledge of English. Over the previous decade or two, the pattern for such mini-businesses had already been established by the Greeks in Chicago and New York. A fruit vendor, for example, could operate either from a cart or from a small leased space. The only required skills were those enabling the entrepreneur to purchase from a wholesaler fruit that was neither too green nor too ripe, to display it attractively, and to sell it at a profitable price the same day. Similarly, the quick lunch and sandwich vendors succeeded by daily selling out all the ingredients purchased at the wholesalers.[91] Bootblacks with shoe-shine stands needed almost no starting capital and hardly any knowledge of English. If longer working hours could increase sales, some of the operators worked longer, then rented better and bigger space, and hired help, usually family members or compatriots.

Unlike in cities with large Greek communities, where most of their patrons were Greeks, the merchants dealt almost exclusively with native local clientage. Daily contact with American customers presented the need and the opportunity to learn better English and imitate local habits. The more the vendors and operators pleased their buying public, the more buyers they attracted and the better they fared financially. Thus quite a few Greek fruit and sandwich vendors, bootblacks, and confectioners parlayed their small investments into busy and lucrative fruit stores, restaurants, ice cream parlors, and shoe and hat cleaning shops. Merchants often purchased the buildings they leased and created the base for better credit and more business. Newly arrived compatriots found work in the already established businesses, absorbed the know-how, gained experience, and in turn started their own undertakings. Selected family members back in Greece, brothers, uncles, and nephews received boat-fare and instructions to come on the understanding they would join the enterprise. Even wives were drafted to assist in the shops, and in larger establishments, depending on the trade, there was also white or black American help.

Perhaps the major and most consequential regional difference between the northern and southern cities was the pervasive existence of African Americans in the South. They anchored the bottom rungs on the social and economic ladder and routinely drew off the stereotypical dislike members of the dominant society might otherwise have had for Greek, Italian, or other immigrants. Unlike in northern cities, the significant presence of blacks tended to raise white immigrants to the next rung, thus easing their entry into the social and commercial circles of the white society. These dynamics, in addition to economic opportunity, may have presented an additional appeal for Greeks to migrate South.[92] Moreover, Greeks were not reluctant to seek opportunities and open quick lunch restaurants and other businesses in black areas. To the extent that most Greek immigrants were self-employed, there existed minimal competition between them and their black neighbors for any specific economic niche. Commercial conditions surely influenced social accommodations. Unlike African Americans, Greek merchants found they could ply their trades both in white or black areas of town. *Adallis' Greek Merchants' Reference Book and Business Guide* (ca. 1912), listed a number of businesses in Atlanta, Jacksonville, and other cities, with a specific notation "for colored," or "colored district."

As employers, Greeks tended to hire relatives or other Greeks first. However, quite a few Greek entrepreneurs hired black workers, who labored side by side with Greek help.[93] Physical proximity, however, did not bring about intergroup solidarity.[94] Although Greek immigrants were not familiar with segregation back home, and their daily contacts with African Americans on the whole remained friendly, they learned very quickly of the limitations that a Jim Crow society imposed on their lives. Just as the Greeks did not reside in black areas, neither did they live next to each other. Unlike in Chicago, New York or other industrial towns, the number of Greek migrants southward never reached such proportions that they could form a "Greektown" or even occupy contiguous blocks along a street. Except for a few men living in the same rooming house, Greek migrants to southern cities resided in the same general district commensurate with their income, but usually well mixed with other white folks. As Greek acculturation proceeded and contacts with the larger white community acquired some depth, Greeks imitated the attitudes of other whites in accepting the racial codes of the dominant society. Businesses provided most Greek merchants with steady earnings, so that their incomes were not conspicuously different from native-born Americans with an income in the middling range. Thus even their skin color helped a large proportion of the first generation Greek migrants to the southern cities to achieve economic progress.

The Greeks integrated relatively easily in the South not only because of their moderate numbers but also because their relative economic stability enhanced and speeded up the establishment of normal family life. Married men brought over their wives from Greece, and the single ones either traveled back to marry or married by proxy and conducted their brides to a home in the New World. Marriages to American women tended to amplify the adaptation of the newcomers and their acceptance by the host society. Nearly 15 percent of Atlanta's Greeks and 25 percent of Jacksonville's Greeks were married in 1910.[95] Compared to the situation in northern cities, Greek family formation in the South was well on the way much earlier. Scourby's research in the North indicated that only when they began arriving in greater numbers, "in the 1920s the presence of Greek women in America made it possible for the male immigrant to think of [America] as a permanent home."[96] Mixed marriages, very rare in the North, were certainly not uncommon in the South. Of the seventeen Greeks who had already married and settled with their families in Jacksonville by 1910, five had married Anglo-American women and the remainder brought wives from the old country. In Atlanta as well, there were six mixed marriages among thirty-three families. Similar proportions of intermarriage existed in most southern cities. Greater exposure to the host culture, and middle class occupations that enhanced acceptance by women of the host society, as well as the men's desire to make a home in the New World, may present likely explanations for the occurrence of exogamous marriages.[97]

Although Greek wives who joined the husbands in the New World confirmed the family's intention to stay here, these wives invariably also delayed the use of English at home. Greek women typically stayed at home and took care of the house and children. Except for those few who helped in their husbands' enterprises, they were slow to learn English. In fact, most of these women learned English only when their own children attended public school.[98] In contrast, Greek men and youngsters encountered customers and school friends daily and these contacts enabled rapid acquisition of English language skills. Of course, households with an English-speaking mother and wife, like the Brown [formerly Bracatzas] household, assumed American ways quicker than those with a Greek-speaking mother.[99]

Whether their adaptation to the New World's different environs proceeded at an accelerated or a retarded rate, a consistent theme in the study of Greek-American social history has been upward mobility or embourgeoisment.[100] Most works place the beginning of this process in the decade of the 1920s. For example, in the 1920s Greek immigrants in the West "moved from the ranks of manual labor to become proprietors of the confectionery stores, flower shops, restaurants, and shoe-shine parlors."[101] In Milwaukee, Wisconsin, Greek immigrants arrived in significant numbers around 1905. Some Greeks worked in tanneries owned by German families, others labored in iron and steel mills, in restaurants as dishwashers and waiters, and in factories of various types. Residents organized the Greek Orthodox Church in Milwaukee in 1906, and some 2,000 Greeks lived in that city in 1912. Even though this population grew over the next decade, by 1920 only about eighty small grocery stores, confectionery shops, coffeehouses, restaurants and shoe-shine parlors had Greek proprietors."[102] In Lowell, Massachusetts, and other places in New England, a flood of Greeks sought jobs in the textile mills. As many as 8,000 Greek immigrants resided in Lowell around 1912, a total exceeded only by the sizable communities in Chicago and New York. "The majority of [Lowell] Greek immigrants found menial jobs in the cotton textile mills and remained there for their entire working lives." A few men left the mills and went into their own businesses during the 1920s but not before.[103] When he wrote about the Greeks of Milwaukee, historian Theodore Saloutos confirmed the cultural inheritance they brought with them from the Mediterranean. Saloutos described the "average Greek" as a "natural-born competitor with a determination to succeed, and to whom "nothing was quite as reprehensible as bringing shame to the family name."[104] But unlike their compatriots elsewhere in the states, only those who migrated to the South found the combination of conditions that led to their early economic and social gains.

Of all the northern cities, by 1910, New York and Chicago had the largest concentrations of Greek immigrants, 20,000 and 15,000 respectively.[105] In Chicago, prominent enterprises attracting Greeks were the confectionery trade and shoe-shine parlors, followed by restaurants.[106] Adding sundry other operations owned by the Greeks, one arrives at a tally of 1,024 businesses. In addition, about 2,000 itinerant fruit peddlers plied their trade in the streets of Chicago, some making upwards of $10 a day. The ratio of Greek-owned businesses, excluding the itinerant vendors, to the total Greek population was 1:14.[107] One 1909 New York survey reported 716 Greek-owned businesses in that city, making the ratio of Greek business-owners to Greek immigrants 1:28.[108] These figures are comparable to the ratio of 1:14 in Boston, 1:23 in Philadelphia, and 1:21 in Milwaukee.[109] Clearly, the proportion of self-employed Greeks to those working for wages was far below that of Jacksonville. In 1910, the River City possessed 63 Greek-owned businesses and a total of 113 Greek immigrants; Atlanta counted 131 Greek enterprises and a Greek community of 446 people, with respective ratios of 1:2 and 1:3.[110] Because of their ability to find relatively uncluttered economic niches for their businesses, Greeks in the South appear not to have engendered competitive animosities from native businessmen. By way of contrast, Greek merchants in northern cities often "incurred the wrath of the non-Greek engaged in a similar enterprise."[111] In at least one situation a native New York businessman advertised "John's Restaurant, Pure American. No Rats, No Greeks."[112] In Milwaukee, Saloutos found "prejudice toward Greek restaurant proprietor[s]" to be "more fact than fancy." He remembered at least one short-order restaurant in his home-town which had a bold sign announcing "Operated by an American."[113]

Such animus may have been caused by the Greeks' resistance and disinclination to adapt to the dominant culture. In northern cities Greeks were numerically strong and felt neither the need nor the pressure to conform quickly. In contrast, substantial numbers of Greeks in southern cities had promptly acquired "American" speech and manners, especially if they had settled in places where few of their compatriots lived. Talking about parents who had settled in the South by 1910, several second-generation Greek Americans claim that except for some individual acts of discrimination, southerners accepted Greeks to a remarkable degree, as neighbors and as fellow businessmen.[114] Adaptation of speech, manners, and outward behavior on the part of so many Greeks engaged in business, however, may have only represented adjustments common to all entrepreneurs anxious to please customers rather than a deep-seated desire to accommodate to American norms.

Milton Gordon concluded that cultural assimilation, or accultura-tion, occurred with little delay among immigrants in the United States.[115] Immigrants changed their manners, language, dress styles, and recreational activities to fit those of the dominant culture. But the deeper and more important realm of structural assimilation, which involved the entry of individual newcomers into primary social groups and organizations, ultimately leading to intermarriage, did not occur quickly or easily, resulting in a persistence of structural pluralism. Gordon's concept of assimilation assumed a nearly static dominant society, to which the various immigrant groups adapted in stages, virtu-ally in a straight line process. His model did not prove helpful in explaining the diversity of Greek immigrant experiences in different regions of the United States, or in justifying the retention of some cultural traditions despite the more rapid "structural assimilation" of Greeks in the South. Gordon's concept has been overshadowed by the work of a number of other historians. Nathan Glazer and Daniel Moynihan attempted to explain the persistence of ethnicity by way of an analysis of five ethnic groups in New York City.[116] They suggested that ethnic groups were not only a source of individual identity, they had also become *interest groups* by which people sought to defend or advance their positions in society. As outlined in Chapter 1 of this work, more recent immigration historians espoused a compatible but more complex view.[117] According to Rudolph Vecoli, after immigrants arrived, they did not shed their culture and traditions. Rather, they proceeded to preserve them as much as the new environment would tolerate. Immigrants engaged in a dynamic process of selective adaptation that included resistance as well as accommodation to the dominant society. In Vecoli's view, American culture sought to shape immigrants, but in trying to do so, the dominant culture itself was also affected and changed by immigrants and their children. Immigrants and their offspring "did not become Americans; rather they became ethnic Americans."[118] Thus the dominant society itself eventually became expressive of the pluralistic, polyglot population that inhabits the United States. The diverse experiences of the Greek immigrant group in America are best understood when explicated by these recent theories.

Those Greeks who migrated southward around the turn of the century and their cohorts who followed them within its first decade, adapted to the southern host society in a relatively short period of time and with comparatively little difficulty. The lack of a large number of compatriots residing nearby, the exposure of Greek immigrants to daily contact with American customers and neighbors, and the pressure to succeed, probably hastened their adjustment to the new environment. Early photographs of local Greek businessmen in well-fitting American suits and straw hats, imitating postures of their American colleagues, their biographical sketches, the changes of polysyllabic Greek names, and the WPA interviews with George Stathis, Cecelia Poulos, and others all provide evidence that Greek newcomers in Atlanta, Jacksonville, Charleston, Savannah, and other southern cities adjusted quickly to the distinct local environment. Such adjustments clearly led to better relations with customers, and ultimately to higher income. These changes could have been motivated by the simple desire to do well in business, accumulate some savings, and to eventually return home. Other, additional factors, however, suggest that these adaptations were more permanent and enduring. When family formation, mixed marriages, name changing patterns, and home acquisitions are considered, a different interpretation emerges. Greek newcomers "of the right kind" soon joined American fraternal orders such as the Elks, the Odd Fellows, Freemasons, Kiwanis, Rotary, Woodmen of the World, and others.[119] While they were included in the fraternal and social life of the host society, at the same time they tried to preserve and maintain transplanted cultural traditions, such as the language and religious practices. Indeed, as Vecoli asserted, the Greeks in the South demonstrated both an acceptance of the host society's culture and way of life, as well as a resistance to it.

Some Greeks who migrated to southern cities demonstrated how much they wished to settle there permanently by the Americanization of their names. Venerable first names like Constantinos and Vasilios mutated into Gus and Bill; Demetrios invariably became Jimmy.[120] Mere contractions of the original name or surname may have equally indicated the desire to be less embarrassed by its length or by the difficulty of pronunciation for Americans. Such temporary accommodations could be discarded when one returned home. However, when the Greek name changed to a wholly English one, the desire to assimilate and completely conceal national origins can be imputed with more conviction. Typical examples, of which there is an abundance in the South, were hotel owner George Brown, saloon owner James Pope, fruit vendor Peter George, ice cream manufacturer George Moore, and others.[121]

Historian Richard Clogg has a theory about changes of names, especially surnames, which holds that name changes by immigrant settlers are only evident when they settle in a society which accepts them to such an extent that a blending takes place. For example, in Germany, where Greeks have been trading and living for over two centuries, no name changes have occurred, because the host society has never allowed Greek settlers to blend in, no matter how few there were or how long they were there.[122] According to Clogg, name changes signify the desire not to stand out, the desire to be an integral part of the host society. However, where the host society is not conducive to the blending process, name changes become useless. Blending is a process very different from the mere friendly acceptance of newcomers by the host society. For example, Clogg pointed out that a number of wealthy Greek merchants in Manchester and Liverpool, such as the Rallis brothers, who were very successful cotton merchants originally from the island of Chios, mingled with the upper class of English society in the 1850s. Although accepted on socio-economic terms, and so part of the English elite, the Rallis brothers never blended into it, never actually became Englishmen of Greek origin, as the Greek businessmen in the southern United States became Americans of Greek origin. On the other end of the scale, there were krypto-Greeks, as well as krypto-Jews in Ottoman Turkey, where one could not be part of the elite unless one blended in and hid or disguised one's origins. To be sure, no matter how good their English or their manners, no Greek could blend into the old southern families, but at a lower level, Greeks in the American South could blend into the local middle-class population.

Displaying another sign of the desire to settle permanently in the South, Greek immigrants engaged in American political activity earlier than their fellow Greeks in northern cities. While most northern Greek communities remained very concerned with political affairs in Greece, southern Greeks avoided intense interest in old country conflicts and they soon shed their commitment to Greek politics and became interested in local issues.[123] As the situation in Mobile demonstrated, there were exceptions to every rule. Sam Felos, son of one of the earliest Greek immigrants to Jacksonville and himself now retired, thought that before 1918 all Greeks in Jacksonville voted Democratic. During this period, no Republican Party organization existed in the city. Atlanta born insurance agency owner Victor Poulos thought that those Greeks who became citizens after 1890 may have disliked William J. Bryan and the National Democratic Party, but they voted Democratic anyway, simply because that was the party of the South.[124] Although Democratic administrations were generally friendlier to immigrants than Republican ones, Felos added that the pro-Democratic leanings of Greek citizens in Jacksonville evolved more strongly from their desire to fit into the political ambience of the wider community than from any espousal of Jeffersonian or Jacksonian ideals.

Although by the 1920s many southern Greek families spoke English at home and copied the appearance of their American neighbors, they nevertheless preserved a number of Greek traditions. They maintained them, however, in a form that had evolved and changed over the course of years. The Greek Orthodox Church, for example, undoubtedly shaped and perpetuated ethnic cohesion, just as the Judaic faith and traditions did for Jewish Americans. But the church adapted to the host society. On the one hand the control and structure of the Greek Orthodox hierarchy could not be duplicated in the New World, and on the other hand the faithful impelled changes at the level of individual communities. In contrast to customs in Greece, lay people in the United States had absolute control over the finances and property of each congregation. The priest and the hierarchy of the religious institution did not decide on the dues, the budget, the handling of physical assets, and the extent of the outreach programs. The new financial arrangements represented but one of the changes in the practice of Greek Orthodoxy in America. Other adjustments and the evolution of the church, particularly in the South, are treated in more detail in chapter three of this work.

In the 1920s, when the flow of fresh immigrants from Greece had ceased, in a number of southern cities Hellenic communities found it necessary to establish church-related parochial or afternoon schools for Greek-American children. Parents wanted organized instruction in Greek for their children. Evidently, even if both parents were of Greek origin and spoke Greek at home, their children were not picking up any of the ancestral language and culture. Instruction took place during the usual school months, according to restaurateur George Stathis, "for two hours each school day after the regular session of the public school [was] over."[125] A teacher hired by the parents taught the children to speak and read Greek and instructed them in Hellenic history. Often the priest would add religious instruction to the simple curriculum. Stathis explained in a 1939 WPA interview that the intention of the first generation parents was to preserve some Greek heritage since the children were not expected to return to Greece. Cecelia Poulos confided to WPA - Writers' Project interviewer Lillian Stedman in 1939 that Greek families sent their children to Greek school because they could learn more Greek there than at home, since "we do not speak so much Greek in our homes [after] everybody in the house [has] learned English."[126]

Another example of the complex dual desires of Greeks who settled in the southern states to fit into their chosen environment as well as to adapt selected traditions is embodied in the establishment of the American Hellenic Educational and Progressive Association (AHEPA). As outlined in another chapter, this fraternal organization was formed in Atlanta, Georgia, and dedicated to the idea of permanent residence and citizenship in America. The stated primary aims of the AHEPA, incorporated in Atlanta in 1922, were to bridge the gap between Americans and Greek immigrants and to help the latter absorb American culture rapidly through contacts, naturalization, and other appropriate means. Members were to learn about and to participate in American life and American democracy. On the one hand, AHEPA members proudly pointed out that Democracy had its beginning in classical Greece. On the other hand, AHEPA rules established English as the official language for all meetings and business affairs. Membership was not limited to Greeks, but was open to anyone who believed in God and desired to promote the Hellenic, and now American, ideas of freedom and democracy. AHEPA's first chapter formed in Atlanta, and within months supporters banded together to form chapters throughout the South.[127] Not all Greeks were eager to join; Angelopoulos explained that although the Americanism of AHEPA moderated prejudice against foreigners, some Greek Americans criticized the organization for neglecting the national heritage.

As happened with other groups, and generally in accord with the interpretation of immigrant adaptation expressed by authors of the landmark article "Invention of Ethnicity: A Perspective From the U. S. A.," Greeks created ethnic customs to preserve and enhance the group image. Rooted in old-world traditions, but strongly influenced by the experiences of subsequent generations in the host country, the transplanted, enduring, and perpetually adapted Greek American ethnic culture and traditions informed "the third and fourth generation and beyond."[128] Examples of this "new ethnicity" abound. One only has to remember the St. Patrick's Day celebrations, Oktoberfests, Columbus Day parades, and the revived Scottish Highland games. More pertinent here are the Greek Festivals—two or three day fairs exhibiting Greek food, music, and history—which were not known in the South until well into the 1960s, when they became an ubiquitous practice, indeed a "tradition" in every southern city with a Greek *kinotis*.[129]

A survey of the major contours of Greek communities in the southern states suggests that the Greek experience in these places fits the typical "southern variant" pattern described by Moskos. The general thrust of Greek immigrant seasoning, like that found with other ethnic groups in America, was a persistent drive toward embourgeoisment. However, in northern and midwestern urban industrial areas, densely settled Greektowns slowed acculturation and enabled the formation of sub-groups based on sectional differences that produced political and cultural feuds and factionalism. In contrast, numerically smaller Greek immigrant communities in southern cities avoided the formation of such limiting enclaves and accelerated the social adaptation of immigrants to an altering and growing host society. A more rapid adaptation by newcomers in turn enhanced the acceptance of individual immigrants by the larger community. Turn-of-the-century Greek immigrants in Atlanta and Savannah, Birmingham and Mobile, Pensacola, Charleston, Charlotte and Raleigh were able to follow their preference and to utilize individual commercial endeavors to earn a living. The presence of distinctive marriage patterns, unobtrusive yet vibrant ethnic communities, comfortable homes in middle class neighborhoods, and the rapid inclusion of Greeks into the business, social, and political life of the wider society all suggest that Greek newcomers adapted to the southern states in special ways. Greeks in the South achieved moderate prosperity and upward mobility decades earlier than their compatriots elsewhere in the United States. One could indeed maintain that Greek immigrants first began to transform into Greek Americans in the South, and that their advancement in the southern cities represented not only the southern variant, but also the paradigm of the wider immigrant experience in America, which followed similar patterns one or more generations later.

Notes

1   In December, 1886, Henry W. Grady, editor of the *Atlanta Constitution*, addressed the New England Society of New York and set forth the vision and creed of the "New South." The "Old South rested everywhere on slavery and agriculture," he said, but "the New South presents a perfect democracy, the oligarchs leading in the popular movement - a social system compact and closely knitted, less splendid on the surface, but stronger at the core - a hundred farms for every plantation, fifty homes for every palace - and a diversified industry that meets the complex need for this complex age." Quoted in Vincent P. DeSantis, *The Shaping of Modern America: 1877-1920*, 2nd ed. (Arlington Heights, Ill., Forum Press, 1989), 32-33. Although Grady's vision never fully materialized, great strides were apparent, such as improvements in transportation, growth of urban population in a number of cities, and the development of industry and commerce.

2   Charles Moskos, "Ethnic Life - The Greeks," in Charles R. Wilson and William Ferris eds., *Encyclopedia of Southern Culture* (Chapel Hill, University of North Carolina Press, 1989), 431.

3   Rudolph J. Vecoli provides a historiographic introduction to this concept of adaptation in "European Americans: From Immigrants to Ethnics," in William H. Cartwright and Richard L. Watson eds., *The Reinterpretation of American History and Culture*, (Washington, D.C., National Council for the Social Studies, 1973), 81-112.

4   Writers' Project, Georgia, *Atlanta, a City of the Modern South* (Atlanta, Atlanta Board of Education, 1942), 31.

5   Among the many new and old products manufactured, note the advent in 1887 of J. S. Pemberton's soft drink "Coca-Cola." Writers' Program, Georgia, *Atlanta, City of the Modern South*, 60.

6   Franklin M. Garrett, *Yesterday's Atlanta* (Miami, Seemann Publishing, 1974), 43.

7   Ibid., 43.

8   *Twelfth Census of the United States, 1900* (Washington, D.C., Government

Printing Office, 1911), Abstract sheets for Atlanta, Fulton County, Georgia.

9   Writers' Program, *Atlanta, a City of the Modern South*, 30-33, 52-53. Atlanta's population according to U.S. Census figures:
     1880 = 37,409, 1900 = 89,872,
     1890 = 65,533, 1910 = 154,839.

10   Dionisys Adallis, *Adallis' Greek Merchants' Reference Book and Business Guide - Atlanta* (n.p., 1911), 26. Original book in possession of Mrs. Mary Farmakis, Atlanta. Copy with author.

11   See Tables 2 and 3. The 1910 (Thirteenth) Federal Census shows a total of 340 Greek immigrant adult males in Atlanta, of whom 125 (37%) were self-employed. Another 121 men worked as waiters and cooks in restaurants, while about 75 Greeks clerked at soda fountains, fruit and grocery stores, made candy, and attended other service businesses all owned by their Greek relatives and compatriots.

12   Adallis, *Adallis' Greek Merchants' Reference Book and Business Guide - Atlanta*, 49

13   Ibid., 48

14   *Twelfth Census of the United States, 1900*, Atlanta, Fulton County.

15   *Greek Orthodox Church of the Annunciation Fiftieth Anniversary Album, 1905-1955* (Atlanta, n.p., 1955), contains some history and a photograph of George Moore. See Table 4.

16   Ibid., also see *Adallis' Greek Merchants' Reference Book - Atlanta*, 7; in 1920, Sparks sold all his movie theaters, and founded The Hotel and Restaurant Supply Company, which he later described as "the oldest and only restaurant supply house in Atlanta to survive under same management the crisis of Depression."

17   *Kinotis* translates into "community" in a secular sense and "congregation" or "parish" if it is a religious public body. In America members of the *kinotis* usually pledge money for the acquisition and maintenance of the church building and to pay the priest, so the *kinotis* served mainly religious purposes although its members often organized social functions as well. Note also that a Greek Orthodox parish includes all the Orthodox faithful who come to that church, even if some of them are not members of the organized *kinotis*; see Appendix 2, which traces the early *kinotites* (plural) in various southern cities, leading to the founding of Greek Orthodox churches.

18   Saloutos, *The Greeks in the United States*, 118.

19   *25th Biennial Clergy-Laity Congress of the Greek Orthodox Archdiocese of North and South America* [commemorative album] (Atlanta, n.p., 1980), 72-73; Mrs. Mary Farmakis [daughter of Gerasimos Algers] oral interview with the author, in Atlanta, June 26, 1992; G. Algers [and partner L. Campbell owned the Blue Seal Ice Cream Company on 23 Peters Street, Atlanta, see Dionysos Adallis, *Adallis' Greek Merchants' Reference Book and Business Guide - Atlanta*, 5, 20. Other Board members were businessmen Constantine

Boutos, Constantine [uncle Charlie] Charalambides, Christos Kotsakos, Nicholas Kouloukes, John Stavropoulos, and Constantine Verghiotes [Gus Verge].

20 *Greek Orthodox Church of the Annunciation, Atlanta, 50th Anniversary Album*; also Commemorative album of the *25th Biennial Clergy-Laity Congress*, 73-75.

21 Robert F. Harney, "Religion and Ethnocultural Communities," *Polyphony* 1 (Summer 1978): 3. Men also met in the *kafenio*-coffee shop. Three were listed in the Adallis *Reference Book*; Also see *Greek Orthodox Church of the Annunciation - Dedication* (Atlanta, n.p., December 20, 1970): in 1928, the community purchased a Jewish Temple on Pryor Street; after additions and changes the building became the "new" Greek Orthodox Church of the Annunciation in Atlanta, until the ever-growing Greek Orthodox community replaced it too, in 1967, with a magnificent structure of 12,650 sq. feet, on 2500 Clairmont Rd.

22 James Esgate, *Jacksonville, the Metropolis of Florida*, cited in James B. Crooks, *Jacksonville After the Fire, 1901-1919: A New South City* (Jacksonville, Florida, University of North Florida Press, 1991), 8.

23 S. Paul Brown, *The Book of Jacksonville: A History*, cited in Crooks, *Jacksonville After the Fire*, 9.

24 T. Frederick Davis, *History of Jacksonville and Vicinity* (Gainesville, University of Florida Press, 1964), 500. Jacksonville's population by decennial Census (excluding suburbs beyond city limits):
1890 = 17,201   1920 = 91,558
1900 = 28,492   1930 = 130,381
1910 = 57,699   1940 = 173,065

25 Crooks, *Jacksonville After the Fire*, 7. The 28,429 residents in the 1900 Census outnumbered the 17,747 people living in Pensacola, 17,114 in Key West, 15,839 in Tampa, 2,841 in Orlando, or 1,681 in recently incorporated Miami.

26 Works Progress Administration (WPA), Writers' Program, Florida, "Biographical Sketches of Greeks in Jacksonville" (the P. K. Yonge Library of Florida History, University of Florida, Gainesville), Gus Panos oral interview by Lillian Stedman, 1939, and George Stathis oral interview by Rose Shepherd, August, 1939.

27 See Table 6. By 1910 the city became the terminus of 8 railroad systems, 5 steamship lines that provided direct access to Baltimore, Philadelphia, New York, and Boston. In the same year Jacksonville boasted of 9 banks, 48 churches, over 15 miles of streetcar tracks, and one enviable railroad bridge in addition to ferries which took passengers to the "South side," across the St. Johns River.

28 See Table 6.

29 Dio Adallis, *Adallis' Greek-American Merchants' Reference Book and Business Guide - Jacksonville* (Atlanta, n.p., ca. 1912), 17.

30   Despite inquiries, records of this society have apparently not survived. See Adallis, *Adallis' Greek Merchants' Reference Book and Business Guide - Jacksonville*, 6.

31   Adallis, *Adallis' Greek Merchants' Reference Book and Business Guide - Jacksonville*, 9.

32   *Thirteenth Census of the US, 1910*, Manuscript for Duval County, Florida; also see Table 5. In Greek-American families the husbands were born in Greece, with American wives born in Alabama and South Carolina, and in one case in Scotland.

33   In Jacksonville, just as in Atlanta and other southern cities (except Tarpon Springs) Greeks clustered first in one general area, then in another, more prosperous one, but never formed a "Greektown" or ghetto. For Atlanta see Ronald Bayor, "Ethnic Residential Patterns in Atlanta, 1880-1940," paper presented at the Georgia Institute of Technology, Atlanta, Georgia.

34   See Table 6; the combined 1910 census manuscripts, the 1911 Jacksonville city directory, and the 1911 *Adallis' Greek Merchants' Reference Book and Business Guide*, Jacksonville section, recorded 63 Greek-owned businesses, including 30 fruit and grocery stores, and 18 restaurants.

35   Saloutos outlined how a "Greektown" in Omaha, Nebraska, invited nativist resentment. One violent incident started when a policeman stopped a Greek on a date with an American girl. The men exchanged words, fought, and the Greek stabbed the policeman. Within hours there was an anti-Greek riot, and "South Omaha's Greek Town was burned down, driving 1,200 Greeks away;" see Theodore Saloutos, "Cultural Persistence and Change: Greeks in the Great Plains and Rocky Mountains West, 1890-1970," *Pacific Historical Review* 49 (February 1980): 85-86.

36   The family's income, as well as its residential and social mobility, served as a convenient definition of an upward movement from the low income ranks into the "middling" mainstream.

37   Costa Carantzas interview. Jerry Felos oral interview by the author in Jacksonville, Florida, April 4, 1990. John Pappas and George Pappas oral interview by the author in Jacksonville, Florida, December 18, 1995.

38   Duval County Circuit Court Public Records, document number 67277, recorded November 2, 1916.

39   Copies of the Jacksonville community charters of 1916 and 1921 are also preserved with the records of St. John the Divine Greek Orthodox Church, 3850 Atlantic Boulevard, Jacksonville.

40   In Eastern Orthodox churches the *iconostasis* is a partition with doors and rows of icons that separates the sanctuary and altar from the nave - the main part of the church where the faithful stand. For a history of the building see Wayne W. Wood, *Jacksonville's Architectural Heritage* (Gainesville, n.p., 1989), 379. In 1968 the community built a larger church, on Atlantic Boulevard; its architectural design won an award for architect Ted Pappas.

41   Although Greek families settled in just about every town and city
      throughout the South, fast-growing urban areas attracted Greek migrants
      in numbers sufficient to form fraternal organizations and church parishes.
      The 1910 Census Manuscripts are, on the whole, lower than numbers
      quoted in Henry Fairchild, *Greek Immigration to the United States*, (Yale
      University Press, New Haven, 1911), 258-260; a 1910 estimated count of
      Greek migrants in some growing southern cities was:

Mobile, Alabama	350	Atlanta, Georgia	500
Tampa, Florida	120	Birmingham	500
Augusta	80	Pensacola	250
Elsey	300	Savannah	500
Jacksonville	150	Garsten	150
Charlotte, N.C.	100	Tarpon Springs	2,000
New Orleans, La.	300		

      Also see Table 1 (Chapter 1 - Introduction).

42   Gary Mormino and George Pozzetta, *The Immigrant World of Ybor City*
      (Urbana, University of Illinois Press, 1987), 322.

43   Charles Masterpolis oral interview by the author in Savannah, August 14,
      1992; Father Aris Metrakos oral interview by the author in Savannah,
      August 14, 1992.

44   *Sholes' Directory of the City of Savannah, 1900*, The Morning News Print,
      Savannah, Georgia; for "Fruits (Retail)" see pp. 863-864, for "Restaurants"
      see p.889.

45   Fannie A. Asselanis, "The Greek Community in Savannah," paper prepared
      for the Friends of the Library, April 19, 1977, 3-5.

46   "The Greek Orthodox Community" in *Official Journal of the 12th Biennial
      Ecclesiastical Congress of the Greek Orthodox Church of North and South
      America* (Savannah, Georgia, n.p., 1954), when St. Paul's of Savannah
      served as the host church; "The History of Our Parish" in *75th Anniversary
      of St. Paul's Greek Orthodox Church - Savannah, Georgia, 1907 - 1982*
      (Savannah, n.p., 1982).

47   In 1942, when it had grown to some 150 families, the community
      purchased the Lawton Memorial Building from the city of Savannah and
      converted it to be the new St. Paul's Greek Orthodox Church. This building,
      fronted by huge classical Greek columns, is located on Bull and Anderson
      Streets in Savannah's historic section, within walking distance of the old
      Cotton Exchange. The building's classical architecture is quite different
      from the usual Byzantine architecture favored by Greek Orthodox churches.
      Until the present time, the building continues to serve as a church for the
      congregants of St. Paul's Greek Orthodox Parish in Savannah. The classical
      columns at the front of the building are similar to the columns on the
      building used by the Greek Orthodox Church of the Annunciation, in
      Atlanta's historic section, located on 522 Pryor Street SW, which served as
      the Greek Orthodox Church from 1928 to 1967, and on the first New

Orleans Greek Orthodox Church, built in 1866. In the chapter on the Greek Orthodox Church more will be said about the significance of choice of classical over Byzantine styles.

48   Greek businessmen in Atlanta, Georgia formed the American Hellenic Educational and Progressive Association (AHEPA) in 1922. Of its first twenty-four chapters, twenty-two were organized in southern cities, among them Solon Chapter #5 in Savannah. *The AHEPA*, Official Organ of the Order of AHEPA, published in Washington, D.C., in its issue of September 1925, 14, had an article headed "Ahepa Society President is in Charlotte to Urge Americanization" and quoted president V. I. Chebithes: "The AHEPA's principal object is to Americanize all Greeks in America by assisting them to become naturalized, and in making them better citizens." More details on this unique fraternal organization follow in this work's chapter on fraternal associations.

49   *60ᵗʰ Anniversary Album of St. Paul's Greek Orthodox Church in Savannah*, n.p., pp. 8, 14, 18, 28, 34, and 44.

50   Epaminondas P. Panagopoulos, *New Smyrna: An Eighteenth Century Greek Odyssey* (Gainesville, Florida, University of Florida Press, 1966). When Florida was a British possession, 1763 to 1783, Andrew Turnbull and several other English investors obtained 100,000 acres in Florida and tried to create an agricultural settlement by bringing boat-loads of Greeks, Italians, Minorcans, and Corsicans. They started clearing the brush and draining the swamps in 1768; by 1778 the Turnbull settlement, named New Smyrna after his wife's birthplace, perished due to disease, death, and finally mutiny, caused by Turnbull's refusal to observe his end of their service contracts. The survivors retired to St. Augustine, while Turnbull's family settled in post-revolutionary Charleston.

51   Dio Adallis, *Adallis' Greek Merchants' Reference Book and Business Guide: Also a General Greek Directory of the City of Charleston, South Carolina*, ca. 1912, n.p., 3-38.

52   Adallis, *Adallis' Greek Merchants' Reference Book and Business Guide*, 30-31.

53   *The 75th Anniversary of Holy Trinity Greek Orthodox Church of Charleston, S.C.* (Charleston, n.p., 1984), 1; Adallis, *Adallis' Greek Merchants' Reference Book and Business Guide*, 21; *The News and Courier*, April 29, 1974, 1B—where the name is spelled "Spero Skiadaresis."

54   *Thirteenth Census of the US, 1910*, Abstract, 213; *In Commemoration of the 75th Anniversary of Holy Trinity Greek Orthodox Church in Charleston, South Carolina*" published by the church council, Charleston, 1984, 1. The journal gave names of some of the earliest families in the city, which included Lamas, Panoutsopoulos, Davis, Demos, Rousso, Lempesis, Christodoulopoulos, Stratakos, Billias, and Milton. Mrs. Alexandra Stefanou, nee Stratakos, oral interview by the author, Charleston, August 16, 1992.

55   *The News and Courier*, Charleston, April 29, 1974, 1B; *The 75th Anniversary*

of Holy Trinity Greek Orthodox Church of Charleston, S.C. reported that seventy people met to form the "Grecian Society;" Adallis, in *Adallis' Greek Merchants' Reference Book and Business Guide - Charleston,* recounted that forty-two men established the "Greek Society."

56 *The News and Courier,* Charleston, February 5, 1968, 1B; Adallis, *Greek Merchants' Reference Book,* 31-33. This account is very similar to the one contained in the commemorative brochure *The 75th Anniversary of the Holy Trinity Greek Orthodox Church, Charleston.* Adallis also enumerated 17 Greek families on pp. 34-36 and referred to several of the wives as "an American lady," or "an Irish lady."

57 *The News and Courier,* Charleston, April 29, 1974, 1B; the same article repeated the tradition that Spero Sciadaresis (sic) was the first Greek migrant to arrive in Charleston, and that his son, Angelo Sciadaresis, was the first "native-born South Carolinian of Greek extraction. This article also referred to a report carried in *The News and Courier* on November 12, 1914, that the first Greek wedding ceremony took place in Charleston, when "Ella Yeitrakis became the wife of John Roussos, a young businessman." Details about the location were obtained in the Nicholas Latto oral interview by the author, in Charleston, August 16, 1992.

58 Nicholas Latto and Mrs. Latto oral interview by the author in Charleston, August 16, 1992.

59 Adallis, *Adallis' Greek Merchants' Reference Book and Business Guide - Charleston,* 10, shows Sofianos Apostolatos as proprietor selling "Groceries, Fruits, Vegetables and Near-Beer" at 229 St. Phillips Street.

60 Nicholas Latto and Mrs. Latto interview.

61 Adallis, *Adallis' Greek Merchants' Reference Book and Business Guide - Augusta,* 4-5, 9-10, 32.

62 Ibid., 6.

63 Ibid., 1-38; Thirteenth Census of the US, 1910, Abstract, 211, enumerated in Augusta 80 people who were born in Greece.

64 Constantine (Gus) Kokenes, "History of the Greek Orthodox Community of Charlotte, N.C.," unpublished paper in possession of Mr. Xenophon Nixon, historian of the Greek community in Charlotte, N.C. The surname "Nixon" was arrived at by contracting the translated original surname "Nikopoulos" = "Nick's son" to Nixon.

65 Bessie Chronaki, "A History of the Greek Community in Charlotte, North Carolina 1908-1988," an unpublished paper, 2-3; Tom Cavalaris's enterprises grew as did Charlotte: he subsequently acquired a hat-cleaning and shoe-shine business, then the Rex Recreation Center, and finally the Cavalaris Skating Rink and Bowling Center; see the Tommy Athans article in *Charlotte Observer* of September 2, 1986, cited in the Chronaki paper.

66 (Constantine) Gus Kokenes, in Charlotte since 1906, fittingly became the first president of the organized parish body. Other members of the first parish council were: Charles Michaels, secretary and George Plumides,

treasurer; Chris Leventis, Charles Anagnos, and Sam Wallace were elected board members. "History of the Greek Community in Charlotte," by Bessie Chronaki, 5-6.

67   Ted Vallas, "A Brief History of the Early Years," in *Holy Trinity Greek Orthodox Church: A Fifty-Year History* (Raleigh, North Carolina, n.p., 1987); Harry John Costa [formerly Kostakou] and Pete George Davis [formerly Bactaris] were partners, first in the Andrews Fruit Stand and later the City Sandwich Shop on South Wilmington Street. Not only were they instrumental in establishing the Greek Orthodox Church in the city, but generations of farmers in and around Wake County came into town Saturdays to visit with Pete and Harry and eat their delicious and famous hot dogs. Other early migrants noted by Vallas were Constantine (Gus) Vournakes, who left his native Sparta in 1895 and within three years managed his own California Fruit Stand on Fayetteville Street, in Raleigh, a block or two from the state capitol. More Greeks in Raleigh were Constantine's two brothers, Leo and Alex; Gus, Nick, and Harry Russos; Pete and Jim Stathacos; Pete Gournas; Nick and George Charles; and others.

68   John Demetrios Stamatelos, "History of the Greek Orthodox Church of Pensacola, Florida, 1909 to 1959," (Pensacola, Florida, n.p., 1959), 4; Ted Carageorge, "The Greeks of Pensacola," in Jerrell H. Shofner and Linda V. Ellsworth, eds., *Ethnic Minorities in Gulf Coast Society*, vol. VIII, proceedings of the Gulf Coast History and Humanities Conference, Pensacola, Florida, 1979, 56-68, at 57.

69   Carageorge, "The Greeks in Pensacola," 57-59.

70   *Pensacola City Directory* (Jacksonville, Florida, R. L. Polk & Co., 1910), 312.

71   Carageorge, "The Greeks of Pensacola," 57; according to Dr. Ted Carageorge, Apostle became the first person of Greek ancestry to be elected mayor in any city in the United States. He bases this conclusion on notes from Theodore Saloutos, *Greeks in the United States*, 240, where that author quotes the Greek newspaper *Atlantis*, which stated (in error) that the first Greek to be elected mayor of an American town was one Antonios Protos, elected in 1895 mayor of Nogales, Arizona.

72   "Consecration Album," Annunciation Greek Orthodox Church, Pensacola, n.p., 1973.

73   Stamatelos, "History of the Greek Orthodox Church of Pensacola," 5, shows that eight of the ten signatories were from the islands and two from mainland Greece; five of the ten were from Skopelos, one each from Aegina, Corfu, and Crete, one man from Macedonia and one from the Peloponnesos. They were respectively: Nicholas Apostolou, John Epifaniou, Demetrios Coucourinis, Nicholas Galatsanos, Savas Stamatiou, Andreas Sahtouris, George Cassimus, Constantine Strategakis, John Gekas, and John Nikolakopoulos.

74   Ibid., 6: Father Joakim Georges served as parish priest for the next six years; he succumbed to the Spanish Flu epidemic in 1918, while in

Mississippi on a fund-raising drive for the church. Father Georges came to Pensacola from Charleston, where he helped to establish, in 1910, the Greek Orthodox Church of the Holy Trinity. See *Adallis' Greek Merchants' Reference Book and Business Guide - Charleston*, 33, for story and photo of Father Georges.

75 George Bokas, son of Victor Bokas, oral interview by the author, in Pensacola, July 8, 1992, confirming story in Carageorge, "The Greeks of Pensacola," 63.

76 Carageorge, "The Greeks of Pensacola," 64.

77 Carageorge, "The Greeks of Pensacola," 66. Also see Rosamonde Ramsay Boyd, *The Social Adjustment of the Greeks in Spartanburg, South Carolina* (Spartanburg, Williams Printing Co., ca. 1950), 69, who found that "[o]ver-attachment to another country, province, town or village... unfit both individuals and groups for successful adjustment to the new locality. Also, absorption with the affairs of the original locality may result in neglect of the new and hence retard adequate adjustment."

78 Theodore Saloutos, *They Remember America: the Story of the Repatriated Greek-Americans* (Berkeley, University of California Press, 1956), 51; Saloutos indicated that "few naturalized citizens of the United States departed for permanent residence in Greece," in the peak year 1920, a total of 20,319 Greek immigrants left the US, of those only 158 were US citizens; on the unusually late formation of an AHEPA chapter in Pensacola, see Ted Carageorge manuscript "The Greeks Come to Pensacola," revised and published as "The Greeks of Pensacola."

79 *75th Anniversary [Album] of the Annunciation Greek Orthodox Church in Mobile, Alabama* (n.p., Mobile, 1987), passim.

80 *75th Anniversary [Album] of the Annunciation Greek Orthodox Church in Mobile*, 23-24, 140.

81 *Ibid.*, 140,142.

82 *Ibid.*, 146, 149; the Tattis - Atherinos marriage contract, executed in Kastellorizo in 1906, is depicted on p. 52 [translation on p. 79].

83 Nick Costarides oral interview by the author, at Tommie's Terminal Restaurant, in Mobile, July 7, 1992; *75th Anniversary [Album] of the Annunciation Greek Orthodox Church in Mobile*, 166-167; Jim Karagan and Rose Karagan oral interview by the author in Mobile, July 8, 1992.

84 *75th Anniversary [Album] of the Annunciation Greek Orthodox Church in Mobile*, 160; Sophia Clikas oral interview by the author, at Tommie's Terminal Restaurant in Mobile, July 7, 1992; in 1938, one of the boys, Steve Clikas, married Sophia, the eldest daughter of Father Seraphim and presvitera Elizabeth Haginas. Steve operated the family restaurant, established in 1916, and upon his death, Sophia took over. When she retired recently, Sophia handed over the thriving restaurant, seating 275 people, to son Steve Jr. (the first Greek American in Alabama to be elected to the state legislature); Tommie's Terminal Restaurant is considered one of the

oldest continuously operated family restaurants in the south-eastern states.

85   Fairchild, *Greek Immigration to the United States*, 259, estimates Mobile's
      "Greek population," in 1908, at 350; *Thirteenth Census of the US, 1910*,
      Abstract, p. 211, shows 142 persons, born in Greece, now domiciled in
      Mobile.

86   *75th Anniversary [Album], Annunciation Greek Orthodox Church, Mobile,
      Alabama, 1912-1987*, n.p., Mobile, 1987, 12; the *Mobile Register*, January 26,
      1912, named the officers elected [bracketed are names as they appear in
      the society's own minutes]: Gus [Constantine] Santis, president; E[vangelos]
      Michael, vice-president; B. [Vasilios] Papailion [Papalios], treasurer;
      N[icholas] Rumpanos, secretary; together with council members
      A[postolos] Giannaros; J[ohn] Brown; D[emetrios] Andreadis; D[emetrios]
      Nichols [Nicholaou]; G[eorge] Poriotis [Panagiotopoulos]; and N[icholas]
      Andros.

87   *75th Anniversary [Album], Annunciation Greek Orthodox Church, Mobile*, 24-
      27.

88   King Constantine, whose wife was the German Kaiser Wilhelm's sister,
      sought to keep Greece neutral during the war. Prime Minister Eleftherios
      Venizelos felt Greece was obliged to enter the war on the allied side and
      actively participate in campaigns against Ottoman Turkey. Venizelos
      prevailed and led the Greeks into the war, but lost the post-war elections.
      The Royalists, however, continued the campaign against Turkey, and in
      1922 suffered a disastrous defeat in Asia Minor.

89   R. R. Boyd, *The Social Adjustment of the Greeks in Spartanburg, South Carolina*,
      69. In Birmingham, Alabama, the intra-congregational conflict became
      so acute over the hiring of a Sunday-school teacher, that one side formed
      a second *kinotis*; see the Birmingham chapter (6) of this work.

90   After entering the US, Greek immigrants generally followed three major
      routes: the majority settled in the large north-eastern New England mill
      towns, from Boston to Haverhill, Lowell, Lynn, and Manchester, to work
      in textile and shoe factories. Another route took them to large cities and
      industrial centers such as New York, Chicago, Cleveland, Detroit, and
      Pittsburgh, where they provided unskilled manufactory labor and also
      entered low-end street trades selling cigars, flowers, sweets, and other arti-
      cles. Finally, many followed a route to the western states, to find work in
      mines and on railroad gangs, from St. Louis to Denver and westward to Salt
      Lake City and Garfield, all the way to Ely, Nevada and from St. Paul west-
      ward to Seattle. Also see Saloutos, *The Greeks in the United States*, 45;
      Moskos, *Greek Americans*, 11-13; Evangelos Vlachos, *The Assimilation of
      Greeks in the United States* (Athens, Greece, National Centre of Social
      Researches, 1968), 62-63 and 74-75. Fewer than 10 percent drifted south.

91   Anthony Hicks oral interview by the author in Jacksonville, Florida,
      October 2, 1992. Costa Carantzas oral interview by the author in
      Jacksonville, Florida, April 12, 1990.

92   Gary R. Mormino and George E. Pozzetta, *The Immigrant World of Ybor City* (University of Illinois Press, Chicago, 1987), 58. The authors confirm "the solid entrenchment of the black community at the lowest end of Tampa's social and economic scale meant that immigrants entered at a level above at least one major segment of the local society, a fact that proved significant in framing the initial reception and mobility of immigrants."

93   Jerry Felos oral interview by the author in Jacksonville, Florida, November 8, 1992. Libby Stathis and Jennie Haramis (nee Stathis) oral interviews by the author in Jacksonville, Florida, April 16, 1990.

94   George E. Pozzetta, "From Rustbelt to Sunbelt: Patterns of Ethnic Migration and Integration in America 1940-1989," in George E. Pozzetta and Randall Miller, eds., *Shades of the Sunbelt: Essays on Race, Ethnicity, and the Urban South* (Westport, Connecticut, Greenwood Press, 1988), 278-279.

95   See Table 2 and Table 5, above.

96   Scourby, *The Greek Americans*, 37.

97   Richard M. Bernard, *The Melting Pot and the Altar* (Minneapolis, University of Minnesota Press, 1980), at 120, found exposure to other cultures and middle class occupations to be the strongest variables relating to mixed marriages. His rates of intermarriage in 1910 Wisconsin range from a low of 2.4% for Austrians to a high of over 50% for Britons and Scandinavians.

98   WPA, "Biographical Sketches," 82, Cecelia Poulos oral interview by writer Lillian Stedman, April 21, 1939. Victor Poulos interview. Dr. Evangeline Papageorge oral interview by the author in Atlanta, Georgia, June 25, 1992.

99   Jerry Felos and John Pappas interviews.

100 Charles Moskos, "Greek American Studies," in Alice Scourby and Harry Psomiades, eds., *The Greek American Community in Transition* (New York, Pella Publishing Co., 1982), 29. Also see Saloutos, *The Greeks in the United States*. Stephanos Zotos, *Hellenic Presence in America* (Wheaton, Illinois, Pilgrimage Press, 1976). Moskos, *Greek Americans*, as well as the two older works, Burgess, *Greeks in America*, and Fairchild, *Greek Immigration to the United States*.

101 Scourby, *Greek Americans*, 37.

102 Theodore Saloutos, "The Greeks of Milwaukee," *UMH* 53 (Spring 1970), 175-193; Scourby, *Greek Americans*, 40.

103 Genevieve Robinson, "The Acropolis of Hellenism in America: First Generation Greeks in Lowell, Massachusetts 1895-1922," Ph.D. dissertation, Boston College, Massachusetts, 1986; 152, 228, 398.

104 Saloutos, "The Greeks of Milwaukee," 177, 181.

105 Fairchild, *Greek Immigration to the United States*, showing the 1909 Greek population in Chicago, Ill., to be about 15,000, and in New York City with Brooklyn about 20,000.

106 Saloutos, *The Greeks in the United States*, 259-260; Fairchild, *Greek*

Immigration to the United States, 122-133.

107   Fairchild, *Greek Immigration to the United States*, 127.

108   Ibid., 150.

109   Monos, "Upward Mobility, Assimilation, and the Achievements of Greeks in the United States With Special Emphasis on Boston and Philadelphia," 126; Saloutos, "Greeks in Milwaukee," 178-179.

110   See Tables 2, 4, 5, and 6 above.

111   Scourby, *The Greek Americans*, 47.

112   Saloutos, *The Greeks in the United States*, 269.

113   Saloutos, "The Greeks of Milwaukee," 180.

114   Libby Stathis and Jennie Haramis (nee Stathis) interview. Sam Felos and Jerry Felos interview.

115   Milton Gordon, *Assimilation in American Life: the Role of Race, Religion and National Origins* (New York, Oxford University Press, 1964), 70-71, 110-112, 242-243; Gordon summarized the then contending theories of Anglo-conformity, Melting Pot, and Cultural Pluralism, and offered his own theory of assimilation, outlined above.

116   Nathan Glazer and Daniel Moynihan, *Beyond the Melting Pot: the Negroes, Puerto Ricans, Jews, Italians, and Irish of New York City* (Cambridge, Massachusetts Institute of Technology Press, 1963); they stated "the point about the Melting Pot is that it did not happen."

117   For example, Rudolph J. Vecoli, George E. Pozzetta, Kathleen Neils Conzen, etc. See Valeria Lerda, ed., *From Melting Pot to Multiculturalism* (Rome, Bulzoni Editore, 1991), passim.

118   Rudolph J. Vecoli, "From The Uprooted to The Transplanted: The Writing of American Immigration History 1951-1989," in Lerda ed., *From Melting Pot to Multiculturalism*, 53.

119   An *Atlanta Constitution* editorialist observed in 1913, "We believe there is plenty of room in America for the right sort of Jews, as for the right sort of Greeks, French, English and Germans." Cited in Herzberg, *Strangers Within the Gate City*, 134.

120   One can understand the anxiety of a mother back in Greece, when she received a letter from the older son, who had written that younger brother "Demetrios is now Jimmy." She agonized over what sort of condition or illness "Jimmy" was. Victor Poulos interview.

121   Adallis, *Adallis' Greek-American Directory and Business Guide; The Thirteenth Census of the US, 1910*, abstract schedules, where one finds the American name and the notation that the said person was born in Greece. Other examples, just in Atlanta, were restaurant owners A. B. Nicol, James Campbell, James Mitchell, and Louis George, confectioner Peter Mitchell, grocer George Lewis, waiter James Brown, moving picture theater owner George Campbell, and huxter Sam George.

122   Dr. Richard Clogg oral interview with the author at the University of Florida, in Gainesville, Florida, November 5, 1993.

123 Sam Felos and Jerry Felos interviews.

124 Victor Poulos oral interview by the author in Atlanta, Georgia, June 26, 1992.

125 Sam Felos, Jerry Felos, as well as John Pappas, Libby Stathis and Jennie Haramis (nee Stathis), second generation sons and daughters of Greek pioneer families, all remember their at times unwilling attendances at the parochial school.

126 WPA, "Biographical Sketches," 81-82, Cecelia Poulos interview.

127 The first chapters were Atlanta, #1; Charlotte, N.C., #2; Birmingham, Ala., #3; Charleston, S.C., #4, Savannah, Ga., #5; Jacksonville, Fla., # 6; etc. See George J. Leber, *The History of the Order of AHEPA* (Washington, D.C., AHEPA, 1972), as well as Table 8 in Chapter 3.

128 Kathleen Neils Conzen, David A. Gerber, Ewa Morawska, George E. Pozzetta, Rudolph J. Vecoli, "The Invention of Ethnicity: A Perspective From The USA," *Journal of American Ethnic History* 12 (1), (Fall 1992), 3-41; also see Werner Sollors, ed., *The Invention of Ethnicity* (New York, Oxford University Press, 1989).

129 Most Greek Festivals in the South began their annual appearance in the 1970s. For example, Jacksonville's Greek Festival has become a "tradition" since 1972, and Atlanta's since 1974.

CHAPTER 3

FRATERNAL BONDING AND CONSERVATISM:

JIMMY JOINED AHEPA[1]

"...with the purpose in view of advancing and promoting
pure and undefiled Americanism among the Greeks of
the United States..."
—Excerpt from the objects of the American Hellenic Educational
and Progressive Association (AHEPA), submitted in 1922
to the County Court of Fulton County, Atlanta, Georgia.

Like other Americans, Greek immigrants were joiners. Part of the
process of settling into the new environment included the establishment
of fraternal, social, religious, and political organizations. Upon their
arrival in the early 1900s, Greeks readily organized or joined voluntary associations of all sorts, promoting a variety of causes. Some of
the Greek societies were short-lived, others showed a remarkable
longevity. Sociologist Dimitrios Monos applied the conventional explanation to the quick growth of Greek voluntary organizations.[2] Some
were designed to perpetuate ties with the place or region of origin, and
thus they eased the inevitable culture shock all immigrants experienced
upon arrival in the new country. Some immigrant ethnic institutions
often paralleled native ones and thus helped their members become
better citizens, more equipped to understand the new environment.
The pattern of formal and informal Greek organizations, together with
the traditional Hellenic culture, and the pressure to succeed, all had a

marked influence on the process of acculturation to the American society.[3] To a degree, the associations tempered rampant Greek individuality through common rules and regulations. Although they may have been founded to perpetuate the customs and culture of the homeland, or to serve economic needs of the common locality back home, they eventually helped[4] unite urbanites in shared interests and promoted cooperation among different Greek groups coming from a variety of places around the Aegean.

There was, however, one Hellenic organization whose members intentionally minimized Old-World-ties and concentrated on succeeding in the new one. Emancipated entrepreneurs, whose livelihood was endangered by sweeping nativism, particularly vicious in the South, formed the American Hellenic Educational and Progressive Association, popularly known by its acronym as the AHEPA. Organized in Atlanta, Georgia, this fellowship emulated American associations, in that English was the language used both on its inception and at all of its formal functions.[5] At first, AHEPA acted as a virtual public relations champion for Greeks who had made their home in the United States and wanted to succeed here. During the 1920s and 1930s, its membership attracted men whose primary concern was to penetrate and find acceptance in the middle strata of American society. Following the example set by Greek entrepreneurs in the South, characterized by young Demetrios who soon adopted the American alias Jimmy, ambitious compatriots in other regions, especially in the north-eastern and midwestern states, swelled the ranks of AHEPA in the hope of improving their status in the wider community.[6] In time, its members became a more conservative segment of that immigrant group, cautious and tending to side with the establishment. AHEPA proved to be the longest-lived, popular, active Greek-American fraternal organization. Its prominence and unique nature in Greek communities, especially in the South, requires further exposition.

Unlike AHEPA, some of the earliest Greek fellowships were based on common habitation back home. Practically every village and parish in the Greek-speaking parts of the Mediterranean yielded immigrants to America. Societies based on a common locality—"topika somateia"—brought together Greeks from a particular area, all devoted to helping each other, aiding those left behind, and collectively perpetuating the culture and kinship of the locality.[7] According to historian Theodore

Saloutos, about one hundred such societies were in existence in the United States as early as 1907; in New York alone there were thirty. "It appears that every village and minute parish in Greece was represented in the United States by a society with an impressive array of banners, lengthy constitutions, and high-sounding names."[8] Manifesting the Greek propensity for flourish, the majority were composed of fifteen to thirty members and governed by councils from twelve to fifteen people. Gold tassels and buttons adorned the officers' uniforms, which were worn on every possible occasion.[9] There were the Lacedemonians, the Macedonians, the Thessalians, the Cretans, the Evrytanian Association, the Chios Society, and many others, based on the Greek mainland, in the numerous Aegean and Ionian islands, as well as in the Greek-speaking areas of Asia Minor.[10]

One more pragmatic reason for the existence of so many local societies was that the members not only helped each other but also provided combined aid to the village they left behind. Saloutos pointed out that a number of local societies sprang from the urgent appeals of village mayors and priests in Greece. By letters and petitions to those "better off" in America, these petty officials succeeded in arousing the immigrants' patriotism, "sometimes to fever pitch."[11] Another reason, working hand in hand with the genuine desire to help, was the innate Mediterranean pursuit of public esteem. What better way to gain respect and admiration in the eyes of the villagers and of all who heard of the persons who so generously extended aid to the folks at home. And here in the states, where they usually held menial jobs, the donors assumed positions of honor which they could hardly achieve otherwise. Many had a chance to bask in the limelight, in the place of honor as the president, vice-president, or secretary-treasurer of the local society. Prolific titles helped in the quest for status and recognition, greatly developed in a society which preferred to focus on the appearance of honor rather than on the reality of immigrant poverty.[12]   The desire to help and conjointly earn high regard was even stronger among those who intended to return home as soon as they scraped together the projected savings. Within about five years of his arrival here, one man returned for every two who came here.[13] To these men, old country politics were of great interest. Not surprisingly, they were the most avid readers of Greek-language tabloids and spent much of their spare time debating Greek military and political successes and failures during the

Balkan Wars, and the turbulent Greek internal strife during the first World War and its aftermath. These men formed the membership of the Panhellenic Union, a very nationalist and patriotic society founded in New York in 1907. It was most active just before and during the Balkan Wars, until about 1913 and developed a large brotherhood in places where one found the greatest number of Greek immigrant workers.[14]

The Panhellenic Union stood on the premise that most Greeks would return to their homeland and for that purpose its members worked hard to perpetuate the Greeks' faith and language in this country.[15] During the Balkan wars, skirting American laws, the Union succeeded in recruiting significant numbers of volunteers for the Greek army. As many as 35,000 Greeks returned to fight for the motherland against Turkey in 1912, and against Bulgaria in 1913. Not all the volunteers were recruited by the Union, but the Union collected close to $375,000 and paid the passage to any volunteer on the way home.[16] Almost without exception, the volunteers were men who had not yet formed families here and, one could surmise, who had not yet decided to remain permanently in the United States. They heeded the Greek government's call to arms, directed to all able-bodied citizens wherever they may be, at home or abroad.

Within a year or two after the end of the 1913 Balkan War, the political situation in Greece became confused, with the basic conflict reflected in the struggle for leadership of the country between the Liberals of Prime Minister Eleftherios Venizelos on the one hand and staunch Royalists loyal to King Constantine on the other hand. Venizelos and his followers desired to align Greece with its traditional Serbian, English, and French allies, whereas those loyal to King Constantine, whose family connections reached to Kaiser Wilhelm of Prussia, intended to keep Greece neutral. The Panhellenic Union in America lapsed into a state of indecision. The prospect that the United States might enter the war on the allied side and the connection of the Union to the Greek Royalist side, at best considered neutral and at worst accused of being pro-German, reduced the organization to a cipher.[17] As the Panhellenic Union waned into oblivion, the Pan-Epirotic Union stepped up its campaign for the annexation of Northern Epirus to Greece.[18] At about the same time, in a fit of nationalist pride, the secretary of the newly formed National Union of the Dodecanesians of America advised Italian Prime Minister Vittorio Orlando that the Greeks considered the presence of Italian armies on the Dodecanese as crusaders who came to pursue the "hated crescent," but that the Italian occupation was just a prelude to national restoration of these islands to Greece.[19]

Fewer such local and patriotic societies branched out to the South. Chapters existed in some Hellenic communities, but on a much smaller scale. Their members in Augusta, Atlanta, Savannah, Birmingham, Mobile, and other southern cities chose to display their insignia and banners very discreetly, if at all. There was always the fear of offending their white Anglo neighbors, who were not friendly to foreigners and who might have considered a foreign uniform or banner to be un-American. Moreover, in many southern cities the manpower to form a local society was lacking. In Florida's Jacksonville of 1910, for example, among only 120 Greeks there, one found people from all parts of the Greek-speaking Mediterranean. There were mainlanders from Epirus as well as from Sparta, islanders from Corfu and Crete, and from the Cyclades and Dodecanese in the Aegean, men from Constantinople and from Smyrna in Asia Minor, too few from any one location to form a local branch.

As outlined in the previous chapter, by the first decade of the 1900s, a high proportion of Greek migrants who settled in the southern cities achieved the status of self-employed businessmen. As entrepreneurs, they did not have to submit to orders from gang-bosses or factory foremen; they made their own decisions and assumed the personal limelight as proprietors of their own businesses. Perhaps the craving to "be somebody," to be the secretary of this fraternal organization or the president of that one was not as pronounced as it would have been if there were no recognition of the individual and his decision-making power in the workplace. To satisfy their craving for public honor, as well as their propensity to join in voluntary and fraternal organizations, these businessmen became members of American organizations and congenial fellowships and associations such as the Masons, Woodmen of the World, the Odd Fellows, Elks, Kiwanis, and Rotary. Finally, a good number of Greek immigrants in the South had found a new home; they had formed families and acquired American citizenship. Their interest in issues of vital importance to Greece may have been strong, but not sufficient to cause overt demonstrations in the new domicile.

In contrast to the political and partisan brotherhoods, whose activ-

ities focused on news and developments back in the old country, more
established immigrants organized associations which enhanced their
social, economic, and spiritual lives here in the new homeland, such as
the associations of Greek florists and restaurant owners and the AHEPA.
In 1910 Birmingham, budding businessmen organized the Young Greeks
Progressive Society, to contract and cultivate a closer relationship
between the members, to help those who desire to become American
citizens, and "to promote mutual friendship between the members
and our American citizens."[20] Surprising for an immigrant group which
generated so much fraternal activity, there were no sodalities organized as a savings and loan society, or a mutual aid and insurance society
that paid out sickness and death benefits. Greeks avoided such mutual
financing activities, prevalent among immigrants of other nationalities, probably because each individual liked to handle his own savings
and investments.

Of the Greek-American fellowships whose members' primary interests were centered in the United States, a most widely spread association
was the "kinotis." Based on the broad, common ethno-religious heritage,
Greeks formed these organized communities in American cities specifically to establish and maintain church parishes. The "kinotis" translates
into "community" in a secular sense, or "parish" if it is a religious
body.[21] For example, Atlanta Greeks formed their kinotis as early as
1902 and named it the Evangelismos Society. Within three years, as it
secured church premises and a priest, the society became the Greek
Orthodox Parish of the Annunciation. The Grecian Society of Charleston,
South Carolina, formed in 1910, leased a church building, hired a priest,
and transformed itself into a parish devoted to the Holy Trinity, all
within one year. In 1913, the Homer Society in Little Rock, Arkansas,
completed a similar transformation into a Greek Orthodox parish also
named for the Annunciation. The following chapter of this work will
specifically consider Hellenic religious life and examine how these
parish entities in the South, entirely organized by the laity, fit into the
structure of the highly hierarchical Greek Orthodox church.

In essence, membership in the topika somateia as well as in the
Panhellenic Union and similar patriotic organizations can be characterized as direct and strong ties to the parochial origin and in that sense
opposed to integration into American life that tended to diminish such
ties. These associations promoted separateness and ethnic survival until

the immigrants' return to the Greek motherland. Conforming to the ebb and flow of immigrants, the mortality rate of these small fellowships was high, but so was their reproductive capacity; new ones emerged from the ashes of the old. The officers attempted to show to their compatriots real or illusory leadership qualities and often the bickering between competing local societies and individual members impeded cooperation and unification for the sake of common activities and kept the wider communities divided.

For example, the *Athena Society* formed in the early 1890s in New York City to organize a religious parish. A common ecclesiastical body would easily accommodate the majority of the Greek Orthodox in New York City, home of over two dozen local societies. Members of *Athena Society* managed to organize the *kinotis* and to form the first Greek Orthodox parish in New York City, the Holy Trinity. Within months, however, the new community experienced internal strife, caused by clashing personalities and contending factions, which was resolved only by a split and subsequent formation of a second Greek Orthodox parish in New York City, the Annunciation.[22] The *Lycurgus Society*, organized by Spartan Greeks in the 1890s in Chicago, Illinois, was representative of voluntary organizations which fostered cooperation among Greeks, leading to the first permanent Greek Orthodox parish in that city, Holy Trinity.[23] But the concord lasted only a few years. A feud fueled by regionalism broke out between the Spartans and a group of Arcadians. When the Spartans threatened to tax the Arcadians who came to worship at Holy Trinity, in 1897 the Arcadians formed their own parish, also named for the Annunciation. In contrast, in Birmingham, Alabama, Jacksonville, Florida, and other southern cities, the mingle of Greeks from several regions of the Mediterranean proceeded directly to form the church parishes, naming the *kinotis* with the same name as the proposed church. There were a number of Greek Orthodox parishes named *Annunciation*; several were dedicated to the *Holy Trinity*.[24]

Chapter two of this work demonstrated that a greater proportion of Greek immigrants to the southern states had decided to settle there around the turn of the century, earlier than their compatriots in the northern and mid-western industrial areas, where they generally committed themselves to America a generation or two later, certainly no earlier than the 1920s.[25] Cities such as New York and Chicago, followed by Boston and San Francisco, all places with large Greek immigrant populations, also spawned many Greek-language newspapers.[26] These papers usually urged their readers to maintain ties to home. Front pages carried stories from Greece; columns covered news and events in specific regions, towns, and villages. The chief purpose of the Greek ethnic press was to keep immigrants informed about the happenings back home. The papers "perpetuated Old World feuds and gave rise to new ones."[27] While popular papers such as the *Atlantís* and *Ethnikos Kyrix* had subscribers in the South, no serious or stable Greek-language newspaper originated here.[28]

Although Greek papers maintained and promoted strong ties to Greece and Greek-populated areas around the Aegean, exceptional editorials periodically urged their subscribers to "Americanize." As early as 1904, on April 15 and again on August 15, *Hellenikos Astir*—the *Hellenic Star*—published an appeal launched by "some Greek community leaders," proclaiming that "Americanization is the star that will guide us to prosperity, success, and progress. Let us adopt this great country as our own. Let us be part of this land of plenty and not remain predatory aliens. America opens her arms to us. Let us embrace her with love and a desire to understand her laws, political and social life."[29] Such appeals, however, were seldom seen. Even in the 1920s, when their subscribers in heavily ethnic regions increasingly opted to apply for American citizenship, sociologist Charles Jaret found that the Greek-language papers in America were "considerably more oriented toward old world news and events than were the Yiddish or Italian presses." Theodore Saloutos confirmed that Greek newspapers were "little inclined to dwell on American issues," and for the most part "sought to capitalize on the partisan Old World preferences of its readers."[30]

After World War I, in the years characterized by 100 percent Americanism, editorials frequently boosted Americanization; some papers even encouraged Greeks to vote for this candidate or for that party.[31] Greek-language newspapers typically used nationalist rhetoric to persuade readers to become American citizens. It was contrary to the character and ideals of a good Greek, they wrote, to remain an alien. All progressive compatriots in America had already become citizens. Editors who thrived on nationalistic discourse earlier, now proclaimed that the American approaches to democratic government and responsible citizenship were derived from the ways of classic Greece. Americanism was but an offspring of Hellenism; the Greek who became a true and ardent American actually promoted Hellenic ideals. While such tirades represented the carrot, both in the South and in many northern localities nativist sentiments exerted pressures on immigrants to be true Americans and, on occasion, the Ku Klux Klan literally provided the stick. In addition, the Immigration Quota Acts of 1921 and 1924 hastened naturalization of eligible newcomers and reduced to a trickle the immigrant influx from the Mediterranean. A naturalized citizen had a much better chance to bring relatives to America; and if an American went home to Greece to marry, he would not be prevented from returning to the United States. Understandably, during the 1920s, membership in the local and patriotic societies markedly decreased.

About this time, in 1922, Greeks residing in Atlanta, Georgia, organized the American Hellenic Educational and Progressive Association [AHEPA]. In many ways the "Order of AHEPA" was a unique fraternal association. Established to check nativist prejudices expressed by the newly revived, fast-growing Ku Klux Klan, and specifically to break the line of prejudgment and discrimination against Greeks in the South, AHEPA sought to facilitate acceptance of Greek immigrant entrepreneurs to their customers and neighbors and to deflect boycotts of businesses owned by non-Protestants.[32] Following its success in the southern cities, the fellowship attracted like-minded Greek immigrants in many other urban areas and within a few years of its inception spread to become a nationwide organization. Its development and maturation deserve distinct attention here, so one can better understand the selective adaptation process experienced by thousands of its members, particularly those Greek-American small businessmen in the South, whose thinking and ideas provided the initial thrust for the association.

Until 1920 Greek store owners in Atlanta and other southern cities had little to fear from the Ku Klux Klan. Their enterprises were supplying needed services; their hard work had endeared them to customers and employees alike. As long as they minded their businesses and did not openly flaunt alien behavior or ideologies, they could prosper and live in any part of town they could afford. By 1921, however, all over the South, imperial wizard William J. Simmons was enrolling new members by the thousands. Organizers Edward Young Clarke and Elizabeth Tyler

managed a vast expansion of the Klan by skillfully manipulating native
fears and prejudices not only against blacks, Catholics, and Jews, but also
against immigrants.

In the fall of that year, newspapers carried reports that estimated the
Klan's strength in the hundreds of thousands and listed murders, tar and
feather parties, and floggings all attributed to the Klan. But despite
Congressional hearings, no Klan action was punished. The Greeks also
noted that the Klan was politically powerful. In Atlanta, prominent
lawyers, members of the city council and the school board were
Klansmen.[33] The Klan succeeded in garnering votes from the mainstream population. People who were in daily contact with the Hellenic
entrepreneurs, both as fellow businessmen, as customers, and as neighbors, people who were concerned with law enforcement, municipal
reform, and the preservation of additional values, voted for Klan candidates.[34] The Klan successfully promoted the election of many members
and sympathizers, including Atlanta mayor Walter A. Sims, Georgia
senator Walter George, Georgia governor Clifford Walker, and Supreme
Court Judge Eugene Thomas.[35]

To deflect the Klan's raw physical power and political strength, early
AHEPA members developed an uncommon strategy, designed to
demonstrate that Greeks were good Americans and good for America,
and therefore desirable business associates and beneficial citizens. Eight
Greek entrepreneurs in Atlanta, Georgia, all already American citizens,
worked out the initial concept. Restaurateurs Nick Chotas and James
Campbell, grocer Harry Angelopoulos, theater owner George Campbell,
and businessmen George Polos, Spiros Stamos, John Angelopoulos,
and James Vlass were concerned about preserving their good fortunes
and agreeable relations with their American neighbors in the face of
increased Klan activity and attacks on anyone Klan members considered
un-American.[36] They saw that nativist hostility was set off by the perception that immigrants were corrupting traditional moral values and 100
percent Americanism, which the Klansmen had sworn to preserve.[37]
As a result, one could be threatened and perhaps whipped for using a
foreign language in public; even worse, one's place of business could be
vandalized, without recourse to the authorities, who frequently agreed
that immigrants came from an inferior society, presented an economic
threat, and undermined American ways.[38] They knew that Klan-induced
boycotts could ruin any business. They also noted the rough treatment

Greeks and other immigrants had already received in Virginia and Oklahoma, and heard that pamphlets were distributed in Jacksonville, Florida, with warnings to Greek and Syrian store owners.[39] Moreover, knowing of the Klan's declared disdain for Catholicism, they perceived the danger that their own Orthodox church, with its iconographic depictions of saints, robed priests, and chanted liturgies might easily be linked by non-discriminating and numerous Klansmen to the Roman Catholic church.

In 1922 eight Greek-American businessmen of Atlanta, Georgia, depicted above, founded the Order of AHEPA [American Hellenic Educational and Progressive Association]. Photo courtesy of AHEPA Headquarters, Washington, D.C.

Like many compatriots, the eight Greek Atlantans had already decided to remain permanently in the Gate City. They had to insure their families' and their own safety; they had to preserve the businesses which provided their livelyhoods. They were not going to be driven away from the place where Greeks had built a community and prospered since the turn of the century. To counter the newly-growing nativist threat and to preserve their enterprises, they had to convince the majority of their fellow Americans, and specifically the Klan, that Greek immigrants would indeed make citizens of the right kind.[40] The founders intended to blunt the increasingly raucous rhetoric and destructive activities of the Klan and its sympathizers with a shrewd strategy: they agreed to form a fraternal organization that would publicly espouse the slogan of 100 percent Americanism, pledge to instill it into all members and compatriots, and thereby convert their southern neighbors—including members and sympathizers of the Klan—to accept the Greeks as good Americans. They needed to loudly proclaim what they had in common with the average American; they could honestly adopt the democratic anti-elite sentiments, the desire to maintain high moral values, and the unabashed patriotism, even as they remained silent on Protestant dominance, white supremacy, and brute force.[41] The creative campaign succeeded, probably because in addition to the novel use of public relations, Greek entrepreneurs actually blended in with the American gospel of success: they worked hard in a society which respected hard work and middle class values, showed they were "white," ambitious, and venturesome, and appeared to accept guidance.[42]

Harry Angelopoulos, one of the AHEPA founders, provided an insight into the group's thinking. One of the reasons for organizing was to come to grips with "the pressure of prejudice against the Greeks," who "deserved better consideration from the American public." Moreover, the group felt they "owed an obligation to [the] adopted country for the abundance of opportunities," and finally owed a duty to instruct and lead their compatriots. "In order to accomplish our objective," Angelopoulos wrote, "it was necessary to organize under the same principles as those whom we intended to convert, and Hutcheson, a member of the KKK knew, so did [George] Polos who had an acquaintance with E[dward] Y[oung] Clarke, the imperial wizard of the KKK."[43] The Greeks retained attorney Carl Franklin Hutcheson, known to them to be a member of the Ku Klux Klan, to draw up the charter and the objects of the proposed association in the "right" way, so that these could not help but warm the heart of every true American. For their astute analysis of the Klan, they may have relied on George Polos, who was employed by the Atlanta Klan "in a confidential capacity" and attended "secret meetings and conferences with the policy makers and high administrators of that then dreadfully powerful group."[44]

Within a week of the initial meeting, Hutcheson had drafted and filed in the Superior Court of Fulton County, Georgia, papers incorporating the American Hellenic Educational Progressive Association. The constitution and specifically the charter of AHEPA disclosed an undeniable desire to conform to American ways.[45] Listing the "Objects, Principles and Ideals," the constitution enumerated the first purpose of the members: "To promote and encourage loyalty to the United States of America; allegiance to its flag; support to its constitution; obedience to its laws and reverence for its history and traditions." Attorney Hutcheson stated the objects of the association even clearer in the charter submitted to the County Court six weeks later: "(T)o form a fraternal order and secure members therefore, with the purpose in view of advancing and promoting pure and undefiled Americanism among the Greeks of the United States..."[46] In accordance with the Order's by-laws, members spoke only English at all formal meetings and functions.

The Order of AHEPA spread rapidly, especially in places where Greek entrepreneurs were concerned about their safety and prosperity. It attracted a great number of Greek small businessmen, who needed to make no changes in their own lives, except to overtly, publicly embrace midstream values and the cause of Americanism, and thus assure continuing patronage by their customers and increased personal respect and acceptance in the community.[47] Judging by the rites adopted for initiation and at meetings and proceedings of the organization, the founders were influenced by the ritual and secrecy of such fraternal orders as the Masons, or Odd Fellows, or such other closed orders familiar to the founders and their lawyer.[48] Of the first 23 chapters 19 were organized in southern cities. By October 1923, AHEPA delegates gathered in Atlanta for the first annual convention. At the convention, the Supreme Secretary reported that the "roster contains more than 1,300 [members'] names and there are more than 1,000 applicants

ready to join our ranks." The individual initiation fee amounted to
$10, and doubled to $20 after January 1923.

Photo of the Jacksonville, Florida, "Socrates" Chapter #6 officers in formal array;
from The AHEPA magazine, August, 1926.

In historian Theodore Saloutos's opinion, from the outset "AHEPA
was middle-class in orientation. It appealed to those who were climbing
the social and economic ladder of success" and extended recognition
to them at banquets, dances, and meetings, where many a businessman
met with compatriots facing identical problems. AHEPA attracted those
who wanted, at least on the surface, to appear and be considered as
Americans. As Saloutos wrote, "the climate was favorable to the growth
of the order."[49] In keeping with the original concept, AHEPA members
in various cities invited American dignitaries, politicians, and other
prominent people to accept membership in the organization and lend
their name and fame to the good causes of the AHEPA and to the
Americanization of the right kind of immigrants.

The first convention took place at the Atlanta Chamber of
Commerce building. Carl Hutcheson was present and gave the dele-
gates a very warm welcome to Atlanta as the representative of the mayor.
AHEPA's outreach to American politicians was also evident by the pres-
ence of Congressman William D. Upshaw and Atlanta councilman
Hooper Alexander, as well as Fred Houser of the Atlanta Convention
Bureau.[50] Upshaw was well acquainted with Hutcheson; most likely
elected with Ku Klux Klan help, he became the Democratic
Representative for three terms, from 1918 until 1926. In 1921, at the

Congressional Hearings on the Klan, he introduced William J. Simmons as a man "incapable of an unworthy, unpatriotic motive, word or deed."[51] The list of the fraternity's own delegates representing various chapters was peppered with Americanized names; there were founders James and George Campbell, and H. I. North of Atlanta, H. G. Link Jr. of Charlotte, Ben Davis and Arthur Greenwood of Birmingham, John Young of Memphis, D. Lorant of Shreveport, C. R. Nixon of Tulsa, Willis Gastaing of Tarpon Springs, Hugh Neal Wells of New York City; John De Mos of Jacksonville, Florida, just elected as Supreme Vice-President, and Charles Kirby, one of several regional Supreme Governors of the Order.[52]

Reports at the convention indicated that quite a few people within the Greek communities opposed the AHEPA strategy, particularly its program of Americanism and use of the English language. Its assertion of "being non-political and non-sectarian" struck many Greek-Americans as being heretical; it was bitterly criticized in many quarters, including the Greek newspapers in America.[53] Saloutos confirmed that "Much of the furor arose over the use of the English language in all official matters. Critics felt this to be a denial of one's cultural roots.[54] On a more personal level, the use of English also prevented those who had not mastered it from full participation in the public arena. A person whose knowledge of English was not good enough to hold an oration would certainly feel deprived and denied the opportunity to exhibit his wisdom to his compatriots. Such people attacked the AHEPA as anti-Greek. Nevertheless, the use of English remained one of the primary planks in the AHEPA strategy.

By September 1924, the organization had grown to 53 chapters and 2,790 members.[55] At the 1924 convention, sponsored by the Washington, D.C., and Baltimore, Maryland chapters in Washington, lawyer V. I. Chebithes became the new supreme president and infused an even greater sense of Americanism into the order.[56] In 1925 and 1926 he edited and arranged for publication several annual convocation issues of The AHEPA magazine. Under Chebithes's leadership the Order of AHEPA spread throughout the northern states, and initiated the now traditional and enduring lobbying efforts, whereby local, state, and national politicians and prominent people not only became speakers and honored attendees at meetings, conventions, banquets, dances, and balls, but also received offers to become honorary members.

Many American friends, politicians, and other elected officials responded positively to these invitations to AHEPA membership. Part of the AHEPA's work was demonstrated by the insistence that all members take out naturalization papers at the earliest opportunity; in fact, continuous failure to do so might mean exclusion from the Order.[57]

By the time the organization's representatives met at the third annual convention in Chicago, some seventy-nine chapters had organized nationwide, and about 7,000 members had paid their $20.00 induction fee. Before this convention, supreme president V. I. Chebithes visited various chapters in his domain. The September 1925 pre-convention issue of the fraternity's magazine, *The AHEPA*, described numerous receptions and meetings to which local Ahepans invited their prominent American friends, mayors, and sundry officials, to hear Chebithes extol the ideals of Americanism and Hellenism. Chebithes's itinerary included St. Louis, Birmingham, Tampa, Tarpon Springs, St. Petersburg, Miami, Jacksonville, and Charlotte, as well as Chicago, Detroit, and Milwaukee. *The Charlotte News* explained that "The AHEPA principal object is to Americanize all Greeks in America by assisting them to become naturalized, and in making them better citizens." *The Jacksonville Journal* noted in a lead article that V. I. Chebithes had been scheduled to speak at a public meeting before the Chamber of Commerce, to show that AHEPA wanted "to promote the spirit of Americanism among the Greeks," to urge them to take out naturalization papers, to study American customs and practices and to "adapt themselves to American methods in commerce and industry."[58]

A reporter for *The Charlotte Observer*, describing the public meeting at that city's Chamber of Commerce, noted the presence of mayor Harvey Moore, Democratic Congressman Alfred L. Bulwinkle, and district solicitor John G. Carpenter. *The Savannah Morning News* enumerated the guests of honor at a banquet in that town, "among them being Mayor Hull, Judge Meldrim, Alderman Carter, all honorary members of the [AHEPA] Solon Chapter [# 5]."[59] In Jacksonville, Florida, Mayor J. T. Alsop "was presented amid a din of applause" and addressed the crowd, which also heard the local AHEPA president, John De Mos [formerly Ioannis Demosthenes] draw a parallel between the Hellenic and Anglo-Saxon characteristics, which showed "striking similarities." V. I. Chebithes followed up with a speech on Americanism, which he asserted, "is nothing more or less than Hellenism transplanted to this rich soil where it has the opportunity to grow and flourish. . .the language, philosophy, architecture, laws, and systems of government of the two civilizations are interrelated and interwoven with each other."[60]

These concerted efforts to show that Greek immigrants can become good Americans created some unexpected results. The Patriotic Order of the Sons of America paid tribute to AHEPA and congratulated its members, "the most thrifty of our citizens [and] all good businessmen," on their "vision of Americanism and the spirit in which [they] seek to exemplify it." They were "making America better by making better Americans."[61] Member Pete [Panos] Peppas, of AHEPA's Asheville, N. C. Chapter [#28], wrote to admonish his chapter's leaders to work harder and be more enthusiastic. Peppas pointed out that in Akron, Ohio, while that AHEPA chapter was in session, "the doors opened and twenty-five to thirty K. K. K. In their uniforms walked in. After a wonderful address by their leader an American flag was presented to the Greeks." Peppas gushed, "That is what I call activity."[62] Peppas's view was probably quite uncommon among Greeks, even among those who had joined the fraternity.

AHEPA's critics and detractors also became more effective. A number of editorials and articles in the Greek-language press publicly censured the fraternal organization for its insistence on speaking English at all formal functions and meetings. The criticism was expected. After all, Greek-language newspapers depended on subscribers who continued to speak Greek. In addition, AHEPA's decision to be a "non-sectarian" organization offended some of the clergy and devout Greek Orthodox faithful. Some of the severest early criticism came from certain sources within the church, despite the fact that selected Greek clergymen were supporters and members. Some clerics in the church hierarchy were vexed because Ahepan leaders linked the "Hellenes" in the United States to classic, Periclean Greece, rather than to Byzantium, the ancestral seat of Greek Orthodoxy.[63] Other priests resented the English-only rules, since they could see that services conducted in archaic church-Greek may not continue to attract those who spoke only English. On the other hand, the newly prospering businessmen were also the biggest donors to the parish treasuries. In his presidential report at the AHEPA convention of 1926, Chebithes said that the attacks, led "by the Hellenic press in America" caused some losses in membership. Greeks "who could not withstand the abuse aimed at the fraternity and its members, also dropped their membership, even though they felt the objectives of the Ahepa were in the best interests of all Americans of Greek descent."[64]

Ahepans defended the use of English on several counts. By using English, they said, discussions would stay on current issues here and avoid Greek-based quarrels. The early 1920s were years of severe political strife in Greece, with Royalists squared off against the supporters of the popular leader of the Democratic Party, Eleftherios Venizelos. As described in chapter four, all of the Greek-language press and most church-parishes reflected that acrimonious old-country conflict; Greek-speaking parishioners and in many cases even their priests took sides. One of the Ahepans warned, "The use of the Greek language in our meetings will turn our meetings into coffeehouse pandemoniums."[65] In addition, guests and American honorary members who attended meetings and celebratory functions were most favorably impressed by the use of English. Moreover, the Order's general secretary pointed out that the vast majority of members in the early years were businessmen, owners of restaurants, diners, candy stores, fruit and flower markets, or employees in these types of businesses, and their greatest asset would be fluency in speaking, reading, and writing English.[66]

Fear that Greek politics might intrude into AHEPA affairs was responsible for postponing the organization of a chapter in Lowell, Massachusetts, where thousands of Greeks made their home. "Greek politics do not permit the establishment of a Chapter of the Ahepa in Lowell, Mass. Every one knows what is meant by 'Greek politics.' The so-called Venizelists and Royalists of Lowell have not yet settled their traditional political differences." Not until passions cooled, well into 1926, did the national office of the AHEPA permit a Chapter to be established in that city. George Demeter, an early AHEPA leader, wrote, "The Ahepa is neither Venizelist, nor Royalist. It is American. It is not a Greek organization. It is an American institution."[67]

AHEPA's opponents, Greek immigrants who wanted to preserve their language and traditions in the New World, formed a rival organization. In December 1923, a group of Greeks met in Pittsburgh, Pennsylvania, and formed the Greek American Progressive Association (GAPA). In Saloutos's opinion the philosophy of GAPA was impractical, having regard to the times and the position of Greeks in the United States. It made no appeal to and found no interest among the more affluent Greek Americans, so it often suffered financial hardships. Its unwillingness to make too radical a break with the past repelled many potential members. As AHEPA had shown, shrewd public relations could well carry the day, but GAPA's leaders did not take that road. GAPA attracted those who felt insecure in the American environment, as well as those who felt that pushing Americanism robbed the Greek Americans of their heritage. GAPA's assumption that Americanization meant an abandonment of Greek traditions was not borne out over the years. However, its unyielding stance lost the next generation.

Most second and third generation Greeks felt more at home with English, yet at the same time most of them have retained the religious faith of their forefathers. To be sure, the Greek Orthodox church has also changed over time and made it easier for them to keep the faith. In the early years, even in the late 1930s, the thinking of the church hierarchy paralelled that of GAPA. To retain all cultural and religious traditions, including the language, history, and way of life, was a holy mission. In 1928, at its peak, the GAPA fraternity claimed over fifty chapters, mostly in the northern and mid-western states, but chapters had formed in some southern cities too. Nevertheless, GAPA was swimming against the current. Unlike the Greek Orthodox church, which adopted and even embraced change, especially when American-born and American-trained Greek Orthodox priests spread to their new parish assignments and remarkably liberal and ecumenical attitudes overtook the Greek church in America, GAPA staunchly fought off influences of assimilation.[68] Without attracting the young, the organization all but disappeared with the passing of its first-generation members.

By 1928, the Klan's power declined. Many of the fears it had used to gain and hold members had faded. The gates had been closed to immigrant hordes. The Klan could not sustain a fight against evils more imagined than real. Above all, the Klan collapsed because of its own lawlessness and acrimonious internal disputes, as the press revealed to an increasingly disillusioned public Klan-inflicted floggings, mutilations, murders, and dissentions between prominent Klansmen.[69] By 1929, AHEPA too had reached a landmark period. Promoting education, philanthropy, and the American dream, its chapters formed into a nationwide organization, with over ten thousand members.[70] Efforts to befriend and lobby prominent public personalities waxed high in February 1929, when outgoing president Calvin Coolidge received a group of AHEPA leaders at the White House, lauded their efforts in educating their compatriots to be good Americans, and posed for photographs with the visitors. Two days later, the organization held its first "AHEPA National Banquet" honoring "the Congress of the United States." Seventy-five assorted senators and representatives had answered their invitations in the affirmative and together with prominent journalists, governors, governmental department heads, and other prominent visitors attended the gathering.[71] United States Senator William H. King served as toastmaster of the evening and delivered "an eloquent oration" praising America's citizens of Hellenic descent and AHEPA as the outstanding patriotic organization. Senator King also expressed his hope that other ethnic groups would follow AHEPA's example.

One month later, in March, the organization achieved another first: a corps of thirty AHEPAns marched in the inaugural parade for president Herbert Hoover. The inaugural committee gave them a place of honor in the division of patriotic organizations, next to the Sons of the American Revolution and the Union and Confederate Veterans, following the men of the American Legion.[72] The American press also recognized the patriotic and philanthropic work; the *Seattle Post Intelligencer*, which called for deportation of undesirable and unassimilable aliens, agreed that there was plenty of room for the type of citizens "turned out of the crucible by the Order of AHEPA," which had undertaken to teach its members loyalty to America, obedience to its laws, respect for traditions, and "the sacred responsibility of citizenship."[73] Franklin Delano Roosevelt became a member of the AHEPA in March 1931, when he was still governor of New York State.

The organization's greatest adaptation to American ways occurred as the leadership divided and formed into a two-party system. The indefatigable V. I. Chebithes had organized well; people loyal to him accepted his authority to such an extent that his will prevailed most of the time. Although there were other able, willing, and fairly affluent Ahepans ready to step up, he and his followers continued to win elective posts on the supreme lodge and subsequent appointments to prominent committees. With their innate resistance to any long-term control, many AHEPA members opposed his style of leadership and formed a vocal opposition. Several oligarchs led the contesting wing of the AHEPA, which managed to outvote the Chebithes party at a number of conventions and assume temporary control.

Chebithes held the supreme presidency for three years, from 1924 to 1927. At the 1927 convention, well-respected and personable men such as Dean Alfange of New York and Harris Booras led the opposition and took over the presidency from V. I. Chebithes until 1934. Then the organized Chebithes delegates formed the majority at the conventions and installed their leader as president again, from 1935 to 1939, when his loyal two-time vice-president, Van Nomikos, moved to the top post. By 1941 the opposition had regrouped; Chebithes's opponents George Vournas and Harris Booras captured the supreme lodge for the duration of the war and until the late 1940s. Very much like the see-saw between American Democrats and Republicans, Chebithes's followers, who in time adopted the name "the New Horizons" party and the Alfange - Booras opposition, later calling themselves "the Ahepa First" party, alternated in leading the nationwide organization.[74]

Differences between the two parties were not philosophical or ideological, but were based almost exclusively on the personalities of the protagonists. Just as in American politics, a number of popular programs and causes espoused by the AHEPA moved forward and changed in time without regard to which side had captured the leadership positions. Party platforms were hammered out at caucuses preceding the open conventions, compromises were achieved or rejected by selected negotiators uninhibited by the opinions of rank-and-file members. The essential philosophy, adopted during the association's early years, to promote American citizenship and loyalty to America and thus be accepted as "real" Americans was espoused by both sides.[75] Similarly, both sides influenced AHEPA's change over time, which clearly reflected the unfolding Greek-American identity adopted by the founders, members, and their second-generation heirs. In the 1940s and 1950s, they were solidly ensconced in the affluent ranks of the middle strata of American society, tending to prefer the status quo and to look at America and life in a notably traditionalist way. Parallel with that process, the history of the AHEPA, including all factions of its leadership, denoted its evolution from a progressive entity, advocating daringly novel ways to succeed in America, into a cautious fraternity, more opposed to innovation and very much in tune with the establishment. A brief overview of some AHEPA activities from the 1940s to the 1960s will clearly show this transformation.

In the 1940s, most Greek Americans were thoroughly involved in the war effort, especially since Greece and the United States ended up on the same side, fighting Italian Fascists, who had invaded Greece in 1940 and German Nazis, who occupied Greece from 1941 to 1944. AHEPA's finest hour came when the Treasury Department authorized the organization as an official agent for the sale of War Savings Bonds and patriotic members raised the initial goal of selling $100,000,000 worth of bonds to $150,000,000 and then surpassed it too, when sales in 1944 reached $162,000,000.

In 1944, at a time when no conventions were held due to the war, the Ahepa First party leaders, headed by George Vournas, decided to purchase a five-story building in Washington, D. C., and make this the permanent headquarters of the Order.[76] The Chebithes forces lodged numerous and vigorous protests, but to no avail. In time, all agreed that the organization ought to have a permanent presence in Washington, where substantive political action occurred. Indeed, in March 1946, at a White House ceremony, president Harry Truman became an honorary member of the Kansas City, Missouri chapter #73.[77]

In the late 1940s, AHEPA leaders of both parties proclaimed the organization's loyalty and support for the American side in the Cold War.[78] In this respect, AHEPA matched the position of the Greek Orthodox Church and approximated the feelings of over 80 percent of Greek America. After the successful elimination of the communist insurgency in Greece, won largely with American aid under the Truman Doctrine, thankful Ahepans commissioned Washington, D. C. sculptor Felix de Weldon to create a large statue of Harry Truman; in May 1963 they placed it on a square in downtown Athens, Greece.[79]

AHEPA now extended its lobbying activities to include more Greek causes. Headquarters in Washington announced the final stage of plans to finance a wing to the Evangelismos Hospital in Athens, adding 400 beds.[80] A lobby-group became active, urging Congress to "return the island of Cyprus to Greece" and to change the Displaced Persons Act, to allow entry into the United States of 50,000 Greeks.[81] Still, it would not do to neglect Americanism. In 1955, during the supreme convention at San Francisco, all factions voted to incorporate the Pledge of Allegiance and a salute to the American flag into the ritual conducted at the opening of all formal AHEPA meetings.[82] Pointedly confirming their patriotism in a period when non-conformity equaled un-Americanism, usually independent-minded members of local chapters, who often questioned most ordinary headquarters directives, accepted the decision and continued reciting the Pledge. Philanthropic causes engaged other members, who became interested in building more Greek Orthodox churches in America and organizing a registry of bone-marrow donors of Mediterranean origin for victims of Cooley's anaemia. In addition, members were urged to establish scholarship funds, to assist an ever greater number of Greek-American youngsters get into universities.

The conservative outlook surfaced again in the 1960s, even though members of specific chapters and even districts found themselves at odds with distinct segments within the fraternal organization. Greek Americans portray themselves as one group of citizens habitually fond of expressing its feelings for democracy and liberty for all people. Despite such resolutions and declarations, at the local level they were strangely reticent to comment on the civil rights struggle, then enveloping the southern states. But action spoke volumes. In the fall of 1963, Alabama governor George Wallace dramatically stood in the doorway of a building of the University of Alabama to block the enroll-ment of several black students; Martin Luther King gave his "I have a dream" speech to the crowd attending the March on Washington. At the August 1963 AHEPA supreme convention, the leadership of the Order "endorsed pending legislation designed to protect all minorities in the United States regardless of race, religion or national origin, to achieve for all groups and people full and complete equality in education, employment, and housing." Notwithstanding this mild nod in the direction of equality, in the spring of 1964, George Wallace became an honorary member of the Birmingham chapter of the Order of AHEPA.[83] In contrast, the once very conservative Greek Orthodox Church, led by Archbishop Iakovos, its hierarch in the United States, placed itself squarely on the side of reform and integration. The Archbishop traveled from New York to Selma and Birmingham and his photograph appeared on the front page of *Life* magazine, standing side by side with Martin Luther King Jr.[84] Of course, in the hierarchical setting of the church, any differences of opinion among the lower ranks tended to remain unheard.

In April 1967, in a bloodless coup, a Greek military junta took control of the nation's government. Droves of Greek Americans agreed with national and international statements deploring the loss of civil liberties in Greece, the "cradle of democracy." AHEPA leaders of both parties as well as a good part of the membership again took the conservative road. The formal statement issued by the AHEPA supreme lodge pointed out that Greece has at all times been a loyal and reliable friend and ally of the United States and urged continuation of all military and economic aid, since "the type of government in Greece is a matter that concerns the Greek people only." AHEPA secretary George Leber wrote, "many of our officers and members have recently visited Greece. They have found that law and order prevail and that conditions for visitors and tourists are most pleasant."[85] Despite these soothing and apologetic words from headquarters, numerous AHEPA members raised their voices in opposition to the military junta. George Vournas, a former supreme president, wrote to William Chirgotis, heading the supreme board of trustees, bitterly complaining that the AHEPA and the Greek Orthodox church must share the guilt for being led by people who act as "spokesmen for the colonels."[86]

By the 1960s there was no doubt that AHEPA had become an American fraternal organization, whose members had decades ago bought into the American dream and who were now struggling to preserve that dream in the face of nationwide change and unrest. In 1964, Saloutos recognized AHEPA as the "greatest single Americanizing force" among the Greeks.[87] In his opinion, it was the most influential lay organization for Greek Americans, in large part because it had mastered the fine art of legislative pressure."[88] It had also changed with the times. The first cycle of history of the organization was that of identifying its members with the greater American community. Once that work was completed, the next cycle dealt with bringing the next, now confidently American generation into closer touch with Greece and their members' Greek heritage. Solid, staid, and affluent Americans of Greek origin sought to foster cultural links that were earlier rejected, but now seemed desireable. Flexibility in strategy and tactics was mandatory for the survival of any viable fraternal organization from one generation to the next. In the 1960s AHEPA was as viable as it was in the 1920s. Its programs consisted of philanthropy and cooperation with the church; its members became influential by their generous donations and activities in the parishes and by their political activity on the local, state, and federal levels.

Early Greek fraternal organizations served a useful purpose. They brought together people who were on the outer fringes of American society and felt uncomfortable in the presence of persons of different backgrounds. They provided a common meeting ground; they aided many worthy causes. Their survival, however, was contingent upon projecting programs that did not draw all support to specific regions in Greece. AHEPA was the only organization designed to operate in the American setting, specifically in the American South. It sought to imitate successful and long-lived fellowships such as the Masons or the Kiwanis. Despite subsequent internal conflicts created by temperamental, stubborn leaders and a contentious membership, through the years AHEPA accomplished more in identifying Greek Americans with the greater American community than did all the other organizations combined.

TABLE 7
THE 1922 CHARTER INCORPORATING THE AMERICAN-HELLENIC EDUCATIONAL PROGRESSIVE ASSOCIATION [AHEPA]

GEORGIA, Fulton County.

To The Superior Court of said County:

The petition of George A. Poulos, Harry Angelopoulos, James Vlass, John Angelopoulos, N. D. Chotas and James Campbell of Fulton County, Georgia shows:

(1) That they desire for themselves, their associates and successors to be incorporated under the name and style of
"The American-Hellenic Educational Progressive Association,"for a period of twenty years, with the privilege of renewal at the expiration of that time.
(2) The object of said association is to form a fraternal order and secure members therefore, with the purpose in view of advancing and promoting pure and undefiled Americanism among the Greeks of the United States, the territorial and colonial possessions thereof; to educate Greeks of the United States in the matter of democracy, and of the government of the United States, and to instill the deepest loyalty and allegiance of the Greeks of this country to the United States, its tenets and institutions and to teach the operation and

meaning of the said government together with its laws, rules and regulations; and to promote American education among the Greeks; and to promote the highest type of American citizenship among the Greeks; and to promote a spirit of fraternity, sociability and benevolence among the members.

(3) Petitioners, already having formed themselves into the "Supreme Lodge," desire the right and power in their corporate name to organize other lodges to be known as "Superior Lodges" and "Subordinate Lodges" in the different cities, towns and hamlets of the different states of the United States, and of the different Territorial and Colonial possessions of the United States if desired, and to provide rules and regulations for said lodges. Said "The American-Hellenic Educational Progressive Association" is to provide a ritual through said "Supreme Lodge," control the ceremonies and to have full and entire control of the said organization, and all matters of complaint between its members, or with superior and subordinate lodges shall be finally settled by its decree. The said "Supreme Lodge" shall be the chief functioning body of said organization. It being the intention of said Association to carry on a fraternal society in conformity with the laws of the State of Georgia.

(4) There shall be no capital stock as none is required or needed in execution of the plans and powers herein sought. Petitioners only desire to organize, and conduct a purely fraternal order based upon the precepts as herein before set forth.

(5) The principal office and place of business of said Association will be in the city of Atlanta, County and State aforesaid, with the privileges of establishing branch offices at any other place desired.

(6) Said Association desired the right to receive donations, make by-laws for the government of itself and its superior and subordinate lodges, sue and be sued, buy, sell or lease real or personal property if beneficial to its organization, or the fund realized therein, and to have all the powers usual or necessary to corporations of like character.

Wherefore, petitioners pray to be made a body corporate, with the privileges and powers herein prayed.

Hutcheson & Morris
Attorneys for Petitioners
Filed in Office, this the 28th day of July, 1922.
Arnold Broyles, C.S.C.

GEORGIA, Fulton County.

In Re: Application of Geo. A. Poulos et al., for incorporation under the name and style of

"The American-Hellenic Educational Progressive Association"

It appearing to the court that the purpose of this incorporation as set forth in the application for incorporation are each and severally within the intent of the laws of Georgia, and all requirements of law have been duly met and complied with including publication as required by law, and this matter coming on to be heard, after full and complete compoliance with all lawful requirements in the premises; and there being no objection thereto,

It is therefore considered, ordered and adjudged that the prayers of petitioners are granted, & that the petitioners are incorporated as prayed, with all the rights, privileges and immunities granted corporations of like character under the laws of Georgia.

This 25 day of September, 1922.

Shepard Bryan

Judge Superior Court Atlanta Circuit

STATE OF GEORGIA,
COUNTY OF FULTON.

I, T. C. Miller, Clerk Superior Court, Fulton County, Georgia, do hereby certify that the within and foregoing is a true and correct copy of the Application of Geo. A. Poulos et al. to be incorporated under the name and style of

"The American-Hellenic Educational Progressive Association,"

with Order thereon granting same, all of which appears of file and record in this office.

Witness my hand and seal of Office,

this the 6th day of July, 1926.

(Signed) T. C. Miller

Clerk Superior Court, Fulton County, Georgia

Seal:

Superior Court.

TABLE 8
**AHEPA CHAPTERS ESTABLISHED 1922-1925, DURING THE FIRST THREE
YEARS OF THE ASSOCIATION'S EXISTENCE [4,992 MEMBERS]**

Chapter No. and Name		City & State
1	Atlanta	Atlanta, Georgia
2	Marathon	Charlotte, N. C.
3	Birmingham	Birmingham, Ala.
4	Plato	Charleston, S. C.
5	Solon	Savannah, Georgia
6	Socrates	Jacksonville, Fla.
7	Memphis	Memphis, Tenn.
8	Shreveport	Shreveport, La.
9	Fayetteville	Fayetteville, N. C.
10	Sir Walter Raleigh	Raleigh, N. C.
11	Wilson	Wilson, N. C.
12	Lycurgus	Tampa, Florida
13	Tulsa	Tulsa, Oklahoma
14	Miami	Miami, Florida
15	Sunshine	St. Petersburg, Fl.
16	Geo. Washington	Tarpon Springs, Fl.
17	St. Augustine	St. Augustine, Fl.
18	Palm Beach	W. Palm Beach, Fl.
19	Fort Worth	Fort Worth, Texas
20	Dallas	Dallas, Texas
21	Fort Smith	Fort Smith, Ark.
22	Eldorado	Eldorado, Ark.
23	Liberty	Montgomery, Ala.
24	Athens	Boston, Mass.
25	Delphi	New York City, N.Y.
26	Hercules	Philadelphia, Penn.
27	Muskogee	Muskogee, Okla.
28	Land of The Sky	Asheville, N. C.
29	Alexander Great	Houston, Texas
30	Worthington	Baltimore, Maryl'd.
31	Washington	Washington, D. C.

32	Winston-Salem	Winston-Salem, N.C.
33	Athene	Johnstown, Penn.
34	Aristoteles	Pittsburgh, Penn.
35	Nashua	Nashua, New H.
36	Cleveland	Cleveland, Ohio
37	Syracuse	Syracuse, N. Y.
38	Samuel Gr. Howe	Brookline, Mass.
39	Acropolis	Haverhill, Mass.
40	Alpha	Detroit, Michigan
41	Brooklyn	Brooklyn, N. Y.
42	Upper Manhattan	New York, N. Y.
43	Milwaukee	Milwaukee, Wisc.
44	Manchester	Manchester, N. H.
45	Daniel Webster	Springfield, Mass.
46	Chicago	Chicago, Illinois
47	Lawrence	Lawrence, Mass.
48	Waterbury	Waterbury, Conn.
49	Fond du Lac	Fond du Lac, Wisc.
50	Aristides	Lynn, Mass.
51	Westchester	Yonkers, New York
52	Eureka	Newark, N. J.
53	St. Louis	St. Louis, Missouri
54	Alexander Hamilton	Paterson, N. J.
55	Black Diamond	Wilkes-Barre, Penn
56	Eastonia	Easton, Penn.
57	Lord Byron	Brockton, Mass.
58	Nathan Hale	Hartford, Conn.
59	Longfellow	Canton, Ohio
60	Lehigh	Allentown, Penn.
61	William Penn	Reading, Penn.
62	Bridgeport	Bridgeport, Conn.
63	Goodfriendship	Akron, Ohio
64	Harrisburg	Harrisburg, Penn.
65	Homer	Bethlehem, Penn.
66	Demosthenes	Minneapolis, Minn.
67	Flower City	Rochester, N. Y.
68	Miltiades	Wheeling, W. Va.
69	Camden	Camden, N. J.

70	Themis	Springfield, Mass.
71	Red Rose	Lancaster, Penn.
72	Trenton	Trenton, N. J.
73	Heart of America	Kansas City, Mo.
74	Philanthropos	Massillon, Ohio
75	Monroe	New Brunswick, N. J.
76	Rainbow	Shamokin, Penn.
77	Leonidas	Binghamton, N. Y.
78	Gary	Gary, Indiana
79	Chester	Chester, Penn.
80	George Jarvis	Worcester, Mass.

[Note: the 1985 yearbook shows 391 active chapters with 28,099 members.]

Notes

1   The American Hellenic Educational and Progressive Association's acronym AHEPA became the popular name for this Greek-American fraternal society, as in "the Order of Ahepa." Members and non-members used the acronym as a noun, for example "AHEPA" and "the Ahepans," or as an adjective, as in "Ahepan principles."

2   Dimitrios Ioannis Monos, "Upward Mobility, Assimilation, and the Achievements of the Greeks in the United States with Special Emphasis on Boston and Philadelphia," (University of Pennsylvania, Ph.D. dissertation, 1976) 83-85. Also see George Pozzetta, ed., *Immigration and Ethnicity* (New York, Garland Publishers, 1991), vol. 5, *Immigrant Institutions: the Organization of Immigrant Life*, passim.

3   Ibid.; Monos believed Greek immigrants aligned themselves with such associations "primarily during the early stages of acculturation" (83-84); he defined "acculturation" as a dynamic process immigrants undergo as they learn the values, traits, and patterns of the dominant host culture (6-7). Monos identified "adaptation" to the host culture to be a process following acculturation; he asserted that successful adaptation, in the context of immigrants to the United States, was judged in terms of adherence to middle-class norms of occupational and social behavior. Monos further held that the time of adaptation might end when neither natives nor newcomers view the latter as "aliens," "foreigners," or "ethnics" and now consider them(selves) as members of the host culture (7).

4   Lubomyr R. Wynar, *Encyclopedic Directory of Ethnic Organizations in the United States* (Littleton, Colorado, Libraries Unlimited, Inc., 1975), xvii: societies and agencies formed by English-speaking nationality groups were regarded as "American;" similar societies created by non-Anglo immi-

grants were classified as "foreign," primarily because non-English languages were used in the organization.

5   Chapter 2 of this work, "Demetrios is Now Jimmy," describes the enterprising and yet equivocal adaptation of Greek immigrants to life in the New South urban areas. The chapter title was derived from the prevalent Americanization of names and simplification of surnames, when every Constantine became Gus, every Demetrios was Jim or Jimmy, every Vasilios answered to Bill, and some of the surnames altered to Johnson, or Moore, where their Greek origin was completely veiled.

6   topika somateia = local societies. The Cretan Brotherhood was one such early "local" society, drafting into membership anyone from the island of Crete; see list of such societies in George Leber, *History of the Order of AHEPA* (Washington, D. C., The Order of AHEPA, 1972), 113, 161.

7   Theodore Saloutos, *The Greeks in the United States* (Cambridge, Harvard University Press, 1964), 75.

8   Ibid., 75, quoting from the Greek language newspaper *Saloniki* of March 6, 1915.

9   Stephanos Zotos, *Hellenic Presence in America* (Wheaton, Illinois, Pilgrimage Publishers, 1976), 136; George J. Leber, *The History of the Order of AHEPA* (Washington, AHEPA publications, 1972), 161, asserts that "the establishment of Greek-American associations on both national and local levels ranks the highest among any immigrant groups." Leber cited no authorities for his assertion, however, he listed a long slate of names of such organizations, which "disappeared over the years."

10   Saloutos, *Greeks in the United States*, 75.

11   See Introduction, pages dealing with honor and shame in the Mediterranean.

12   Immigration History Research Center, University of Minnesota at Minneapolis, the Theodore Saloutos Collection [hereinafter referred to as IHRC, T. Saloutos Collection], Box 20, Folder 123.

13   Zotos, *Hellenic Presence in America*, 137.

14   Saloutos, *Greeks in the United States*, 77, 100-101.

15   Babis Malafouris, *Greeks in America 1528-1948* (New York, Isaac Goldman Company, 1948) .

16   Ibid.

17   Saloutos, *Greeks in America*, 171.

18   The Dodecanese islands, populated by Greeks, were occupied by Ottoman Turks 1522-1912, then by Italy until their liberation by the Allies in World War II. In 1947 the islands finally became part of Greece. Inhabitants of the islands Symi, Kalymnos, and Halki dived for sponges since ancient times, and formed the majority of the Greek population in the early days of sponging in Florida's Tarpon Springs; see chapter 6.

19   *Dedication: Holy Trinity Greek Orthodox Church 1906-1956* yearbook on the occasion of the 50th anniversary of the parish (Birmingham, n.p., 1956),

"Brief History of the Greek parish of Birmingham," 2.

20   See chapter 2, and Table 9 (chapter 4); the *kinotis* denotes an organized community or congregation or parish which could be incorporated. Members of the *kinotis* usually pledged money for the acquisition and maintenance of the church building and to pay the priest, so the *kinotis* served mainly religious purposes, although its members often organized social functions, such as dances and luncheons. Note also that a parish includes all Eastern Orthodox faithful who attend that church, even if some of them are not members of the organized *kinotis*.

21   "Factional Strife Marked Cathedral's Earliest Years," *Orthodox Observer* 57 (November 1992), 24, [New York, Greek Archdiocese Publication].

22   *Orthodox Observer* 59 (June 1994), citing Andrew Kopan's article "Hellenism in Chicago," published in 1984 by the United Hellenic American Congress (UHAC); the Spartans founded the Annunciation parish in 1892;the Arcadians established Holy Trinity in 1897; see "Chicago's Church Marks 100th Anniversary," in *OrthodoxObserver* 62 (October 1997), 20.

23   See chapter 2 of this work, as well as Table 9 of chapter 4, both show the establishment of *kinotites* in various southern cities, leading to the founding of a church parishes.

24   Saloutos, *Greeks in the United States*, 237-240, indicates that in the North "the peak of naturalization" was reached in the late 1920s.

25   Zotos, *Hellenic Presence in America*, at 178-179 has a listing of early Greek-language newspapers, as does Saloutos, *Greeks in the United States*, 89-90; neither list shows any newspapers published in the South. The presence of few potential subscribers probably explains the fact that there were no notable Greek-language papers published in the South; however, many Greeks living in the South subscribed to the *Hellenikos Astir* [the Hellenic Star] from Chicago, *Atlantis* from New York [very much pro-Royalist], or *Kalifornia* from San Francisco, and after 1914 to the *Ethnikos Kyrix* [National Herald, which favored the Venizelos side during the great schism].

26   Saloutos, *Greeks in the United States*, 88.

27   Although Babis Malafouris, *Hellenes in America 1528-1948* (New York, Isaac Goldman Co., 1948), at 230 mentions an Atlanta bi-weekly paper, *to Vima=The Tribune*, he did not state in what year the paper might have been published nor for how long; all attempts to find a copy failed; by courtesy of Dr. Gary Mormino, this writer saw one issue of a four-page paper, *The Florida Greek Review*, of June 1, 1942, written in Greek and poor English, edited, printed, and distributed by a Tampa man, who referred to himself as "Mr. Sakelracos;" the issue was marked "Vol. 26-No.1;" see Box 26 of the Spessard Holland papers, P. K. Yonge Library, University of Florida; some solid papers have been established lately, such as *The Greek American Herald*, published in Hollywood, Florida, since 1991.

28   Zotos, *Hellenic Presence in America*, 117.

29   Charles Jaret, "The Greek, Italian, and Jewish American Ethnic Press,"

Journal of American Ethnic Studies 7 (#2), (Summer 1979), 47-70, at 53; Theodore Saloutos, *Greeks in the United States,* 183; Jaret disagreed with Saloutos, in that he, Jaret, saw *some* evidence of Greek press involvement in American issues and quoted some Chicago Greek papers' advocating naturalization and voting, of course all in Greek; on page 64, however, Jaret admits that "editorial after editorial" selected Greek language and religion to be "the essentials of Greekness" and advocated that one had to remain loyal to these "central Greek symbols" even as one Americanized.

30 Charles Jaret, "The Greek, Italian and Jewish American Ethnic Press: A Comparative Analysis," 56-57; Jaret found that the Yiddish press was indeed a vital factor in educating its readers to an American point of view and a most powerful "Americanizing agency operative on the Jewish scene," pp.48-49; the Italian press made few efforts to instruct its readers on the American political system, and devoted abundant space to defend the good name of Italians against accusations and prejudicial allegations connecting all Italians with the Mafia, pp. 51-52; The Greek press touched on American issues, but spent much more space on local and regional issues and events in Greece, pp. 54-55.

31 Kenneth T. Jackson, *The Ku Klux Klan in the City 1915-1930* (New York, Oxford University Press, 1967), 7-12.

32 David M. Chalmers, *Hooded Americanism: the History of the Ku Klux Klan* (New York, Franklin Watts, 3rd ed., 1981), 71; it is quite likely that astute Greek Americans also knew when the House of Representatives in Washington investigated the Klan in 1921, Georgia Congressman William D. Upshaw and Senator Tom Watkins defended 'Colonel' William Simmons.

33 This mainstream side of the Klan is best represented in Leonard J. Moore, *Citizen Klansmen: The Ku Klux Klan in Indiana, 1921-1928* (Chapel Hill, University of North Carolina Press, 1991); although Moore deals with the mainstream nature of the hooded order in Indiana, one can argue that the same situation existed in Georgia, in that most of the state's voters, just as in Indiana, rejected violent vigilantism. Also see Nancy MacLean, *Behind the Mask of Chivalry: The Making of the Second Ku Klux Klan* (New York, Oxford University Press, 1994), 53, where MacLean finds that Klansmen in Athens, Georgia, are "middling men," part of the same stratum of society as the Greek small businessmen in the South.

34 Kenneth Jackson, *The Ku Klux Klan in the City 1915-1930,* 35, 39.

35 George J. Leber, *The History of the Order of AHEPA 1922-1972* (Washington, D.C., The Order of AHEPA, 1972), v, 150.

36 Kenneth Jackson, *The Ku Klux Klan in the City 1915-1930,* 10; professional Klan recruiters arranged for Klan lecturers to speak "on the principles of 'one hundred per cent Americanism'," adding 48,000 members to Klan rosters in three months; organizers retained $4.00 of each recruit's $10.00 initiation fee.

37   Lubomyr Wynar, *Ethnic Organizations in the United States*, xvi, outlined
      that the Americanization movement was, in part, based on ethnocentri-
      cism; since ethnic non-Anglo cultures were perceived as being "inferior"
      to the Anglo cultures, it followed that ethnics were "inferior," "unpatriotic,"
      and "un-American." In order to overcome these problems, AHEPA organ-
      izers had to show themselves as "American," "patriotic," and "equal."

38   Harry Angelopoulos letter to Georgia Chotas, January 1965; thanks to Dr.
      David Chalmers, professor of History at the University of Florida [retired
      1996], the author received a copy of Harry Angelopoulos's letter to his
      daughter, Mrs. Georgia Chotas, nee Angelopoulos, written in 1965, when
      Harry A. felt moved to describe for his daughter and for posterity the
      founding of the organization.

39   An *Atlanta Constitution* editor observed in 1913, "We believe there is plenty
      of room in America for the right sort of Jews, as for the right sort of Greeks,
      French, English and Germans;" cited in Steven Herzberg, *Strangers Within
      the Gate City* (Philadelphia, Jewish Publication Society of America, 1978),
      134.

40   Nancy MacLean, in *Behind the Mask of Chivalry*, and Leonard Moore, in
      Citizen Klansmen, both assert that concerns for the public good, not irra-
      tional bigotry, sustained the popularity of the Klan during the early 1920s.

41   IHRC, T. Saloutos Collection, Box 37, Folder 272.

42   Harry Angelopoulos letter to Georgia Chotas. In fact, E. Y. Clarke was the
      Imperial Kleagle = organizer and recruiting director in charge of the
      "Propagation Department;" also see Table 7.

43   Peter N. Mantzoros, *AHEPA and I Across the Years* (Glenview, Illinois, Pnyx
      Publications, 1966), 9-11; Mantzoros gave short biographies of the eight
      founders, including James Vlass [Demetrios Nicholau Vlassopoulos] and
      George A. Polos [Nickopoulos], who was, the author wrote, "employed by
      the Imperial Palace of the Ku Klux Klan in a confidential capacity...was
      present and participated in its secret meetings and conferences..."; the
      author gave no source for his information linking Polos to the Klan, but
      the founders evidently knew of it and used it. In 1939 Peter Mantzoros
      established the English language newspaper *Chicago Pnyx*, "An Independent
      Monthly Newspaper Interpreting The Nation's Hellenic Thought;" he was
      its publisher and editor for over fifty years.

44   Leber, *History of the Order of AHEPA*, 147-151; see Table 7 for the complete
      text of the AHEPA Charter.

45   Ibid., 150: paragraph (2) of the AHEPA charter contains the words cited
      above, as well as the intention "to educate Greeks of the United States in
      the matter of democracy, and of the government of the United States, and
      to instill the deepest loyalty and allegiance of the Greeks of this country
      to the United States, . . . and to promote American education among the
      Greeks; and to promote the highest type of American citizenship among
      the Greeks; and to promote a spirit of fraternity, sociability and benevo-

lence among the members."

46 Ibid., 160; see Table 8 for a record of the first 32 AHEPA lodges established between July 1922 and October 1923.

47 Harry Angelopoulos letter to Georgia Chotas: founder Nick Chotas [a senior relative to Georgia's husband] had "experience in fraternal orders" as past Worshipful Master of the Masons; founder James Campbell was a Mason; See also: Mark Christopher Carnes, *Secret Rituals and Manhood in Victorian America* (New Haven, Yale University Press, 1989).

48 Theodore Saloutos, *Greeks in the United States*, 250.

49 George Leber, *History of the Order of AHEPA*, 162-164.

50 Robert M. Fogelson and Richard E. Rubenstein eds., *Hearings on the Ku Klux Klan 1921* (New York, Arno Press & The New York Times, 1969, with a text of "The Ku-Klux Klan Hearings before the Committee On Rules of the House of Representatives," 67th Congress, First Session; earlier, in 1906 in Atlanta, Upshaw published *The Golden Age*, a militant Christian magazine; later, in 1932, Upshaw was nominated as the presidential candidate for the Prohibition Party: *Biographical Directory of the American Congress* (Washington, D.C., US Government Printing Office, 1950), 1944.

51 Peter Mantzoros, *AHEPA and I Across the Years*, 70-72; George Leber, *History of the Order of AHEPA*, 170-172.

52 George Leber, *History of the Order of AHEPA*, 161.

53 Ibid. , 161.

54 Ibid., 168, 170, 178.

55 Ibid., 252-254; Vasilios Isidorou [V. I.] Chebithes came to America in 1906, when he was fifteen, and settled in Somerset, Kentucky. After completing high school, he attended Center College at Danville, Kentucky, where he became a member of the Chamberlain Literary Society, the Athletic Council, and the College Publicity Board, won inter-collegiate debating and oratorical prizes and was elected the orator of his class. He also took an active part in politics and worked in campaigns for William Howard Taft, Theodore Roosevelt, Charles Evans Hughes, congressman King Swope, and governor Edwin P. Morrow. During World War I he served with the American Army overseas. On his return he studied law at the George Washington University. Since 1923, he practiced law in Washington, D.C.

56 Ibid., 197.

57 IHRC, T. Saloutos Collection, *The Charlotte Observer* and *The Charlotte News*, both of August 20, 1925, cited in *The AHEPA*, September 1925, 14; *The Jacksonville Journal*, August 5, 1925, cited in *ibid.*, 29.

58 IHRC, T. Saloutos Collection, *The Savannah Morning News*, August 10, 1925, cited in *The AHEPA*, September 1925, 25.

59 IHRC, T. Saloutos Collection, *The AHEPA*, September 1925, 29; see also article in the *Jacksonville Journal*, August 5, 1925,

60 George Leber, *History of the Order of AHEPA*, 198-199.

61   *The AHEPA*, September 1925, 166.

62   George Leber, *History of the Order of AHEPA*, at 185, the "Springfield, Massachusetts, chapter [#45] noted five reverend brothers among their membership;" in Chicago, Illinois, reverend Mark Petrakis [father of Greek-American author Harry Petrakis] was the chapter's treasurer, while Bishop Philaretos Johannides was on that chapter's Board of Governors; page 212: reverend S. S. Spathy, of Richmond, Virginia Greek Orthodox Church of Sts. Constantine and Helen was a member of that AHEPA chapter [#83] and delegate to the 4th convention; page 202: in 1926, reverend Louis Rocca, of the Holy Trinity Episcopal Church, in Fort Wayne, Indiana, was a member of AHEPA's Fort Wayne chapter #81.

63   Ibid., 206-207.

64   *Archon Magazine* of August, 1927, cited in Zotos, *Hellenic Presence in America*, 143.

65   George Leber, *History of the Order of AHEPA*, 209-210.

66   George Demeter, "Why Greek Organizations Fail," special 1924 AHEPA Convention magazine, cited in George Leber, *History of the Order of AHEPA*, 173-175.

67   In 1933, the Greek Orthodox Archdiocese of North and South America, led by Archbishop Athenagoras, purchased an estate in Pomfret, Connecticut, and in 1937 established the first Greek Orthodox theological school in the United States; AHEPA contributed $10,000 to the purchase monies for the Pomfret property; by 1942 this institution began graduating American-born, English-speaking priests, who were also expected to speak fluent Greek, and who were quickly appointed to Greek Orthodox parishes throughout the United States. The new priesthood, together with enlightened leadership by Archbishops Athenagoras and Iakovos, contributed in large measure to the liberalization and modernization of the church in the Americas. See chapter 4, dealing with religious life in Greek-American communities.

68   David Chalmers, *Hooded Americanism*, 291-298.

69   See Table 8. A survey prepared for the Supreme Lodge of the AHEPA in 1977, shows that the organizations actual membership, in good standing as of December 1975, amounted to 22,082 members nationwide.

70   George Leber, *History of the Order of AHEPA*, 228-232; Leber's notes cite a bulletin which shows "that great Philhellene, United States Senator William H. King" as the toastmaster of the evening, with an incomplete guest list, including Senators: James A. Reed [D] of Missouri; Thomas F. Bayard [D] and Daniel Oren Hastings [R] of Delaware; Clarence C. Dill [D] of Washington; Walter F. George [D] of Georgia; Matthew M. Neely [D] of West Virginia; Key Pittman [D] of Nevada; Arthur R. Robinson [R] of Indiana; Ellison DuRant Smith [D] of South Carolina; David I. Walsh [D] of Massachusetts; Park Trammel [D] of Florida, and many others; the AHEPA still holds a Congressional Banquet every two years—up to and

including 2006—by inviting all Congressmen and honoring those politicians who contributed in any way to causes espoused by the AHEPA.

71   George Leber, *History of the Order of AHEPA*, 232.

72   *The Post Intelligencer* of Seattle, Washington, November 7, 1930, cited in George Leber, *History of the Order of AHEPA*, 263.

73   From the early 1960s to the present, the AHEPA leadership is still divided into opposing camps; from time to time wings of one or the other party cooperate with other independently-minded members to create temporary third-party situations; see, for example, a series of articles named "The Birth and Growth of the AHEPA First Party: An Ahepan's Odyssey," by past supreme president Dr. Peter V. Paulus, and the "Ahepa Update" column in *Hellenic Pilgrimage*, June 1988 to December 1989, or editorials by Peter Mantzoros and articles by Nicholas Limperis in *The Chicago Pnyx*, both English-language Greek-American newspapers. This author is grateful to Dr. Paulus, now retired in Ocala, Florida, for making available his papers covering some AHEPA political and philanthropic activities in the 1970s and 1980s.

74   George Leber, *History of the Order of AHEPA*, 213; after his election victory, Dean Alfange echoed V. I. Chebithes on the need to unite for the good of the organization, "AHEPA has profited from the sad experiences of the past. It has eliminated from its organic make-up all those factors which in the past contributed to the inability of the Greek people to unite...It speaks the English language. It follows American methods. It vibrates with the spirit of progress. It has none of the earmarks of the Greek organizations of the past. This is the secret of its success."

75   The five-story building was located at 1420 K Street North-West in downtown Washington, adjacent to the Ambassador Hotel.

76   George Leber, *History of the Order of AHEPA*, 367; in 1945, mayor of Minneapolis, Hubert Humphrey, future senator and vice president, joined the Demosthenes chapter #66 in the twin cities; late in 1946, two senators from Vermont, George D. Aiken and Ralph E. Flanders and Vermont governor Ernest W. Gibson were added to the membership roster of the Rutland, Vermont, chapter #244; senator William Knowland of California became a member of the Oakland, California, chapter #171.

77   Despite united efforts, during World War II, of both the Greek communist and Greek nationalist underground forces to free the country from German occupation, the two sides fell out in 1945 and by 1946 a civil war enveloped Greece. The communist strongholds were in the northern part of the country, close to the borders of then communist Albania, Yugoslavia and Bulgaria; nationalists had some British aid, but prevailed only after the Truman Doctrine went into effect and several hundred American "observers" brought massive military supplies and trained Greek government troops. A majority of Greek Americans favored the nationalist side.

78   IHRC, T. Saloutos Collection, Box 47, Folder 374, contains a picture of the

statue, also depicted in the *New York Times* of Sunday, May 5, 1963, as well as a twelve-page pamphlet, printed by the AHEPA on the occasion of the dedication of the Truman Memorial in Athens, Greece, May 29, 1963; the ceremony included AHEPA supreme president George J. Margoles, Greek prime minister Constantine Caramanlis, US ambassador to Greece Henry Labouisse, mayor of Athens Angel Tsoukalas, Archbishop Chrysostomos of Athens and all Greece, Archbishop Iakovos of the Greek Orthodox Church in the Americas.

79   George Leber, *History of the Order of AHEPA*, 367, 370-371; in addition, the AHEPA financed a hospital in Salonika and six AHEPA health centers at Chryssoupolis, Kalavryta, Paramythia, Molai, Meligala, and Ierapetra.

80   Ibid., 383, also see 390-392; the Displaced Persons Act was created to allow World War II refugees, from countries behind the iron curtain, to immigrate into the United States; since Greece was not behind the iron curtain, its nationals were not included; however, pursuant to AHEPA's lobbying efforts, Congress allowed the immigration of 10,000 Greek displaced persons, provided the AHEPA accepted responsibility for their placement in the US; all were taken care of. In 1953, the new US Refugee Relief Act included special non-quota immigrant visas for 214,000 refugees, among them were 15,000 Greeks.

81   Ibid., 401.

82   Ibid., 452; on page 442 Leber notes the convention resolution endorsing pending legislation to protect minorities. At page 443 one can see the strength of the AHEPA factions at the 1963 convention fairly evenly divided: The Ahepa First party captured the offices of supreme president and supreme secretary [John Plumides and Nick Smyrnis] and the New Horizons party elected the supreme vice president and supreme treasurer [Nicholas Chirekos and Xenophon Microutsikos].

83   IHRC, T. Saloutos Collection, *Life* magazine, March 26, 1965, depicts on its front page Archbishop Iakovos in full regalia standing next to Martin Luther King Jr., with Walter Reuther just behind them, at the ceremony commemorating reverend James Reeb.

84   George Leber, *History of the Order of AHEPA*, 478-481; Leber's own comments were in the same vein: after 1964, the political struggle between the dozen or more parties caused chaotic situation close to anarchy. "...we offer no apologies for the actions taken by the Greek Colonels, but logic does demand that the onlooker take into account...the tragic suffering of the people." Since April 1967, economic conditions "improved considerably, benefits and services to the people had increased tremendously, people were all working, and life was good, pleasant, and calm. There were fewer tensions, and very little insecurity."

85   IHRC, Theodore Saloutos Collection, Box 83, Folder 284: letter, August 8, 1975, George C. Vournas to William G. Chirgotis, complains that AHEPA is "willing handmaiden to the Greek Orthodox Archdiocese of America,"

and therefore not non-sectarian in religion, and must assume with Archbishop Iakovos guilt for being spokesman for the colonels." Also see *Washington Post* of December 7, 1972, A1 and A16, write-up about lawyer George C. Vournas, 71, who arrived in 1916, in time became member of AHEPA and an American in outlook and way of life, "My 'we' had changed. How imperceptibly that moment had arrived." The *Washington Post* of December 12, 1972 carried a reply written by reverend Demetrios G. Kalivis.

86   IHRC, Theodore Saloutos Papers, Box 24, Folder 172, "Greeks in the United States," unpublished article written in 1945; Box 36, Folder 269, Saloutos, himself a member of the AHEPA, confirmed this opinion in a speech made in 1964.
87   Theodore Saloutos, *Greeks in the United States*, 375.
88   Ibid., AHEPA pamphlet cited at 383.

CHAPTER 4

FROM BYZANTINE RITES TO CIVIL RIGHTS:

THE GREEK ORTHODOX CHURCH IN THE SOUTHERN STATES

Once they arrived in America, most immigrants asserted their ancestral faith. The parish, the congregation, or the shul became places where people with similar backgrounds regrouped after immigrating. The church or the synagogue was part of their spiritual heritage and the adjoining hall served not just as part of a religious entity, but also as a social gathering place.[1] With Greek immigrants, in addition to religious conviction and social need, national sentiment was another important motive to organize early parishes and remain loyal to the Greek Orthodox church. This held especially true with ethnic Greeks who came from areas outside Greece, for example, Asia Minor, Thrace, Epirus, and islands such as Crete.[2] Greek clergy, raised and trained in the Balkans and in the Middle East, were as much concerned with political affairs as they were with the spiritual needs of the people.[3] For example, during and after World War I, the royalist - liberal schism, essentially a political clash based in Greece, directly affected Greek immigrants and their nascent church parishes in America. Moreover, this conflict retarded the institutional organization of the church in the United States and tainted relations between Greek Orthodox hierarchs at the Holy Synod in Athens and those at the Patriarchate in Constantinople. Byzantine-like threads of the discord straightened out only after hierarchical authority over the Americas shifted to church primates resident in the United States.[4] Inasmuch as the Greek Orthodox hierarchs in America ultimately answered to the Patriarchate in Constantinople, their position approximated that of the Roman Catholic hierarchy in the states, who still answered to the pope in Rome. Despite its insecure start, the Greek Orthodox Church in America matured and transformed from a conservative, conflict-ridden ethnic denomination to a progressive religious force and a spiritual and ecclesiastical home for millions of Americans.

At least on the surface, religion had a firm hold on the Greeks.[5] Thus whenever Hellenic immigrants settled in a city, even if they came from a variety of regions around the Aegean and the Mediterranean, they tended to get together and form a *kinotis*, an organized community. *Kinotis* translates into "community" in a secular sense and "congregation" or "parish" if it is a religious public body. One cannot easily determine just when there were "enough" Greeks, how many families made up the critical mass, to form a parish. By tradition, at times captured in parish year-books or commemorative albums, usually the gathering of a few successful businessmen was sufficient. They would invite other local Greeks to a meeting, either at a larger private home or a Greek-owned coffee shop or restaurant, for the purpose of discussing the possibility of forming the *kinotis*. From as few as fifteen to as many as over one hundred men attended, agreed with the need to enhance their families' and their own religious and spiritual life in the new place, and outlined practical ideas about location and finances.[6] If a general accord crowned the meeting, those present usually agreed upon an appropriate name for the new entity, signed the first roster and elected the first officers. From time to time, members of an already existing fraternal or social association formed the nucleus of the extended *kinotis*. The Grecian Society of Charleston, South Carolina or the Homer Society in Little Rock, Arkansas were respective examples of such a beginning for the Greek Orthodox churches of the Holy Trinity and the Annunciation.

Members of the *kinotis* usually pledged money for the acquisition and maintenance of the church building and for the salary of a priest. As soon as these were secured, members dedicated their organized *kinotis* to a saint or to a holy day. A number of southern congregations were dedicated to "the Holy Trinity," as well as to "St. John the Divine," or to "St. Nicholas." Another popular name was "The Annunciation."[7] The earliest parishes in the South, established by fewer than 150 Greeks in each city, were Holy Trinity in Birmingham, Alabama and Annunciation in Atlanta, Georgia, both organized in 1902.[8]

TABLE 9
Showing the establishment of a kinotis—a church parish—in various southern cities; year in brackets denotes when church building secured, if not secured same year.

CITY	Year established	Name of church parish	Approximate # of faithful
New Orleans, Louisiana	1864 (1866)	Holy Trinity	wealthy merchants
Birmingham, Alabama	1902	HolyTrinity; (1953) Holy Trinity-HolyCross	100-130
Atlanta, Georgia	1902 (1906)	Annunciation	140-150
Savannah, Georgia	1905 (1907)	St. Paul	150-200
Tarpon Springs, Florida	1905 (1907)	St. Nicholas	400
Memphis, Tennessee	1905 (1908)	Annunciation	20-30
Baltimore, Maryland	1906 (1909)	Annunciation	
Montgomery, Alabama	1908	Annunciation	
Pensacola, Florida	1908 (1910)	Annunciation	50
Charleston, South Carolina	1908 (1910)	Holy Trinity	175
Augusta, Georgia	1911	Holy Trinity	115
Mobile, Alabama	1912 (1924)	Annunciation	125
Little Rock, Arkansas	1913 (1920)	Annunciation	
Jacksonville, Florida	1916 (1917)	St. John the Divine	165
Nashville, Tennessee	1917 (1919)	Holy Trinity	
Charlotte, North Carolina	1917	Holy Trinity	50-95
Hopewell, Virginia	1917	St. Elpis (Hope)	1,400
Richmond, Virginia	1917 (1919)	Sts. Constantine and Helen	

Clarksburg, West Virginia	1918 (1920)	St. Spyridon	300 families
Raleigh, North Carolina	1924	Holy Trinity	
Miami, Florida	1925	St. Sophia	

NOTE: some of the above parishes, for example those in Virginia, Tennessee, and Arkansas, are outside the present scope of this work (see Chapter 1).

In fact, the earliest Greek Orthodox church ever established in the United States was Holy Trinity of New Orleans.[9] But unlike parishes formed in the turn-of-the-century South, where groups of rising Greek entrepreneurs organized a *kinotis*, the New Orleans parish, organized in 1864, had only a few wealthy merchants as its founders. By 1866 they financed the building of a simple one-story edifice, which accommodated the small number of well-to-do Greek Orthodox New Orleanians and their families, and from time to time some Greek sailors, whose ships anchored long enough to refit and pick up new cargo.[10] With the onset of mass immigration from south-eastern Europe, during the first decade of the new century, enterprising new Greek settlers had arrived in New Orleans. As in other cities throughout the South, they became dominant in the Hellenic *kinotis* and replaced the oligarchy which had built the church and established the first parish.[11]

The act of organizing a Greek Orthodox church parish in southern cities usually enhanced the harmony within the upwardly mobile Greek immigrant group. One of the reasons contributing to the apparent solidarity may have been the fact that the more economically successful merchants gave the largest contributions and won the greatest number of votes in elections to the parish council. These merchants undoubtedly utilized the skills of negotiation and compromise that assured their own success in the larger dominant society. They tended to avoid taking uncompromising positions that usually led to stubborn battles and the formation of factions. In addition, relatively small numbers of Greeks in these southern cities possibly prevented the usual regional rivalries from taking hold. There were simply too few Greeks from Smyrna or Thrace to feud with a group from Sparta or Achaia, too few from the island of Chios to quarrel within the *kinotis* with people from Cyprus or Crete. With economic success and incipient acceptance by the dominant society, the upwardly mobile individuals perhaps had no need to prove their mettle and to look for honors inside the parish.

By comparison, in a much larger Hellenic community in New York

City, numbering over 1,000 compatriots, Solon J. Vlastos, future publisher of the Greek-language newspaper *Atlantis*, began organizing a *kinotis* as early as 1892. According to researcher Peter Kourides, feuds, factionalism, and power politics plagued the New York congregation of Holy Trinity. During the first year many members broke away and formed the splinter Annunciation parish. Each group managed to find and employ its own priest. [12] A similar feud between the Spartans and the Arcadians in Chicago resulted in the formation of a second parish in that city's large Hellenic community. In 1892, the Lycurgus Society, obviously a Spartan group, formed the Annunciation parish. Although the parish purported to accommodate all Greek Orthodox in the area, disagreements abounded. By 1897, a group of immigrants from Arcadia formed the Holy Trinity parish, served by a priest whom several Arcadians, returning from the 1897 Greco-Turkish War, hired in the port of Piraeus and conducted to Chicago. [13]

For years, the most significant problem facing the members of a newly organized *kinotis* was where to get a suitable priest. Unlike in Greece, where the government paid for the upkeep of churches and salaries to the clergy, in America all costs were sustained by private donations and by pledges of the faithful. Particularly in the southern cities, business-oriented congregants easily calculated and covered the cost of leasing or building church premises, but they encountered great difficulties in the early years in finding and securing a priest. The Greek Orthodox church had no organized hierarchy in the United States, so Greeks tended to contact the Holy Synod in Athens, or the Ecumenical Patriarchate in Constantinople, to request the appointment of a priest. [14] There were always risks involved with this approach: members of the *kinotis* knew nothing about their proposed spiritual leader; they had to worry that he might embarrass them in a social ambience which might ridicule or resent a stranger adorned with untrimmed hair and beard, clad in a long black robe and an unusual stove-pipe hat. It was therefore always better to make contact back home with a Bishop, or some other influential member of the clergy known to at least a few parishioners, who could be relied upon to represent the needs of the new congregation to the church authorities back home and to influence the choice of a younger and more pliable priest, unencumbered by wife and children. [15]

Priests sent by the Synod or the Patriarchate were usually learned and devoted men, who served their parishioners well. But there were clergymen who often came from the same poorer, rural strata as the immigrants. Despite inferior training, they sold their services to some-times desperate communities. At times, some parishioner knew a priest in the village back home, who was willing to undertake the journey, and persuaded his compatriots here to hire the *papás* and pay his way to the states.[16] On occasion, members of the *kinotis* heard of a priest already in the United States, perhaps traveling from city to city offering to perform the needed rites, such as marriages and christenings, and offered him a steady position. In 1912, more enterprising brethren of the Annunciation parish in Los Angeles whisked Father Koutousis off the train en route to Florida and conducted him into the waiting arms of his new community.[17] That situation also posed problems, since some of these traveling men of the cloth "were not ordained or recog-nized as canonical clergymen." It was hard to check ecclesiastical credentials without an organized administration, without an estab-lished bishopric in the United States.[18] In addition, monks who for one reason or another left their Orthodox monasteries spread throughout the Mediterranean, often visited parishes that were left without a priest and offered services at bargain prices. Since neither side was subject to any formal hierarchical restraints, the communi-ties negotiated the hiring of priests as best they could.[19] Just as there were no established procedures for hiring priests, there was no set process for dismissing them. In essence, priests became employees, dependent for their job on the whim of the same people to whom they were spiritual leaders.

There was also the problem of jurisdiction.[20] The Holy Synod in Athens only ministered to the Greeks within the then independent Kingdom of Greece. Hellenes who lived outside sovereign Greece, in regions still controlled by the Ottoman Empire, such as northern Epirus, Macedonia, northern Thessaly, Thrace and the whole Aegean coast of Asia Minor, belonged to the Orthodox Christian millets headed by the Great Church of the Ecumenical Patriarchate in Constantinople. It was the governing religious center for all Greeks in the diaspora.[21] As Greeks from these regions emigrated to America, the Patriarch in Constantinople also received numerous requests, asking for priests to be appointed, both to newly established and to already existing parishes in the states. Both branches of Greek Orthodoxy, the Synod in Athens and the Patriarchate in Constantinople, were mindful of the Russian Orthodox Church, which at the turn of the century claimed hegemony over all Orthodox in America.[22]

Since the late 1700s, Russian Orthodox traders and settlers had migrated to Alaska and in the following years spread down the west coast. The church had thousands of faithful, Russians, Aleuts, and others, from Alaska to San Francisco, and claimed ecclesiastical jurisdiction over all adherents in North America. With a growth of immigration late in the 19th century, the Russian church shifted its headquarters eastward in an effort to minister more effectively to the needs of newcomers. For the first three decades of its existence, the Holy Trinity Greek Orthodox Church of New Orleans, built in 1867, remained in the domain of the Russian Orthodox Church. In fact, a Russian priest, Father Agapius Honcharenko, served as the first pastor, and the Russian czarist court donated a variety of liturgical vessels and candelabra to the Orthodox parish in the Crescent City.[23] According to historian Theodore Saloutos, Russian ecclesiastical supremacy helps to explain, at least in part, "the indecisiveness and tardiness of the Ecumenical Patriarchate and the Church of Greece" to designate a bishop in America, despite strong demands by Greeks in the United States to have their own hierarch.[24]

Meanwhile, the growing number of Greek Orthodox congregations formed by the settlers refused to submit to Russian hegemony.[25] Locally autonomous parishes, functioning far from the spiritual direction of any central authority, nurtured the same spirit of independence that influenced the ancient Greek city states, when each unit was a democracy unto itself. Petty entrepreneurs, who manned the board of trustees or council which headed each *kinotis*, took control of most aspects of the church administration and frequently assumed commanding and proprietary airs so typical of self-made men from the Mediterranean.

The better-led, better-financed and stronger Russian Orthodox Church pressed the Ecumenical Patriarchate in Constantinople formally to cede its spiritual jurisdiction over the faithful in this part of the diaspora to the Russian church. At about the same time, Ecumenical Patriarch Ioacheim III must have been aware of the renewed surge of Turkish nationalism, driven by Ottoman army officers, especially those centered in the army contingents around Salonika, where the revolution of Young Turks against Sultan Abdul Hamid began.[26] The Sultan abdicated in July, 1908, leaving the reformers free to institute a massive thrust toward Ottomanization and centralization, accompanied by an ever increasing pressure on the minorities to submit to obligations of "full citizenship."[27] Under prospects adverse for non-Muslims, an Orthodox Patriarch based in Constantinople could not provide responsible leadership for his people and churches on a far-away continent. In the spring 1908, the Patriarch formally turned over the nominal jurisdiction over the Greeks in America to the Holy Synod in Athens.[28] The Synod was slow to establish its presence in the states; before it could do so, a political conflict disordered its own ranks. For another decade, Greek communities in America remained without any coherent religious leadership.[29]

In areas where they arrived in large numbers in the first two decades of the new century, Greek newcomers organized dozens of communities; those in Boston, Lowell, Milwaukee, Newark, Philadelphia, and San Francisco rivaled in size and number the diverse parishes around Chicago and New York. Once they established a pattern for parish formation, Greek settlers continued to organize a multitude of local churches in the urban industrial regions east of the Mississippi. In the New England states, without central guidance and planning, the obsession for church founding reached a point where migrants organized churches in communities that were only fifteen to twenty minutes apart in travel time. Historian Theodore Saloutos agrees that this proliferation proved how nationalism and "provincialism of the Old World was being reborn in the New."[30] Ambitious but unsophisticated individuals often expressed their pretentious desires in economically unsound decisions that strained the ability of members to maintain these churches. In contrast, by the end of 1918, just over a dozen Greek Orthodox parishes had formed in the southern cities.[31] Partially due to their better economic judgment and smaller numbers, Hellenes in the southern states established church parishes at a far slower rate.[32]

The sense of ecclesiastical disorder, caused by the lack of a common spiritual center in the states, grew and intensified when the Synod in Athens, which had at least nominal jurisdiction over many churches in America, became embroiled in a political conflict that rocked Greece. The old-country disruption spread to most Greek communities in the diaspora. The conflict was driven by the idealistic dream to unite all Greeks in an independent Greece, a dream that could be achieved only by carving out the ethnically Hellenic regions from the Ottoman Empire and joining them to the sovereign kingdom of Greece. Nationalism among Greeks reached a climax during the Balkan wars. Internal conflict arose only in 1914, when King Constantine, whose wife was the German Kaiser Wilhelm's sister, sought to prevent Greece from entering World War I. His prime minister, Eleftherios Venizelos, leader of the Greek Liberals, supported especially by the Greek populace in the "unredeemed" areas still ruled by the decrepit Ottoman Empire, saw Greek destiny fulfilled by joining Greece's traditional allies, England, France, Russia, and Serbia.

Greeks throughout the diaspora supported their compatriots back home and fractured into two political factions: Venizelists and royalists. The Greek Orthodox church did not escape the discord. Archbishop Theoklitos in Athens, a staunch royalist, removed from positions of power and influence all clergy sympathetic to the prime minister. Late in 1916, in conformity "to an ancient ceremony," the Archbishop excommunicated Venizelos.[33] However, the political tables soon turned. In 1917, under pressure from the allies, the King abdicated and Venizelos assumed sole authority over the divided country. Within days, he led a "united" Greece into the war against Turkey and Germany. Archbishop Meletios, acceptable to Venizelos, replaced Theoklitos as the Metropolitan of Athens. Theoklitos's appointees resigned or were reassigned to less desirable outposts.

The division engulfed the Greeks in the United States, taking chaotic, sometimes violent turns. At times, council members had to call local police to maintain order as parishioners entered and left church premises. In their sermons, royalist clergy upheld constitutional authority, represented by the king. Liberal priests, supporting the policies of Venizelos, refused to mention the name of the king in church liturgies. In many communities the council divided into vociferous royalist and Venizelist factions, with the priest often having to abide by the demands of the majority.[34] Some communities became so fractured that they divided into separate parishes.[35] Unlike in the South, in large Greek settlements factions formed early, and the church-halls served as a veritable battleground for Greeks with conflicting ideas and purposes. The contest was most pronounced in the populous Greek communities in the north-eastern and mid-western parts of the United States. The Chicago, New York, Milwaukee, and Lowell communities experienced

not only verbal but also physical clashes. Royalists broke away from
the Annunciation church in Baltimore, Maryland; St. Sophia's in
Washington, D. C.; and St. Mary's in Minneapolis, and formed their
own respective parishes of Holy Trinity, Saints Constantine and Helen,
and St. George's.[36] Sociologist Alice Scourby described the formation
of eleven different Greek communities in Chicago. "In 1915 the United
Greek Parishes of Chicago sought to bring unity out of the chaos that
separated Greek from Greek, parish from parish. The attempt met with
frustration, as each faction, obsessed with the issue of political turmoil
in Greece, failed to meet substantive issues confronting them as a
marginal community in the United States."[37] In May 1918, in New
York, Venizelist supporters established the new parish of St. Eleftherios
and hired a liberal-leaning priest away from the royalist-dominated St.
Constantine's church in Brooklyn.

In an attempt to overcome this confusion and dissention, just as the
war was ending in Europe, Archbishop Meletios visited the faithful in
the United States. Since he was elected to head the Holy Synod in Athens
at the time Eleftherios Venizelos was in power, his visit evoked a very
disunited reaction. Nevertheless, he appointed a Synodical Vicar,
Archbishop Alexander, to administer all the Greek Orthodox churches in
the states.[38] Of course, the royalist side ignored the appointment.[39]
Meletios persevered and in September 1921 returned to the states to
convene the first ever clergy-laity congress, with all parishes invited to
send representatives to attend and ratify the formation of the Greek
Orthodox Archdiocese of North and South America, headquartered in
New York.[40] Over fifty royalist-led church communities and their priests
resisted and simply refused to acknowledge the new authority. Lay and
clergy representing about 130 communities attended the congress. They
confirmed the new constitution, which held, among other provisions, that
all physical church properties purchased by the parishioners will remain
the ownership of each individual parish, with members of each parish
retaining the right to dispose and acquire the moveable and immove-
able physical property of the *kinotis*. Ecclesiastically the new Archdiocese
had an almost independent status in that all decisions regarding its
internal administration originated with the new Archbishop and four
Bishops, who were to be elected by the clergy and lay representatives at
the Diocesan congresses.[41] For the first time, Greek Orthodoxy had an
established hierarchy in the United States, although only two-thirds of its

adherents in America agreed to abide by its spiritual guidance.

Meanwhile, post-war elections in Greece unseated Venizelos and returned the royalists to office. In November 1921, the ecclesiasts in Constantinople, perhaps in answer to Theoklitos's return to power in Athens, selected Meletios to be the new Ecumenical Patriarch.[42] He was enthroned in January 1922. Two months after his installation, the new leader of eastern Christianity issued a decree and restored the jurisdiction over the Greek churches in America to the Patriarchate. Later the same year, the royalists countered with the formation of an "autocephalous Exarchate" of the Greek Orthodox church in America. They petitioned Archbishop Theoklitos of Athens to send a Bishop to lead the newly-formed entity. The Archbishop readily complied and sent a very dynamic and charismatic churchman, Metropolitan Germanos of Sparta, who established his new diocesan headquarters in Lowell, Massachusetts, and undertook to shepherd the dissident group. There followed jurisdictional disputes and quarrels about properties, sometimes resulting in lengthy lawsuits.[43]

The friction was compounded in 1924, when both the Ecumenical Patriarchate in Constantinople, directed by the indefatigable Meletios, and the Orthodox Church of Greece, now headed by Archbishop Chrysostomos, a man devoted to peace and unity, both adopted the more modern Gregorian calendar for use by the church.[44] The royalist clergy and adherents in the United States retained the inaccurate Julian calendar in spite of all entreaties to maintain a unified religious practice in the Greek Orthodox Church. As a rule, the southern communities did not experience these deep ruptures. As elaborated in chapter two of this work, since the turn of the century, the process of adaptation and involvement into American ways and habits proceeded there at a more rapid rate. In addition, throughout the South, with the exception of Mobile, Alabama, Venizelist sympathizers seemed to be in the majority. Elsewhere in the states, measured calm did not return until well into the 1930s, when time blunted the intensity of the conflict and the great Depression became a more immediate concern.[45]

In Greek Orthodox parishes from Virginia and the Carolinas to Florida, and across the deep South westerly to Louisiana, the strife seen elsewhere seemed much better contained. Individuals and even groups of *kinotis* members may have been offended by the political opinions of fellow parishioners, but lack of larger numbers placed the disagreements on a personal rather than institutional level. Southern parishes may have temporarily lost good members who decided not to attend church rather than to continue meeting political adversaries, but much more numerous were those members who placed religion above politics. These parishioners may have been deeply concerned with the conflict in Greece; they must have been disheartened by the fights and splits experienced in large Greek communities, but they were not caught up in the strife to the point of litigation or violence within the parish. Mobile's Hellenic community represents perhaps the only southern parish where the two sides matched their strength at parish meetings. The Greek Orthodox *kinotis* of the Annunciation formed in Mobile in 1912, but it was not until November 1926 that the Venizelist faction of the parish finally rented space to hold church services and hired father John Santorineos at a monthly salary of $150.00. By carefully reading the abstract of the "official minute book of the community," one can detect the strong conflicts that plagued it.[46] Although the minutes did not say so, the priest's appointment must have been questioned. Certainly opponents managed to cancel his pay at the meeting of the following month, since the record disclosed that in December, devoted member Jason Malbis stepped forward to undertake, "along with his co-workers," to personally pay the priest's salary for the following year.

In addition, Jason Malbis offered to donate a large lot, 170 feet by 216 feet, to build a church. Parishioners who attended the assembly in December 1926 accepted the donation "with 102 votes." Six months later, at the May 1927 general assembly meeting, "with 22 members present," the assembly rejected "all prior decisions" and voted to purchase an existing building from the "First Christian Church" Protestant congregation. This transaction closed in July 1927 and the Mobile Greeks finally had a church to call their own. After this success, however, at the October general assembly meeting, attended by hierarch Metropolitan Vasilios from Lowell, "it was requested that the priest [father Santorineos] be transferred."[47] The Metropolitan obliged, assigned a new priest, and persuaded the faithful to switch from the new, Gregorian calendar to the old Julian calendar. Metropolitan Vasilios was a staunch royalist, and found sufficient support in the ranks of the Mobile community to undertake a visit.[48] From November 1926 to January 1936, eight Greek Orthodox priests were hired, came, and left the Mobile parish. Only in May 1929, did the Mobile congregation revert to the new calendar and again celebrate Christmas on the 25th of December, at the same time as their American neighbors.[49]

In May 1930, the church leadership in the Balkans cooperated in a welcome example of unity to the faithful: the Patriarchate in Constantinople and the Synod in Athens jointly agreed that the Patriarchal appointee, Metropolitan Athenagoras of Kerkyra, take over in the United States administration of the 133 communities guided by the Patriarchate and the 50 communities in communion with the Synod. He arrived in New York the following year and set about reuniting the communities under one spiritual and jurisdictional hierarchy. Athenagoras prevailed in this endeavor, but not before his sponsors in Constantinople and Athens recalled most of the feuding church leaders from America back to the Mediterranean. In addition, the Patriarchate in Constantinople approved a new constitution for the American Archdiocese, one that placed the administrative authority over the church here "wholly in the hands of the Archbishop."[50] The four Bishoprics created by the first constitution of 1922 remained as mere geographic subdivisions; their bishops were no longer to administer them independently, but merely as auxiliaries of the archbishop. Moreover, the bishops were no longer elected by the parish representatives, but appointed by the archbishop, now the chief Orthodox hierarch in North and South America.

The church in the whole United States now had one central authority to guide it and this arrangement proved beneficial for the archdiocese. Athenagoras's eighteen-year tenure of office brought most of the dissident and recalcitrant churches back to the fold.[51] Having worked singly and sometimes against each other for many years, each parish resisted submerging even a part of local independence to the common cause. A uniquely American solution bridged the contentious and often suspicious lay membership on the one hand, and the hierarchy of the venerable and tradition-strapped Orthodox Church on the other hand. Although the spiritual dominion of the church in general was never questioned, specific decrees intended to bring order into the administration of a large, new, rapidly but haphazardly growing diocese could not be practically enforced without the cooperation of the parishes. The parishes, in turn, depended on their existence and physical assets entirely on the parishioners, individual voluntary members of each *kinotis* and their donations. Feuding and discord cut down on voluntary donations and weakened both the secular and the spiritual fabric of the communities. Some blame for the turmoil had to be placed with the clergy, who seemed unable to keep the ecclesiastical life of the institution apart from the secular, political influences.[52] The new archbishop for America, assisted by the new constitution, brought about substantial order and unity.

A majority of parishes accepted the right of the hierarch to select bishops and to have the major say in the training and placement of clergymen. Clergy and the bishops received their appointments from Archbishop Athenagoras, and he, in turn, answered to the Ecumenical Patriarchate. As of old, the Patriarchs of eastern Christianity remained the unquestioned interpreters of all religious and dogmatic matters. But the new archbishop also knew that decisions reached without community representation could only create new tensions. Most importantly, the elected councils or trustees in every *kinotis* retained control over all physical property and financial matters in each individual parish.[53] In essence, the church administration could not operate without the cooperation and money which came only from willingly given gifts and offerings of the faithful. An unprecedented democratic arrangement gave each individual parishioner a "vote" by way of voluntary pledges, budgeted by the council to maintain the physical assets of the parish and ultimately the Greek Orthodox Archdiocese. Clergy - laity congresses, where each individual parish had lay representation, a complete novelty in any Orthodox jurisdiction, had the obligation to address questions of common interest and to decide them by majority vote. Moreover, the Patriarchate always remained receptive to direct representations and visits by wealthy members of its most influential archdiocese in the diaspora. Although future clergy - laity congresses made further adjustments to the basic arrangement, for the first time in ages, in the crucible of the new American environment, the Greek Orthodox church adapted its archaic ways of ministering and exercising authority over its faithful. Even with the changes, the church had a problem engaging the disaffected second generation of Greek Americans.[54]

Although the basic jurisdictional and political disputes were out of the way, the Greek Orthodox church in the United States continued to resist tendencies to adapt some of its venerable traditions, tendencies displayed and desired by a significant part of the faithful. The parish priests were invariably born in Greece or other Greek-speaking parts of the Mediterranean. They were trained in theological seminaries in Athens or in Halki.[55] They learned only enough English to get by, especially in the South; however, in the large Greek communities such as New York, Lowell, Chicago, or Pittsburgh, a priest could easily live without the need to speak any English. Although devoted to their calling and traditional ways of the ancient church, few priests could give counsel and really minister to the needs of their younger American parishioners. By the 1930s, influenced by the laity, the church hierarchy clearly perceived, as never before, the need for change.

Especially in the southern cities, where they mingled with their white Anglo neighbors, the maturing second generation of the Greek Orthodox were concerned to have the church present a front as compatible as possible to other churches in their neighborhoods. In the 1920s, the days of 100 percent Americanism, and in the 1930s, when assimilation seemed the only way for all newcomers, Greek Americans wanted their priests to look like those of other denominations, so white collars and black suits replaced the long robes and monastic hats usually worn by Orthodox clergy in the Mediterranean. Pews, never used in Greek Orthodox churches back home, made their appearance. To be sure, individual members of the parish strenuously argued against this westernization and corruption of the ancient traditions, but the desire to fit in prevailed. By 1949, when Archbishop Athenagoras left America to take up his Patriarchal staff in Constantinople, Greek Orthodox church buildings, from Raleigh and Charlotte in North Carolina to Austin and San Antonio in Texas, had pews.

Perhaps the best evidence of pressure exerted on the church by its American parishioners occurred when they no longer observed the strictly gendered space divisions inside the church.[56] For the early Greek immigrants, gender inequality was a fundamental part of the rural way of life they left behind.[57] Where for ages men had stood on the right and women on the left side of the center aisle of the church, in response to pressures from the growing American-born population, men and women now sat intermixed, clearly expressing rejection of the gender-based demarcation which prevailed in the old country. With the formation of an active church-related Ladies' Auxiliary Society—Philoptochos—women were taking a much more public role in the affairs of the Greek Orthodox Church in the states. Women still usually discharged the "female" duties of cooking and serving meals at church-sponsored luncheons, suppers, and even formal banquets. But they also participated in the choirs, became elected members of the governing councils or boards of trustees, represented their parish at clergy - laity meetings, and partook in the raising and management of money for the parishes.[58] Orthodox adherents, upwardly mobile men and women, led by Greek Americans in the southern states, urged on and encouraged the all-male conservative Greek-Byzantine institution in the United States, given to preservation of form and language of time-honored eastern Christianity, to change into an American institution.[59]

In a number of parishes, especially in southern cities, the desire of non-Greek speaking parishioners to understand, and participate in the liturgy, as well as the American-trained priests' desire to retain parishioners who were drifting away, resulted in a variety of translations into English of parts of the liturgy and sacraments such as marriages and christenings, all without a formal permission from the archdiocesan authorities. Clergy - laity congresses, which continued to provide to the Greek Orthodox parishes a venue to democratized decisions respecting the church in America, deliberated the question of using English in the liturgy. Despite resistance by the Greek-oriented clergy, parishioners, who were themselves experiencing the process of adaptation and Americanization, turned on inescapable pressure in favor of using English. After its formation in the 1920s, the American Hellenic Educational Progressive Association—AHEPA—gave another thrust to the inevitable transformation of the church. AHEPA members were among the more generous donors to the church as well as loyal attendees; at the same time they soft-pedaled the idea of maintaining Greek National identity in the United States, they advocated naturalization and participation in American community affairs and politics, and extensive use of the English language.[60]

Unlike most priests who hailed from the Mediterranean and considered the preservation of one's nationality as an integral part of the Orthodox religion, a notable number of congregants in America did not view mixed marriages with horror. For years, priests had discouraged and denounced such nuptials as a threat to the Greek Orthodox way of life. Mixed marriages took place often enough for young Greek Americans to ask that parts of the elaborate and impressive wedding ceremony be spoken or chanted in English. As early as 1926, Bishop Ioachim of

Boston estimated that 20 out of every 100 Greek families in the United States were involved in mixed marriages.[61] Even if the majority of the children born of such marriages were baptized in the Orthodox churches, they might not speak Greek at home. And even children reared in homes where Greek was spoken may not be comfortable in using Greek, the bishop thought, because they would not speak it on the playground, in the classroom, and in the neighborhood.

Holy Cross Chapel, on campus of the Holy Cross Greek Orthodox School of Theology, at Brookline, Massachusetts. From the Commemorative Book of the 25th Clergy Laity Congress held in Atlanta in 1980, courtesy of Father Homer P. Goumenis, Dean, Greek Orthodox Cathedral of the Annunciation, Atlanta.

Conduct of the liturgy and other services in English became an area of contest between those who wanted to preserve unchanged practices and traditions even if it meant losing members, and those who desired to perpetuate their Orthodox religion, by adapting its ways to the New World. The contest was resolved in favor of change when Archbishop Athenagoras and other leading clergy decided to establish a theological school in America. Rather than depending on importing priests, the archdiocese decided to meet the need for more parish priests by training them and ordaining them here. In 1937, with donations raised mostly from the Greek Orthodox of New England, the archdiocese purchased a suitable building and property in Pomfret, Connecticut and assembled a teaching staff.[62] The freshman class of fourteen theological students, all but two born in the United States, began its studies in 1942, and graduated in 1946. Twelve graduates found immediate placement in parishes throughout the nation, as twenty more communities marked time, waiting for the next class to graduate. [63] The following year the seminary moved to larger premises in Brookline, Massachusetts and continued to prepare American-born young men for Orthodox priesthood in the states. The curriculum extended to six years and included a three-year college pre-theological preparatory program, designed to fulfill the future priests' knowledge of liberal arts.[64]

The impact of American-born priests on Orthodox religious life in the states was indeed significant. Above all, they could communicate effortlessly in English and so provided new leadership and guidance especially in the religious and spiritual life of the second and third generation Greek Orthodox and their spouses; they eagerly joined in the administration and organization to meet a variety of needs of a modern parish, unlike their counterparts from the old country, who were used to leaving such mundane things to governmental care, which did not exist in the United States. By 1965, 292 students had graduated from the Holy Cross seminary in Brookline, of whom 245 became ordained priests. In the opinion of historian Theodore Saloutos, the training of American-born youth for Orthodox priesthood was an unmistakable "admission that the church was responding to the needs of the American environment."[65]

Archbishop Michael, appointed in 1949 to replace Athenagoras, continued to yield to assimilative pressures. To enhance the financial situation of the archdiocese, he started the *dekadollarion*, the ten-dollar-per-member drive, authorized by the tenth biennial clergy - laity congress. Although individual Greeks gave to the church generously, the majority did not consider financial needs of the church past the immediate requirements of the parish. For most Greek Americans, the archdiocese did not present significant concerns. The imposition of an annual ten-dollar fee per church member was in fact resented by many, and formal membership in the parishes declined, even as more funds flowed into the coffers of the archdiocese.[66] In fact, some parishes made little effort to collect the *dekadollarion* and simply refused to be bound by this mandate of the clergy - laity congress.

Archbishop Michael also started the Greek Orthodox Youth Association (GOYA), created the Archdiocesan Office of Information and Public Relations, and promoted uniform parish by-laws. Under his leadership, for the first time, the Greek Orthodox church joined the National Council of Churches in the United States [NCC] and the World Council of Churches [WCC]. Recognition that the church counted as one of the American denominations came in the form of an invitation by president Dwight Eisenhower's inauguration organizers, who asked Archbishop Michael to deliver the invocation at the inauguration cere- monies in January 1957. During the same years, Greek Americans leveled criticism at the archdiocese, that is to say at the archbishop, for his failure to appoint American-born, American-educated, and American-oriented bishops. Many rank-and-file priests who had received their theological training and education at Holy Cross in Brookline and who were sympa- thetic and understanding to the needs of their American-born parishioners, felt that their hierarchical superiors misunderstood their participation in many undertakings that furthered civic, educational, and philanthropic causes and needlessly chided them for involvement in modern, trendy activities and outreach in the parishes.[67]

The most significant changes in the American Orthodox Archdiocese came with the enthronement of the new Archbishop Iakovos, in 1959. His predecessors had still accepted the idea that the Greek Orthodox church in the United States was but an extension of the church in the Mediterranean. In the 1960s this thinking changed with the realiza- tion that the church was to an ever greater extent ministering to Americans, albeit Americans of Greek ethnic origin. Moreover, increas- ingly mixed marriages brought into the church spouses who were unfamiliar with Orthodox traditions. The church in the United States was becoming an indigenous church, affected by the happenings in the United States, interested in participating in the lives of its American parishioners. In 1964, at the seventeenth clergy - laity congress,

Archbishop Iakovos urged those attending to remove the church "from the sidelines of life."[68] The same reformist Congress decided to involve the church in social action, such as neighborhood community work, and to clearly and unmistakably show its position against abortion, discrimination, and drugs, and for civil rights and environment.[69]

Perhaps the most prominent evidence of the hierarchy's desire to involve the church in American life and ecumenicism came during the civil rights struggles in the 1960s. The church leadership adopted a far more liberal position with respect to integration and equality than some of its southern congregants. In March 1965, Archbishop Iakovos participated in the civil rights march to Selma, Alabama, with Reverend Martin Luther King, and looked defiantly at the cameras of *Life* magazine, as he appeared on that publication's front page standing next to King and other black leaders in Selma, commemorating "the martyred Reverend James Reeb."[70] One has no way to determine actual numbers, but this unrestricted support for the civil rights cause clearly infuriated more than a few parishioners in southern cities. They had long ago become accustomed to southern culture. With their neighbors, many considered the influx of civil rights activists from the North to be an unwanted and unnecessary intrusion into states' rights and the segregated status quo. [71] Just in the previous spring of 1964, after he had dramatically stood in the doorway of the University of Alabama to prevent the enrollment of several black students, governor George Wallace became an honorary member of the Birmingham chapter of the Order of AHEPA.[72]

The 1970 Clergy - Laity Congress in New York adopted a formal resolution to accept an English translation of the Liturgy and other sacramental services.[73] In fact, the resolution simply confirmed the practice in use for years, especially in the southern churches, and sought to have one approved translation prevail over dozens of others, which had been used in individual churches for the past three decades. The influx of some 86,000 Greeks between 1965 and 1971, made possible by the new 1965 Immigration Act did not retard the thrust toward English, probably because the newcomers stayed in large communities in the north-eastern urban areas, where they were outnumbered by Greek Americans.[74] Especially after 1960, while the church was in theory urging the study of Greek, in practice it encouraged in many parishes the use of English as a means of retaining some hold on the young and adults who did not understand Greek.[75]

American born, American educated clergy: Bishop John of Amorion, a native of
Chicago, Illinois. As Bishop of the Greek Orthodox Diocese of Atlanta (now retired), he
was responsible for all Greek Orthodox parishes in Georgia, Alabama, Florida, Louisiana,
North Carolina, South Carolina, Mississippi, and Tennessee. From the Commemorative
Book of the 25th Clergy Laity Congress, held in Atlanta in 1980, courtesy of Father
Homer P. Goumenis, Dean, Greek Orthodox Cathedral of the Annunciation, Atlanta.

Joining its southern sister parishes in the use of English and led by
the second and third generation Greek Orthodox, Mobile's ethnic-
based conflicts subsided; the Annunciation parish became a model of
ecumenical cooperation with other area churches. Several constituents
of the now large congregation pointed out that over the past decade, 80
percent of its new members were converts to Orthodoxy. Sophia Clikas,
living in Mobile and active in the church since 1936, described the
transformed parish by stating that the biggest difference between

southern and other Greek Americans was that the southern ones do not have the "compound barricade" mentality about their church, evident elsewhere.[76]

Indeed, under the tutelage of Archbishop Iakovos, the Greek Orthodox church in America shed much of its ethnic image.[77] No longer an immigrant Greek-speaking religious enclave, by the 1980s, the Greek Orthodox Archdiocese of America had become a complex bureaucratic institution with an increasingly ethnically diverse community of believers. Throughout the South, the majority of its congregants were monolingual English-speakers, mostly second, third, and even fourth-generation Greek Americans, boosted by converts, mostly married to Greek-origin spouses, and by Eastern Orthodox of other than Greek origins.[78] Sixty-six percent of all marriages were to non-Greek Orthodox, but still Christian spouses.[79]

The clergy was indigenous and American trained; almost without exception the priests had graduated from the Holy Cross Theological School in Brookline. Their most natural way to communicate and give sermons was in English, which predominated in liturgical services.[80] Despite the first generation's resistance to innovations, especially the use of English in choral music, mixed choirs were intoning "Lord have mercy" as often as "Kyrie Eleison."[81] Moreover, some choirs were now accompanied by sounds of organ music, until a few years ago considered a sacrilege, heard only in Roman Catholic and Protestant churches. All the meetings of the parishioners and their councils were now conducted in English. Teachers and pupils in Sunday schools used English and followed a modernized curriculum. The church offices have embraced English as the primary and in most parishes the only language used in church governance. Church-bulletins, encyclicals and all correspondence between the parishes, diocesan offices, and the archdiocese in New York were written in English—the legal language of the archdiocese according to the constitution updated in 1977.[82] Moreover, reflecting present-day struggles, the clergy prepared sermons and clerical activities designed to fulfill the current religious, spiritual, and sacramental needs of the faithful, to speak out against the lack of absolutes promoted by the New Age religion, to save children from the idea that any form of discipline is to be ridiculed, to suppress pornography, alcohol, marijuana, hard drugs, gambling; to continue the church's uncompromising stand against homosexuality and abortion.

Statistics point to a conclusion that the archdiocese has become an indigenous American institution, rapidly growing toward ever greater similarity with its national denominational counterparts.[83]

On the other hand, clerical and lay leaders of the American archdiocese retain solid ties with the revered and sage Ecumenical Patriarchate. Despite its uncomfortable position in Moslem Istanbul and physical quarters that are constrained by Turkish authorities, the largest and richest part of the Patriarchate's domain—the archdiocese in America—still submits its constitutional amendments and suggestions for appointments to high clerical offices to headquarters on the Bosphorus. Invariably, the Patriarchate approves submissions and endorses all recommendations and proposals, limiting its supremacy to a spiritual rather than a mundane level. For the time being, the vast majority of the ethnically increasingly diverse parishioners of the Greek Orthodox Archdiocese of America are not anxious to relinquish the ethnic tie and to become organized, with other formerly ethnic Orthodox churches, as an indigenous, all-embracing, universal Orthodox church of America. Consequently, as long as other Americans see the "Greek" in any Greek-Orthodox church and in the name of the religion, they will probably continue to consider this particular religious body to be part of a religion circumscribed by identification with a specific nationality and thus limited to only a select ethnic segment of the general American population.

TABLE 10
THE GREEK ORTHODOX CHURCH IN THE UNITED STATES
AND ITS HIERARCHY : A CHRONOLOGICAL OVERVIEW

Traditionally, the Ecumenical Patriarchate in Constantinople had jurisdiction over all Greek Orthodox churches in the diaspora, outside the borders of Greece. Within Greece, the church was administered by the Holy Synod in Athens.

Until 1908 the Russian Patriarchate [in Moscow] claimed jurisdiction over all Orthodox churches in North America, by extending its 18th century claim for jurisdiction over Alaska and the West Coast. In 1908, the Ecumenical Patriarch decided to place the Greek Orthodox churches in the Americas under the jurisdiction of the Holy Synod in Athens. Although the Synod accepted jurisdiction, until 1918 no Greek Orthodox hierarch resided in the

United States.

In 1918, while visiting the faithful in the United States, Archbishop of the Holy Synod in Athens, Meletios Metaxakis, appointed [on October 29] Bishop Alexander of Rodostolon as the Synodical Vicar for the Greek Orthodox Churches in America, to reside in New York. Archbishop Meletios returned to Athens to find he had been deposed and replaced by the royalist Archbishop Theoklitos. Meletios returned to the US, convened [with Bishop Alexander] the first ever clergy-laity congress in September 1921. Although only Venizelist sympathizers attended, the congress ratified the creation and the constitution of a Greek Orthodox Archdiocese for North and South America.

In 1922, Meletios was elected as the Ecumenical Patriarch of Constantinople; he transferred the jurisdiction over the church in America, now formed into an Archdiocese, from the Holy Synod in Athens to the Patriarchate in Constantinople.

Under the aegis of the Patriarchate in Constantinople, from 1922 to 1930, Bishop Alexander, with headquarters in New York, headed the Greek Orthodox church in America, comprised of about 130 parishes, leaning to Venizelos.

1922 the royalist parishes in the United States formed the Synodical Autocephalous Exarchate of the Greek Orthodox Church in America. 1922-1930, on behalf of the Holy Synod in Athens, at first Metropolitan Germanos, then Archbishop Vasilios, with headquarters in Lowell, Massachusetts, headed the Exarchate in America, comprised of about 55 parishes where the majority of faithful favored the royalists and King Constantine.

May 1930, Patriarch Photios of Constantinople and Archbishop Chrysostomos of the Holy Synod in Athens jointly dispatched Metropolitan Damaskenos of Corinth to assume temporary administration of all American parishes. Damaskenos recommended the recall of all hierarchs from America and replacement with a new top echelon. As a result, archbishops Alexander [on the Venizelist side] and Vasilios [on the royalist side], as well as Bishops Philaretos of Chicago and Joachim of Boston were recalled to serve in various archbishoprics in the Mediterranean.

1931 the Patriarchate, with consent of the Holy Synod in Athens, appointed Archbishop Athenagoras Spyrou of Kerkyra, to be the new Greek Orthodox primate in America. He arrived in February 1931 in the United States to take over and unite all parishes, with the help of a new constitution for the Greek Orthodox Archdiocese of North and South America. In November 1948 the ecclesia elected Athenagoras to be the new Ecumenical Patriarch of Constantinople.

1949-1958 Archbishop Michael of Corinth succeeded Athenagoras in the United States.

1959-1996 Archbishop Iakovos [born Demetrios Coucouzis] succeeded Archbishop Michael and led the American archdiocese for 37 years. During these years, the Greek Orthodox Church in America reached a peak in ecumenical activity and became an American denomination. The church grew to 488 parishes [in 1994], administered by the archbishop, who divided the American archbishopric into Diocesan Districts and who appointed 15 auxiliary bishops to assist him.

Within the archdiocesan structure in the United States, the archbishop divided his domain into several dioceses and appointed bishops [actually suggested clerics to be appointed by the Patriarchate] to administer on his behalf:*

the Archdiocesan District**	Diocese of Chicago
Diocese of Boston	Diocese of Atlanta***
Diocese of Pittsburgh	Diocese of San Francisco
Diocese of Detroit	Diocese of Denver
Diocese of New Jersey	

In September 1996 Archbishop Spyridon replaced Iakovos. Spyridon was born George Papageorgiou in Warren, Ohio; he was raised and went to public school in Tarpon Springs, Florida, served a number of years in ecclesial functions in Europe as representative of the Patriarchate, until he became the first American-born hierarch of the church in the United States.

Coinciding with Archbishop Spyridon's appointment, the Ecumenical Patriarchate divided the Archdiocese of North and South America into four parts = the Archdiocese of the United States, seated in New York and now headed by Archbishop Spyridon; the Metropolis of Canada [centered in Toronto]; the Metropolis of Mexico, Central America and the Caribbean [headquartered in Mexico City]; and the Metropolis of South America [centered in Buenos Aires].

Despite a congenial beginning, Spyridon's tendency to dominate the clergy and to control the work of laity in the parishes, even to by-pass Diocesan Bishops, created conflict and controversy. Bountiful donations of the faithful became less generous; by 1998, most regional Bishops [now Metropolitans] resisted his dominance. Under considerable pressure, both within the USA and from the Patriarchy, Archbishop Spyridon resigned his post in August 1999.

The Patriarchate next selected a scholar, Bishop Demetrios, to be the new Primate of the Greek Orthodox Church in the United States. Demetrios [Trakatellis] was born in Thessaloniki, in Greece. He was ordained a priest in 1964 and moved to the United States in 1965. He spent the next few years at Harvard, where he received his Ph.D. in 1972. From 1983 to 1993, Demetrios taught at Holy Cross School of Theology, in Brookline, Massachusetts, as professor of Biblical Studies. In September 1999, Archbishop Demetrios was enthroned as the sixth leader of America's Greek Orthodox Christians

* James Steve Counelis, "Greek Orthodox Church Statistics of the United States, 1949-1989: Some Ecclesial and Social Patterns," Journal of the Hellenic Diaspora 16 (No's 1-4, 1989), 152.

** This area was traditionally the local responsibility of the Archbishop and consists of greater New York City, upstate New York and Long Island, the western half of Connecticut, and Washington, D. C.

*** The Diocese of Atlanta includes most of the parishes examined in this work and extends through North Carolina, South Carolina, Georgia, Florida, Alabama, Mississippi, and several parishes in eastern Louisiana and Tennessee. See Charleston News and Courier of October 29, 1981, 2B.

TABLE 11
SOME STATISTICAL DATA RELATING TO
THE GREEK ORTHODOX CHURCH IN THE UNITED STATES:

The American Archdiocese is an autonomous [not autocephalous] church within the purview of the Ecumenical Patriarchate of Constantinople and New Rome [Charter, articles I, II];* the Patriarchate has the authority to select the American Archbishop and his Bishops [Charter, articles XII, XIV]; further, the Patriarchate approves the legislation of the Clergy-Laity Congress and the Holy Synod of the Archdiocese, whose seat is in New York [Charter, articles VI, XI] and provides the holy *myron* for the archdiocese [Charter, article VIII]; the Patriarchate also directs all interchurch and external affairs for the archdiocese [Charter, articles II, VII, Sec.8]; however, the American archdiocese governs itself internally [Charter, article IV].

Establishment of Greek Orthodox church-parishes in the United States:**

1864-1866	1 [New Orleans community established in 1864, church built in 1866]		
1890-1899	4		
1900-1909	37	1940-1949	33
1910-1919	90	1950-1959	48
1920-1929	79	1960-1966	25
1930-1939	51	1966-1988	*98*
		total	466

As to total numbers of Greek Orthodox in the USA: one can never be sure, because actual paid-up membership in the community-parishes varies from one year to the next. One could calculate that at the time of the *dekadollarion* some 55,000 to 60,000 membership fees actually reached the archdiocese. Clearly there were a good number of parishes which did not enforce the collection from its members, and one could guess that about 1/3 more members donated no fees to the archdiocese, thus one can calculate with some certainty that there were 100,000 active Greek Orthodox families and single members in parishes around 1955-1960. In addition, there are the Greek Orthodox throughout America who are not regular parish members, but attend the church now and then, perhaps twice a year. The total, including families and descendants, bring the Greek Orthodox population of the US, in the 1960s, to about 1,750,000. This estimate does not include converts, nor any other Eastern Orthodox church parishes, such as those formed by Americans of Russian, Romanian, Serbian, Bulgarian, and other origins.

In the *St. Nicholas Greek Orthodox Church in St. Louis, Missouri* yearbook for 1962, the article "The Greek Orthodox Church in America" stated: when he was enthroned, in 1959, Archbishop Iakovos became "administrative leader of 1,500,000 Greek Orthodox communicants in the New World"

Newsweek July 13, 1964, 52: "[the Greek Orthodox] church can claim some 1,750,000 U.S. communicants and status as the "fourth faith" in the United States."

* *Charter of the Greek Orthodox Archdiocese of North and South America* (Brookline, Massachusetts, Holy Orthodox Press, 1978).

** James Steve Counelis, "Greek Orthodox Church Statistics of the United States, 1949-1989: Some Ecclesial and Social Patterns," *Journal of the Hellenic Diaspora* 16, (No's 1-4, 1989), 152-153.

Notes

1   Robert F. Harney, "Religion in Ethnocultural Communities," *Polyphony* 1 (2), (Summer 1978), 3-10, at 3; the "community" here conforms to one described by Kathleen Neils Conzen, who found that immigrants belong to a community even if they did not reside in spatial proximity; see K. N. Conzen, "Immigrants, Immigrant Neighborhoods, and Ethnic Identity: Historical Issues," *Journal of American History* 66 (December 1979), 603-615.

2   Lord Kinross, *The Ottoman Centuries: The Rise and Fall of the Turkish Empire* (New York, Morrow Quill Paperbacks, 1977), 112; during the Ottoman Muslim rule around the Mediterranean, religious minorities were *rayas*, literally "flocks," organized into *millets*, or nations, virtually self-governing communities under their own religious leaders, responsible to the central power for administration and good behavior of the people. Ottoman Turks held leading Greek priests in various regions, as well as the Greek Orthodox Patriarch in Constantinople (renamed Istanbul in 1930) accountable for order in the Greek millet.

3   Theodore Saloutos, *The Greeks in the United States* (Cambridge, Massachusetts, Harvard University Press, 1964), 18-19; Saloutos points out that the hierarchy and priests of the Greek Orthodox Church actively participated in the national and political life of their faithful during the War of Independence, the Balkan Wars 1912 and 1913, and the King Constantine v. prime minister Eleftherios Venizelos conflict right up to the disastrous 1922 campaign in Asia Minor.

4   See Table 10; Archbishop Athenagoras headed the Greek Orthodox church in America from 1930 to 1948. Over the years, he united the feuding factions, then became the first and only American citizen selected to the position of the most exalted ecclesiast in the Orthodox church, the Ecumenical Patriarch in Constantinople. For the following ten years, Archbishop Michael was the chief hierarch of the Greek Orthodox Church in the Americas, until 1959, when Metropolitan Iakovos became head of the American Archdiocese and presided over its "Americanization" until his retirement in 1996.

5   Ninety-seven percent of all ethnic Greeks are nominally Greek Orthodox; see Henry Pratt Fairchild, *Greek Immigration to the United States* (New Haven, Yale University Press, 1911), at 46: "A Greek is born to his religion

just as he is to his nationality. It would be hard to find one who would not profess to be Greek Orthodox."

6   Commemorative Album *25th Biennial Clergy-Laity Congress of the Greek Orthodox Archdiocese of North and South America* (Atlanta, n.p., 1980), 72-73; *Greek Orthodox Church of the Annunciation, Atlanta, 1905-1955, Fiftieth Anniversary Album* (Atlanta, n.p., 1955); "The History of our Parish," in *75th Anniversary of St. Paul's Greek Orthodox Church - Savannah, Georgia, 1907-1982* (Savannah, n.p., 1982).

7   See Table 9, cataloguing the names of Greek Orthodox parishes in the South, as well as the date each was organized; "the Annunciation" was not only popular because it honored the *Theotokos*, Mother of God, but also because on that day, in 1821, an uprising against the Turks had taken place in the Peloponnesus, that eventually led to independence for at least one part of the Greek population. Note that by 1910 Greek Orthodox parishes existed in a number of major southern cities.

8   For other Greek Orthodox parishes in the South see Table 7; Bishop John of Amorion, the first American-born Bishop of the Greek Orthodox Church and retired Bishop of the Greek Orthodox Diocese of Atlanta, now president of the St. Photios Shrine in St. Augustine, Florida, very kindly provided this writer with informative materials from his personal historical archives; Bishop John is the author of a number of scholarly works, including "The Greek Orthodox Church in the South," in Samuel S. Hill, ed., *Encyclopedia of Religion in the South* (Mercer University Press, 1984), 313.

9   See Chapter 5 of this work, specifically dealing with the Greek community in New Orleans; also see Theodore Saloutos, *Greeks in the United States*, 121-122.

10   Seraphim Canoutas, *Hellenism In America* (New York, Kosmos Printers, 1918), 159-162; Cotton merchant Nicholas Benachi(s) donated the lot for the church as early as 1864, but the church building was erected, at his direction, in 1868; also see Chapter 5 of this work.

11   Theodore Saloutos, *Greeks in the United States*, 121-122; Seraphim Canoutas, *Hellenism in America*, 160-161; also see "The First Greek Orthodox Church in America," *31st Biennial Clergy-Laity Congress, New Orleans, 1992* commemorative album (New Orleans, Holy Trinity Cathedral, 1992).

12   Peter J. Kourides, "Factional Strife Marked Cathedral's Earliest Years," *Orthodox Observer*, November 1992: 24 [New York, Greek Orthodox Archdiocese Publication.]

13   Theodore Saloutos, *Greeks in the United States*, 123-125.

14   Theodore Saloutos, "The Greek Orthodox Church in the United States and Assimilation," *The International Migration Review*, 7 (#4, winter 1973), 395-407, at 397.

15   Eastern Orthodox priests, who aspired to spend most of their lives active in the parishes, were allowed to marry and indeed expected to marry and

have families and thus serve as examples to the faithful; however, those members of the clergy who aspired to higher offices in the church hierarchy had to remain celibate, although they too could serve in parishes for a time. All Orthodox clergy of the rank of Archimandrite to Bishop and up to Patriarch were therefore unmarried, celibate men, observing monastic disciplines.

16   Papás = father, priest; also see Immigration History Research Center [hereinafter IHRC], Theodore Saloutos collection, Box 35, Folder 132.

17   *32nd Biennial Clergy-Laity Congress, July 3-7, Chicago [commemorative album]* (Chicago, Album Committee of the Congress, 1994), St. Sophia Cathedral - Los Angeles Greek Orthodox Community page.

18   Theodore Saloutos, *Greeks in the United States*, 126.

19   IHRC, Theodore Saloutos collection, Boxes 35-37; see specifically notes on the confusion about control over credentials of priests; also see Seraphim G. Canoutas, *Hellenism in America*, describing the establishment of first Greek Orthodox churches in the United States, 158-168, 190-203.

20   IHRC, the Theodore Saloutos collection, Box 35, at the University of Minnesota; the Eastern Orthodox Church is the eastern branch of the Christian religion and an entity comprised of autonomous national Orthodox churches. Its counterpart in the western world is the Roman Catholic Church, headed by the Pope in Rome. Since the days of the Apostles, Bishops were named in the East, in Jerusalem, Antioch, Alexandria, and Constantinople, and in the West, in Rome. Ever since the fifth century, when the Roman Empire divided, the once united Christian Church started drifting apart politically and dogmatically. In 1054 A.D., the Bishop of Rome parted company with the other Bishops over theological issues, including Rome's intention to be the universal head of the whole church. Ecclesiastical rulers in Constantinople [Byzantium], the seat of the eastern branch, and in Rome, seat of the western branch, excommunicated each other and thus finalized the split in the universal Christian church. Although the primates of the eastern branch, including those heading the Orthodox churches in eastern Europe, retained full autonomy over their regions, they considered the Patriarch in Constantinople *primus inter pares*, the first among equals. In contrast, the Pope in Rome assumed the autonomous spiritual reign over *all* the Roman Catholic faithful in the world. Both sides lost ground to the Muslim surge that started in the 14th century and subsided only after absorbing most of the Middle East and parts of Southern Europe. Constantinople, seat of the leading Patriarch and the crown city of the Byzantine Empire, fell to the Ottomans in 1453, followed by the Balkans, northern Africa, and most of Spain. Practically all ethnic Greeks, the Orthodox Christian backbone of Byzantium, became subjects of the Sultan; the Patriarchs and clerics were compelled to administer their various *millets* of Christian Orthodox. By the 19th century, the Ottoman power was in retreat and the Orthodox churches in the Balkans

and elsewhere, aided by the powerful Orthodox church in Russia, headed by the Patriarch in Moscow, established their separate national autonomies. Following a successful uprising against the Ottomans in 1821, the Greek Orthodox Church in newly independent Greece also claimed autonomy, separate and apart from the Patriarchate in Constantinople.

21 The Greek Orthodox Church in Athens became the primary spiritual care-taker for the Greek Orthodox living on those parts of the mainland that had newly gained independence, but against the wishes of the Patriarchate in Constantinople, which was most reluctant to divest itself of direct authority over an adjacent area. For seventeen years, from 1833 to 1850, the Patriarch excommunicated the prelates in Greece. Conciliation lifted the ban in 1850, but even today, the Holy Synod in Athens heads the Orthodox church within the borders of Greece, all other Greek Orthodox in the Aegean and Mediterranean answer to the Patriarchate in Constantinople [Istanbul since 1930]. In this century, Orthodox Patriarchs continue to hold their ecumenical brother in Constantinople in high esteem. He is still the first among equals and has exceptional spiritual influence in the Eastern Orthodox world. His temporal existence, however, is sorely pressed by the Turkish state. For example, since 1923 the Turkish state required the Patriarch to be a Turkish citizen, permits to repair Patriarchal buildings are often withheld; in 1955 Turkish rioters ransacked Greek church buildings, expelled and killed Greek priests and laity; in 1972 the Turkish authorities closed the seminary at Halki; see *Orthodox Observer*, October 1991, September 1995, July-August 1996.

22 Stephen J. Sfekos and George E. Matsoukas eds., *Project for Orthodox Renewal: Key Issues Facing Orthodox Christians in America* (Chicago, Orthodox Christian Laity, 1993); since the late 1700s, when Russian traders brought Eastern Orthodoxy to Alaska, and even after 1867, when the United States purchased Alaska from the Russia, all of the United States was considered part of the see of the Russian Patriarch. However, Orthodox faithful of the Greek, Serbian, Bulgarian, Macedonian, Romanian, and other Orthodox ethnic groups broke this monopoly, as they all sought their own priests. Consequently, there are now literally dozens of Orthodox hierarchies in the United States, all claiming to be "spiritually" united by the dogma and canons set forth by the first seven Ecumenical Councils. The administration of this extensive network of national churches can be compared to that of a large religious confederation. A number of discus-sions were held, and attempts made to unite the Orthodox into one religious body in the United States, with little real progress evident to date. Also see Lila Ross, "Creating a New Identity: Orthodox Church in U. S. developing its own character," *Florida Times Union*, January 6, 1995, A-14.

23 See chapter 5 of this work, dealing with the Hellenic community in New Orleans, Louisiana; Steven Phillips, "Paths in the Greek Orthodoxy in

America," *Odyssey*, July August 1996, 29.

24 Theodore Saloutos, *The Greeks in the United States* , 119.

25 Although the Roman Catholic Church in the United States was hierar-chically united, since all authority emanated from the Vatican, numerous problems materialized because of the different national origins of the faithful, for example the Irish, the Poles, and the Italians; see Rudolph J. Vecoli, "Prelates and Peasants: Italian Immigrants and the Catholic Church," *Journal of Social History*, 2 (Spring 1969), No.3, 217-268, at 237, 242-245, 250, 258.

26 Ferdinand Schevill, *A History of the Balkans* (New York, Dorset Press, 1991), 450-453, 462.

27 In fact, within the year several thousand Armenian Orthodox were massa-cred in Cilicia; and an Arab rebellion took place, which aimed at nothing less than complete Arab independence; see Ferdinand Schevill, *A History of the Balkans*, 462.

28 Father George Nicozisin, "The Mission of the Greek Orthodox Parish in America," *Loghxa*, 2.

29 Rev. Constantine Andrews, Speros B. Boudoures, and George J. Frangoulis, "The Greek Orthodox Church in America," Yearbook, St. Nicholas Greek Orthodox Church, St. Louis, Missouri.

30 Theodore Saloutos, *Greeks in the United States*, 128-129; by 1918, when the "first cycle" of the Greek Orthodox church in the US came to an end, about 130 church communities had been established, including 61 from 1914 through 1918 alone, a record that was never again duplicated during any 5-year period; also see Appendix 6.

31 See Table 9.

32 In the West, between 1907 and 1909, Greek Orthodox churches appeared in San Francisco, Galveston, St. Louis, Pueblo, Salt Lake City, Omaha, Los Angeles, Kansas City, and Portland, see Saloutos, *Greeks in the United States*, 128

33 Theodore Saloutos, *Greeks in the United States*, 136; also see *New York Times*, October 16, 1916; and Doros Alastos, *Venizelos* (London, 1942), 175.

34 Theodore Saloutos, *Greeks in the United States*, 136.

35 Father George Nicozisin, "The Mission of the Greek Orthodox Parish in America," *Loghxa* 2 (March 1994), 2, a publication of the Greek Orthodox Archdiocese of North and South America, New York.

36 IHRC, Theodore Saloutos collection, Box 47, Folder 377 contains copy of *Minneapolis Tribune* of October 16, 1921, reporting on "warring factions:" Peter Boosalis requested police protection from disturbances caused by new (Venizelist) priest trying to assume duties while old (Royalist) priest refused to give up "his" church; IHRC, T. Saloutos collection, Karen Bruce paper (1961); *Orthodox Observer*, November 1992, 21, reported on Baltimore *kinotis*, established in 1906, split as above in 1922 and re-united

in 1929.

37   Alice Scourby, *The Greek Americans* (Boston, Twayne Publishers, 1984), 45.

38   Father George Nicozisin, "The Mission of the Greek Orthodox Parish in America," *Loghʋa*, 2; on October 29, 1918, Archbishop Meletios appointed Bishop Alexander of Rodostolon as the Synodical Vicar. Archbishop Meletios returned to the United States in 1921, called together the first ever Clergy - Laity Congress in September 1921, which ratified the formation of the Greek Orthodox Archdiocese of North and South America. On November 25, 1921, Meletios was elected as the new Ecumenical Patriarch and left for Constantinople. There, he rescinded the 1908 Tome and so returned the nominal jurisdiction of the Greek churches in America to the Ecumenical Patriarchate, where it remains to date.

39   Stephanos Zotos, *The Hellenic Presence in America* (Wheaton, Illinois, Pilgrimage, 1976), 202.

40   Meanwhile, in 1921, while Venizelos attended the prolonged sessions of the peace conference in Paris and lobbied to have the Greek army occupy parts of eastern Thrace and the western coast of Asia minor, the royalists won the elections held in postwar Greece; as a result, King Constantine returned to the throne of Greece, Venizelos was no longer the prime minister, Archbishop Theoklitos was reinstated and all his ecclesiastical appointees replaced all Venizelist clergy throughout Greece.

41   Father George Papaioannou, "The Founding of the Archdiocese and its Administration," *Orthodox Observer*, May 5, 1997; the archdiocese was divided into four Dioceses: Boston, Chicago, San Francisco, and New York; clergy and laity representatives from the entire Archdiocese met at a biennial conference; the Archbishop and the Bishops shared authority collectively. This "Synodical System" of shared authority was soon replaced: in 1931 the newly appointed Archbishop Athenagoras successfully sought to amend the Archdiocesan constitution to make the Bishops auxiliary ecclesiasts, appointed by the Archbishop alone, to carry out his directions. This certainly unified the Archdiocese, but gave a lot of power to the Archbishop alone. One more amendment to the charter, in 1977, sought to adjust this balance, to give separate rights and responsibilities to the Bishops to administer their Dioceses, and yet preserve the unity of the Archdiocese under the Archbishop.

42   Father George Papaioannou, "The Founding of the Archdiocese and its Administration," *Orthodox Observer*, May 1997.

43   Father George Nicozisin, "The Mission of the Greek Orthodox Parish in America," *Loghia*, March 1994, 2; also see IHRC, Theodore Saloutos collection, in Box 35-37: John Papas, *The Greek Church in Courts* (Sanford, Maine, by author, n.d.), passim.

44   Lewis Patsavos, "The Calendar Adopted by the Church," *Orthodox Observer*, November 1991; the Julian calendar was introduced by Julius Caesar in 46

B. C. Slightly inaccurate, it was corrected in 1582 A. D. Since the correction was introduced during the time of Pope Gregory XIII, it is called the Gregorian calendar. Because the correction emanated from Rome, no Eastern Orthodox church adopted it then. Due to its inherent and cumulative inaccuracy, at present the Julian calendar is about 13 days late. After lengthy discussions at an Inter-Orthodox Congress, convened in 1923 by Ecumenical Patriarch Meletios, the Orthodox churches of Constantinople, Alexandria, Antioch, Greece, Cyprus, and Romania adopted the new calendar. The Orthodox Churches of Jerusalem, Russia, Serbia, and a Greek contingent refused to switch and continue using the "old calendar." Most recently, in 1968, the Orthodox church of Bulgaria switched to the new calendar.

45 IHRC, Theodore Saloutos collection, Box 35-37, notes point out that even in the 1970s there were still five parishes in Massachusetts, New York, and New Jersey which continued to follow the old calendar, and thus refused to submit to either the Ecumenical Patriarchate in Constantinople or the Holy Synod in Athens, but sought nominal shelter with the Russian Orthodox Church in the United States, which continued to observe the old calendar.

46 *75th Anniversary [Album], Annunciation Greek Orthodox Church, Mobile, Alabama, 1912-1987* (n.p., Mobile, 1987), 24-27.

47 *Ibid.*, 26-27.

48 In the mid-1920s, Metropolitan Vasilios replaced Germanos as head of the autocephalous Exarchate of the Greek Orthodox Church in America, headquartered in Lowell, Massachusetts = the group of parishes with royalist majorities, which refused to participate in the clergy-laity congress organized by Archbishop Meletios.

49 *75th Anniversary [Album] of the Annunciation Greek Orthodox Church in Mobile*, 27; since it was 13 days late, the Gregorian calendar showed 25th December to fall on a day which the new, more accurate Julian calendar showed as the 7th of January. Accordingly, some Eastern Orthodox Churches, which still adhere to the "old" calendar, celebrate Christmas 13 days "later" than their Christian co-religionists who now use the "new" Julian calendar; see Lewis Patsavos, "The Calendar Adopted by the Church," *Orthodox Observer*, November 1991; also see by the same author "Determining Easter's Date," *Orthodox Observer*, March 1995.

50 Father George Papaioannou, "The Founding of the Archdiocese and its Foundation," *Orthodox Observer*, May 20, 1997, 15.

51 Father George Nicozisin, "The Mission of the Greek Orthodox Parish in America," *Loghia*, 2; in May 1930 Patriarch Photios of Constantinople and Archbishop Chrysostomos of Athens jointly dispatched Metropolitan Damaskinos of Corinth to assume temporary administration of all parishes in America and break the path for a new Archbishop. The Patriarchate, with agreement of the Holy Synod in Athens, then selected Metropolitan

Athenagoras of Kerkyra to assume the duties as the Primate of the "Greek Orthodox Archdiocese of North and South America." He arrived in the United States on February 24, 1931. After a successful eighteen-year reign, in 1949, Athenagoras became the second "American" Archbishop to be elected the Ecumenical Patriarch in Constantinople.

52   John Papas *The Greek Church in Courts* (Sanford, Maine, n.p., 1944?).

53   James Steve Counelis, "Greek Orthodox Church Statistics of the United States, 1949-1989: some Ecclesial and Social Patterns," *Journal of the Hellenic Diaspora* 16 (1-4, Spring-Summer-Fall-Winter 1989), 155-156, even to this day, parish corporations are solely under legal control of the parish membership and these non-profit entities are the owners of all parish assets.

54   Theodore Saloutos, *Greeks in the United States*, 304-309.

55   Halki is an island in the Bosphorus, just off Constantinople; in 1972, Turkish authorities closed the Greek Orthodox Theological School on Halki, see *Orthodox Observer* of October 1996, 5, 27; and *ibid.* of October 1994, 18.

56   Dr. Michael Herzfeld, oral interview by the author, in Gainesville, April 10, 1997, when the interviewee confirmed that although women were still barred from any pastoral positions, and still cannot enter the altar area behind the iconostasis, Greek Orthodox women in America assumed much larger and more significant roles in the management of the church than their catechumen counterparts in the Mediterranean.

57   Vasilikie Demos, "Maintenance and Loss of Traditional Gender Boundaries in Two Greek Orthodox Communities," *Journal of the Hellenic Diaspora* 16 (Nos. 1-4, 1989), 77-93, at 77.

58   Dimitrios Ioannis Monos, "Upward Mobility, Assimilation, and the Achievements of Greeks in the United States with Special Emphasis on Boston and Philadelphia," (University of Pennsylvania, Ph.D. dissertation, 1976), 91-94, where Monos claims that with a group's increased upward social mobility, the group's members increasingly observe the religious traditions but neglect national and ethnic ones; moreover, the church-factionalism in Greek communities impaired the nationalistic function of the Greek Orthodox Church as a resistant force to assimilation.

59   Theodore Saloutos, "The Greek Orthodox Church and Assimilation," *International Migration Review*, reprinted in George E. Pozzetta ed., *American Immigration and Ethnicity*, volume 19, *The Immigrant Religious Experience* (New York, Garland Publishing, 1991), 307.

60   See chapter 3 of this work.

61   Theodore Saloutos, "The Greek Orthodox Church in the United States," 311.

62   *Greek Orthodox Theological School "Holy Cross"* (Pomfret, Connecticut, n.p., 1952?).

63   Reverend Milton Efthimiou, "Where it Began: Roots of Holy Cross at

Pomfret," *Orthodox Observer*, June 1992, 19.

64   Theodore Saloutos, "The Greek Orthodox Church in the United States," 314.

65   Theodore Saloutos, *Greeks in the United States*, 314.

66   Ibid., 371-372; archdiocesan income before the *dekadollarion*, 1945-1950, when each church member should have contributed through the parish $1 for the archdiocese, hovered between $80,000 and $100,000 per year ; in 1951, during the first year of the new revenues, archdiocesan income amounted to $329,726, or fewer than 33,000 paying members; by 1958, the total annual income had risen to $585,698. As outlined above, a significant number of parishioners simply chose not to pay their $10 assessment.

67   Theodore Saloutos, *Greeks in the United States*, 373-375; Greek Americans, together with other Eastern Orthodox faithful, wanted to have Orthodoxy recognized as a major faith in the United States; prodded by the Federation of Orthodox Churches (a body formed by the Syrian, Greek, Russian, and Serbian Orthodox church jurisdictions in the US), by 1955 seven states had made provisions for incorporation of Eastern Orthodox churches and by 1959 twenty state legislatures had enacted resolutions to grant the Eastern Orthodox Church the status of a major faith. It took another united campaign to have dog-tags issued to Orthodox soldiers in the US armed forces; after much resistance by the Pentagon, Senator Leverett Saltonstall of Massachusetts introduced a special bill providing for inclusion of "E. O." (Eastern Orthodox) on the tags; finally on June 6, 1955, Secretary of Defence Charles E. Wilson issued a directive ordering the new label.

68   *Newsweek*, July 13, 1964, 52; the 17th congress took place in Denver, Colorado; delegates partook in a long and sometimes biting discussion on the use of English in services; the Archbishop sided with the reformers, as 60 percent of the then membership consisted of third-generation Greeks, children of US-born parents. The formal decision to use English came at the 1970 clergy - laity congress, the decision coupled with the admonition to use only the approved Diocesan translation. By that time there were dozens of English translations in use in different regions and even individual churches throughout the Archdiocese.

69   Theodore Saloutos, "The Greek Orthodox Church in the United States," *International Migration Review* 7 (Winter 1973), 395-407, cited in George E. Pozzetta ed., *American Immigration and Ethnicity* (New York, Garland Publishing, 1991), volume 19, *The Immigrant Religious Experience*, 318-319.

70   *Life* magazine, March 26, 1965, front page; also see *Mobile Press Register* of January 31, 1976, 7-B, confirming Archbishop Iakovos's stay in Selma, "where he participated in the late Martin Luther King's justice walk to Montgomery;" also see "A Remarkable 37-Year Ministry," *Orthodox Observer*, July-August 1996, 5-9.

71   See chapter 6 of this work, dealing with Greeks in Birmingham, Alabama.

72   George Leber, *History of the Order of AHEPA,* 452; also see chapter 3 of this work on Greek fraternal associations.

73   *Orthodox Observer,* September 1970; also see *New York Times,* June 30, 1970

74   Theodore Saloutos, *Greeks in the United States,* 316.

75   Theodore Saloutos, "The Greek Orthodox Church in the United States," 313; also see at 317 citation from Nicon D. Patrinacos, "The Truth About Our Historic 20th Congress," *Orthodox Observer,* September 1970: "Even during the tenure of the late Archbishop Michael (1949-1958), an English translation of the Liturgy was openly sold by the Archdiocese and... used by non-Greek understanding Greek Americans to follow the ritual and...by priests for rendering certain parts of the Liturgy."

76   Nick Costarides and Sophia Clikas oral interview by the author on July 7, 1992, in Mobile, Alabama; both are active veteran members of the Annunciation, involved in preserving the history of the parish.

77   Stephanos Zotos, *Hellenic Presence in America,* 204-209, despite criticism from the Church of Greece and some Orthodox faithful in the United States, under Archbishop Iakovos relations that American Orthodoxy has with other faiths are greatly improved; two of his bishops are in Geneva as permanent representatives at the World Council of Churches; Iakovos himself served as one of the presidents of WCC; in his report to the 17th biennial clergy - laity congress in July 1965, he promoted "our dialogue...with the Church of Rome, with the Anglican Church, and with the national Council of Churches of Christ."

78   James Steve Counelis, "Greek Orthodox Church Statistics of the United States, 1949-1989: Some Ecclesial and Social Patterns," *Journal of the Hellenic Diaspora* 16 (Nos. 1-4, Spring-Summer-Fall-Winter 1989) 158.

79   Ibid., 157 = of these, however, inter-Christian weddings outnumber intra-Orthodox weddings by 2:1; see also Jim Golding's report "Mixed Marriages Issue of Major Concern," in *Orthodox Observer,* September 1995, where Archdiocesan Council president Demitrios Moschos indicated that at this time "Over 80 percent of the marriages are mixed..."

80   *Orthodox Observer,* January 1996, see "English in the Liturgy" by Dr. Theodore Bogdanos, who pointed out that although prayers and hymns in English guarantee instant understanding by the worshipers, the Roman Catholic Church went through the same dilemma a generation ago, with disastrous results. Led by the same concerns as the Orthodox church at present, the Catholics replaced Latin with English, and as a result lost their Gregorian Chant and choral polyphony. The vacuum was soon filled by less ritualistic and more casual elements, popular religious songs and musical hits, which in turn brought in guitar accompaniment and even dancing. The act of worship became a parody of the solemnity and mysticism of the old Latin mass. To retain some of its liturgical dignity, the Roman Catholic Church borrowed anthems from the Protestant hymnal

and thus by conformity and assimilation lost its spiritual identity. Many Catholics left the church because it had lost its unique traditional worship. And the children, for whom parents made all these changes, did not stay in the church; they could no longer distinguish it from the Unitarian or Evangelical churches down the street.

81   James Steve Counelis, "Greek Orthodox Church Statistics in the United States, 1949-1989: Some Ecclesial and Social Patterns," *Journal of the Hellenic Diaspora* 16 (Nos 1-4, 1989), 131; see also *Orthodox Observer*, July-August 1996 [and in other issues], "Letters to the Editor," where one can see a clear note of dissent: from both a traditional and artistic standpoint many Greek Orthodox wish to retain the treasured Byzantine modal music in the original Greek - untranslated and unspoiled.

82   James Steve Counelis, "Greek Orthodox Church Statistics of the United States, 1949-1989: Some Ecclesial and Social Patterns," *Journal of the Hellenic Diaspora* 16 (Nos. 1-4, 1989), 153; also see Lewis J. Patsavos, "History of the Charters: the Structure of the Archdiocese According to the Charters of 1922, 1927, 1931 and 1977," in Miltiades Efthimiou and George Christopoulos eds., *History of the Greek Orthodox Church in America*, 67-92.

83   James S. Counelis, "Greek Orthodox Church Statistics of the United States, 1949-1989: Some Ecclesial and Social Patterns," *Journal of the Hellenic Diaspora* 16 (Nos. 1-4, 1989) 158.

CHAPTER 5

SOCIAL DIVISIONS IN NEW ORLEANS, THE CRESCENT CITY

New Orleans was a cosmopolitan center, built and populated by the Spanish and French before it became, in the mid-1850s, the third-largest city of the American Republic. This jewel of the South, occupied by Union forces in the second year of the war between the states, provided the home for the first Greek Orthodox church-community ever formed in the United States, in 1864. The initially small congregation reflected the city's international flavor: although Greek merchants predominated, other Eastern Orthodox, primarily Serbs, Russians, and Syrians also participated in this *kinotis*. The complexity of this Orthodox community was magnified by the frequent presence of Greek sailors in the city, who from time to time sought spiritual solace, but more often searched the city for comforts that mariners everywhere expect to enjoy in port. The principal segment of the city's Hellenic community, secure in the commercial life of New Orleans and residing in its better suburbs, had little contact with the thousands of seafaring Greeks who sailed into port every year. During the 1960s and 1970s, a high tide of ethnic expression engulfed the nation. Young ethnic Americans sported buttons proclaiming "Greek Power - Spiro Agnew for VP," or "Thank God I'm Polish," and "I'm glad I'm Latvian." Greek Americans in New Orleans inaugurated three-day annual Greek festivals and a Greek Night, but excluded from these events any help from Greeks who had just sailed in from the Mediterranean.

Unity did not always elude the Hellenes who settled in the exotic
port city. Nicholas Marinos Benakis, a Greek entrepreneur originally
from the island of Chios, found a home in *antebellum* New Orleans
and made a fortune operating a line of steamers out of the Crescent
City.[1] He was only one of a handful of wealthier Greek traders, businessmen, and cotton merchants who had settled in the colorful
commercial and maritime hub on the Mississippi. The Greek government appointed Benakis to its consulship, to look after scores of Greek
vessels that docked there carrying European and American cargoes.
Demetrios and John Botassis, and representatives of the Greek merchant
house of the Rallis Brothers also carried on lucrative businesses in New
Orleans.[2] They were in turn acquainted with Greek and Serbian businessmen Constantine Kilili, Nicholas Panzios, Michael Draskovich,
Marco Popovich, and others. All were interested in building an
Orthodox church, where their families, sundry Orthodox employees,
and transient Greek sailors could worship.[3]

In 1864, two years after General Benjamin Butler's occupation of
New Orleans, the group met, formed a congregation, and elected
Constantine Kilili as its president.[4] The parishioners soon secured the
services of a Russian-trained Orthodox priest, father Agapios
Honcharenko, who held religious services at several locations, until
Benachi agreed to sell to the parish a parcel of his land, fronting ninety
feet on North Dorgenois Street. With generous donations from the
Botassis brothers and other merchants made possible by the revival of
trade, the church building took place within the year. By 1866, father
Agapios "officiated in the first Eastern Orthodox Church of America,"
a modest rectangular, one-story structure, with its front just over twenty
feet wide and about sixty feet long, graced in the southern plantation
style with four wooden Doric columns across the front elevation that
supported a fancy gable.[5]

Although its exterior was unpretentious, the congregants soon
furnished the interior with icons and sacred images characteristic of
Greek Orthodox churches.[6] In June 1867, Nicholas Benakis signed over
the deed of the property to two trustees, Constantine Kilili and Michael
Draskovich, who represented the "congregation (not yet incorporated)
of the members" of the Eastern Orthodox Church.[7] Marco Popovich, a
young Crescent City businessman, took on the responsibilities of the
first cantor, or *psaltis*.[8] Affirming their respective interests in the new

Orthodox house of worship, the Czar of Russia contributed a new communion chalice and Queen Olga of Greece presented a gold-plated Holy Bible.[9] Reflecting the variety of his congregants, father Agapios celebrated the liturgy in Greek, church-Slavonic, and English.[10] Within the next few years the congregation acquired a parish house, a library, and a cemetery.

In 1866, the small Greek congregation in New Orleans erected the first Greek Orthodox Church in the United States, with generous donations from cotton merchants such as Nicholas Benachi and Demetrios and John Botassis. Membership consisted of Greek, Serbian, Russian, and Syrian Orthodox faithful. In 1901, the State of Louisiana chartered the church as the Eastern Orthodox Church of Holy Trinity. In 1992, the author received this photo [origin unknown] courtesy of Father Nicholas W. Jonas, Dean of the Holy Trinity cathedral in New Orleans and Mr. and Mrs. Harry and Mary Zaharis, New Orleans, Louisiana.

New Orleans continued to grow during the years of the Gilded Age and just as other New South cities, it attracted newly arriving Greek settlers. They were the same impecunious but ambitious, enterprising, and industrious young men, who filled a variety of commercial niches. As best they could they linked their fortunes to their wealthier compatriots in Louisiana's capital. The port expanded when engineer James B. Eads built a jetty that created a thirty-foot deep channel in the river, enabling large ships to reach the docks.[11] The Pontchartrain Railroad extended its tracks to Canal Street, and the city council leased the Jackson Square riverfront for use as a freight depot. The rapid recovery of the sugar and cotton industries did not halt the massive exodus of former plantation slaves, who looked for better opportunities elsewhere. To replace the missing labor, the Louisiana Bureau of Immigration and the Sugar Planters' Association encouraged European immigrants, mostly Italians, Spanish, and Portugese, to work the fields.[12] Many ended up in the city, providing more population, and thus more customers and trade for the Greek entrepreneurs. By 1900, the city had grown to just under 300,000 inhabitants, nearly half of them immigrants or born to immigrants.[13] The city's growth paralelled the growth of mass immigration from the Old World, particularly from southern and eastern Europe.

A few new Greek settlers were former sailors, who had decided to exchange the confined and at times dangerous life at sea for a less exciting but more gainful living in a thriving port. Others arrived from eastern and mid-western American industrial cities, as well as directly from the Mediterranean, drawn by reports from friends and relatives who praised the open markets and the chances to earn good money in a place with flourishing trade and commerce. In this respect, the influx of Greek newcomers into New Orleans conformed to their arrival in other growing New South cities described in chapter two. In much the same way, New Orleans Greeks, probably guided by their wealthier and respected compatriots, quickly adapted to the segregated society and made sure they stayed on the "right," white side of the tracks. Moreover, the Greeks avoided the censure suffered by the entire law-abiding Italian community in New Orleans, when the police incriminated a few Sicilian immigrants in the fatal shooting of police chief David Hennessy.[14]

By 1910, over 400 Greeks had settled in the city. Most were self-employed or working for self-employed relatives or compatriots.[15] In addition, true to patterns noted in the South, a number of the newer Greek settlers had established families. Typical of those was Gus (Constantine) Pelias, who arrived in New Orleans in 1903 and operated a tiny tobacco store. By the start of World War I, he was heading a size-able business enterprise he named the "Imperial Trading Company and Wholesale Grocery," grossing $2,000,000 annually.[16] Pelias was also active in the parish as well as in the wider community, where he had joined the Elks, the Athletic Club of New Orleans, and sundry other sodalities. Nicholas Bellamore was another active member of both the business and Hellenic communities in the Crescent City. Upon settling there in 1901, he attracted customers to his optical store with the enterprising slogan "See me to see right." He was elected as presi-dent of the Holy Trinity Greek Orthodox parish in 1912 and again in 1926, and was a "popular member of the Elks, the Chess, Checkers and Whist Club and numerous other fraternal and social organiza-tions."[17]

There were no direct references about the political leanings of the early Orthodox merchants who first formed the *kinotis* and built the Holy Trinity church. Nevertheless, they probably steered a middle course between the radical Republicans and southern Democrats during the turbulent and sometimes lawless Reconstruction period. After all, their main purpose was not politics but trade and commerce, so the less openly they sympathized with the Confederate side and the White Leaguers until the Hayes - Tilden compromise and the election of governor Francis Nicholls, and the less they overtly fraternized with northern businessmen after that, the better off they were. Similarly, newly-arriving Greeks were likely to be much more interested in commercial activities in the Canal Street district than in the political activities around Jackson Square and the State House. In spite of the occasional riot, labor unrest, and corruption in government in the late 19th and early 20th centuries, the city's population grew and business escalated, undeterred by the political rivalry between the Regular Democratic Organization of mayor Martin Behrman and the reformers of Luther E. Hall and John M. Parker.[18] Business boosters continued to brag about the city's commercial prosperity, its cotton and sugar exchanges, its port where bananas and coffee from Latin America arrived in greater quantities than anywhere else in the world, and its expanding railroad network. Holy Trinity parish also prospered: in 1913 the congregation authorized its president Nicholas Bellamore to arrange a $2,000 loan with the Hibernia Bank of New Orleans for a new rectory for the priest; in 1914 the parishioners voted unanimously to change the church chandeliers from oil to electricity.[19]

The parish continued its cautious modernizing along with the city. By the time Huey Long became governor, the Levee Board completed plans to improve the lakefront and protect the city's expansion by building a stepped concrete seawall along the shore of lake Pontchartrain.[20] The congregation decided to install pews and to introduce a regular membership fee; father John Zografos organized the first mixed church choir, and two AHEPA chapters formed—the first one in Shreveport, followed by the one in New Orleans, appropriately named after Andrew Jackson.[21] In 1938, the chapter hosted its first national convention of this popular Greek-American fraternal organization, whose members were chiefly businessmen. Despite hardships imposed by the Depression, hard-working owners of small enterprises such as shoeshine and hat-cleaning parlors, hamburger and sandwich shops, restaurants and sundry other businesses, representative of Greek settlers in the South, generally survived quite well the economic adversities of the 1930s. And during the 1940s, while most of their sons - the second generation - were fighting the war, the Hellenic entrepreneurs sold War Bonds, collected donations for Greek War Relief, and enjoyed the additional boost the war bestowed on the economy of the largest port city in the Gulf.

In fact, during the war, when Greeks, along with sundry other nationals in the Mediterranean became American allies in the contest against the same Nazi enemy, Greek Americans in New Orleans felt less concerned in disclosing their old-country origins. Although occupied by German troops, Greece was firmly in the allied camp and her people were suffering for "freedom and democracy," the same causes America was fighting for. A transfer of United States fighting vessels to sailors of the Greek Royal Navy, that took place in New Orleans in 1943, highlighted the alliance. Subsequent governments in Athens and Washington later adapted this coalition to subdue communist insurgents in northern Greece, a struggle won by Athens with extensive American economic and military help received under the Truman Doctrine. George Pappas, who resided in New Orleans since 1930, when he was twelve, remembered that before the war, and even later, in the 1950s, the fact that one was "Greek" American was "not advertised."[22] One did not overtly reject assimilative pressures; if one wanted to be accepted as an equal in social and business circles, one reduced ethnic differences only to attendance, on Sundays, at the Greek Orthodox Christian church instead of the Protestant or Roman Catholic Christian houses of worship. Pappas, who had graduated in accounting and finance at Loyola University in 1941, and who spent the war years building PT boats for the navy, found it most appealing to describe himself as an American; then, depending on the particular situation, he might add the detail that he was an American "of Greek origin." In his opinion, "the whole ethnic situation opened up" only in the early 1970s.

Soon after the war ended, the congregation sought to enlarge the church, which had become too small for the parish now numbering nearly one thousand souls.[23] Even though only a fraction of that number attended church regularly, at Christmas or during the Easter Holy Week, the old building could not accommodate those who came to worship regularly. Since 1946, the congregation had purchased additional property on the corner of North Dorgenois and Governor Nicholls Streets, to erect a new church edifice.[24] However, if a new church were to be built on the property, the old one had to be razed. Led by the hierarchs of the Archdiocese, many parishes urged the New Orleans congregants to preserve the oldest Greek Orthodox church in America as a shrine to Orthodoxy. But at a landmark meeting in April 1949, the congregation rejected the pleas.[25] As George Pappas explained, the building was simply too ridden with termites and too decrepit to be saved; demolition was unavoidable.[26] Bishop Germanos of New York represented the Archdiocese when leading members of the parish laid the corner-stone in November 1950. The new Holy Trinity church, this time built of red brick and steel, with two impressive cupola-towers on either side of the front entry, stretching just under 100 feet in length, with wings extending on either side to form a cross, stood ready for dedication by July 1951.

Cornerstone Ceremonies of New Greek Orthodox Church
NOV. 19th, 1950

By the late 1940s, the oldest Greek Orthodox church in the US, built in 1866 on Dorgenois Street and dedicated to the Holy Trinity, became termite infested and was demolished to make room for a larger church. Mr. George W. Pappas kindly supplied the author with this photo, taken during cornerstone laying ceremonies for the new Holy Trinity church, in 1950. Participants depicted and numbered from left to right: George W. Pappas; a Gulfport, Mississippi guest; George Konos; Constantine (Gus) Christakis; Gerasimos C. Pelias; a Gulfport, Mississippi guest; His Grace Bishop Germanos; Emanuel Ioannides; Reverend Vasilios Bouterakos; Ernest Couloheras; Frank Vloutis; Alex Castrinos; Eleftherios C. Tzavellas; Louis Malachias.

Less than a decade later, the new hierarch in America, Archbishop Iakovos, elevated the church to the rank of a cathedral, and named its local priest, father William Gaines, to be the dean of the new cathedral of Holy Trinity. New Orleans now became the seat of an auxiliary Bishop, whose duties consisted of assisting the Archbishop, the hierarch of the church in America, to administer a newly created diocese, which included churches and parishes in Louisiana, Arkansas, Mississippi,

Alabama, Memphis, Tennessee, and the entire Republic of Mexico.[27] Another chapter of this work deals in more detail with the transformation of the Greek Orthodox church in America from a conservative, ethnic creed to a progressive and American religious denomination. One should note here however, that the ceremonies surrounding the establishment of a new diocese also served to strengthen some ecumenical ties in New Orleans between the Orthodox on the one hand and the Anglican Communion and the Protestant Evangelical churches of the area on the other hand. Reverend Canon Donald Wattley, canon missioner of the Episcopal diocese of Louisiana participated for the Anglicans, and Reverend George Wilson represented the Protestants at the traditional services establishing the Orthodox bishopric. One month later, in November 1960, the same Reverend Wilson, in his capacity as the executive secretary of the Greater New Orleans Federation of Churches, wrote to father William Gaines to inform him that Holy Trinity's application to join the Federation had been approved.[28] At that time, neither the Holy Trinity nor the Federation seemed to have any formal relations with the city's Roman Catholic or Jewish religious bodies.

The 1960s also brought into focus the rather tenuous link between the regular Hellenic community in New Orleans, congregating around Holy Trinity church, and the always changing but numerous fraternity of Greek sailors, who sometimes visited the church, but who more often could be found in taverns, clubs, and restaurants surrounding the harbor area. Tradition had it that the Orthodox merchants who built Holy Trinity in 1866 welcomed the attendance in church of Greek mariners and any other Orthodox travelers. Sailors have been part of New Orleanian life ever since there was a port. International shipping increased since the turn of the century, when the city's Dock Board acquired authority over all water frontage in Orleans Parish and during the first decade of the 1900s rebuilt the port with cotton warehouses, bulk storage facilities, and one of the biggest grain elevators in the world.[29] Not surprisingly, America's second largest port attracted ships from Greece, which had the largest merchant marine in the world. By the 1960s, over 1,000 Greek-registered vessels docked in New Orleans each year. As a matter of policy, Greek ships carried more than 50 percent Greek crews, so roughly 20,000 Greek sailors reached New Orleans in any one year. One must add to this figure those Greek sailors who worked on ships under non-Greek flags. For a long time, Liberia was a convenient Greek shipping center due to relaxed regulations and lucrative tax breaks. "Liberian" shipping corporations located at addresses in the capital city of Monrovia were actually owned and operated from Piraeus, London, or New York by Greek ship owners, who hired thousands of Greek crew members for their world-wide voyages. There are no statistics on the exact number of Greeks on non-Greek ships arriving in New Orleans, but it seems safe to estimate that they brought the total number of Greek sailors in Louisiana each year to about 25,000 men.[30]

Although particular New Orleanian Greek merchants always catered to Greek sailors, after the war, the Hellenic community that had settled in New Orleans had little contact with their seafaring, transient compatriots. Partly, this gap between the two groups can be explained by practical realities: most of the permanent population was engaged in businesses, and had little free time to fraternize with transient seamen. Sailors, on the other hand, were here today and gone within a week or two, with scanty opportunities to form lasting friendships. Traditionally ship owners and sailors came from the Aegean islands, and usually the home island of the owners determined the make-up of the crew. Islands such as Andros, Chios, Hydra, and Lesbos, though small in population, have produced shipping empires whose "wealth and tonnage surpass that of most countries."[31] Until recent times, being a sailor was a viable and lucrative way for an uneducated islander to support himself and a family, and most sailors were married and had families. To spend a Sunday morning in the Greek Orthodox church located not too far from port was not an unusual pastime for some married seamen, especially if there was a chance that one might meet an acquaintance from an earlier voyage. For the most part, these Greek sailors took pride in their profession and remained at sea for the better part of their working lives.

With the present generation, however, a noticeable change occurred. Second and third generation New Orleanian Hellenes, while no strangers to the Greek language, considered themselves more American than Greek. Over the same period, since the mid-1950s, Greek merchant shipping hired an ever-increasing percentage of younger, less-experienced, less serious-minded, non-family oriented sailors, who have signed up for a few years of adventure before trying something else.

They were the *tihodiotis*, the "luck-chasers."[32] No longer did they necessarily come from the islands. In fact it was now common to find sailors from Athens, and from inland mountain villages where the sea has never been an integral part of their culture. Economic developments accelerated this change. Island economies have improved; young men who would have set sail years ago now found they could make a living at home and thus remained with the family.[33] The "new" Greek seamen were also younger than their counterparts of earlier days. If years ago most sailors fitted into the 30-50-year-old category, in the 1970s, they were predominantly in the 18-30 group. Their interests seldom included meetings with mostly family-oriented and more staid second- and third-generation Greeks, who are much more comfortable conversing in English, and whose interests run to business, local Louisiana politics, and sports. The new seamen perceived a general negative attitude on part of the settled Hellenic populace, based on the view that transient and lewd sailors only wanted a good time in port and that no women were safe from them. Conversely, the notion prevailed among mariners that they will not be well-regarded among compatriots who emphasized their "American" status and who only wanted to show their superiority, evident by their patronizing ways, even as they pretended to be friendly.[34]

Nevertheless, interviews with Greek seamen disclose that New Orleans was their favorite American city. They liked the climate, the moderate size of the city, the proximity of the port to the center of town, and above all the easy-going and welcoming atmosphere in the several "Greek" bistros and lounges on upper Decatur Street near Canal Street.[35] Although parts of Decatur Street sometimes seem to serve as a place where prostitutes exhibited their attractions, what really drew the Greek sailors to this area was the jovial mood prevailing in the Greek clubs and bars operated and staffed by Greeks, such as the Scorpios, the Athenian Room, or the Habana Bar. There was male camaraderie, female companionship, and a "Greek" environment, including bouzouki music, singers, food, ouzo, and wine. Most of the sailors realized that prices may be cheaper in other French Quarter bars, but they felt most comfortable with their own people at a place like the Athenian, where a *parea* [party] of sailors from the same ship can find a form of release from tensions, pressures, and frustrations, and within the familiar cultural attitude realize that certain feeling, combining bravado and joy, described as "kefi."[36] In addition, that area had a number of Greek-owned shops, such as the noted Casa Angelo, that sold electronic equipment, cameras, blue jeans, and tourist souvenirs.[37] Clearly these establishments served as the center of activity for transient Greek sailors, but with the exception of the owners and waiters, seldom attracted the Greek-American population.

One place consciously designed for Greek seamen to meet local compatriots and to relax in, was the Saint Nicholas Maritime Center, organized and directed by father William Gaines.[38] Although every sailor knew of the Casa Angelo, only a minority were familiar with the Center, despite its proximity to Angelo's emporium. Father Gaines, who served as the regular priest at Holy Trinity from 1955 to 1972, persuaded the Greek Archdiocesan authorities to support the maintenance of an outreach facility that would enhance the fellowship between local and transient Hellenes, and fill a void in the mariners' existence in a port of call. A small chapel provided the seamen an opportunity to attend services, and the whole Center presented a haven for fraternization, to counteract the seamen's feelings of loneliness and privation. It was to be a place where the visitors might meet compatriots in the lounge, play billiards in the game room, watch a movie, play basketball, use the swimming pool, receive and send mail home, and generally spend time while in port, without the attendant pressure to purchase goods or to consume alcoholic beverages.

The Saint Nicholas Maritime Center could be considered a partial success, if one were to look at the five or six thousand sailors' signatures logged in its guest-book annually. It may also be considered a partial failure, since it reached only about one fifth of the men it was intended for, and especially because very few local Hellenes came to meet the transient seafarers, to extend the traditional hospitality. In fact, father Gaines volunteered so much of his time to the seamen and, with ship-owner Lucas Christakis, to activities in the Maritime Center, that the majority of his parishioners felt neglected. In 1971, Dennis Georges, the then president of the church-community, together with the whole council, asked father Gaines to make a choice between the parish and the sailors. The matter eventually ended up with the Archbishop in New York. He chose father Demetrios Katerlis as the new priest acceptable to the parish and appointed father Gaines to be the Chaplain of the Seaport, thus enabling him to continue in the outreach to the seamen.[39]

The two communities, the permanent Greek American parish in New Orleans and the transient Greek sailors remained separate even when the wider American society no longer rejected those whose origins did not fit into a standard mold. In the 1970s New Orleans, as in other cities, maintenance of cultural diversity became socially acceptable even for those whose forefathers were neither Anglo, nor French, nor Spanish. As George Pappas and author Ethelyn Orso pointed out, by the early 1970s, the New Orleanian Greek American ethnics "revitalized" their cultural heritage.[40] In fact, Crescent City's ethnic revitalization was part of a larger nationwide experience, chronicled by a group of American historians, who asserted that after half a century of pressure on generations of immigrants to become 100 percent Americans, their offspring "ceased to be 'foreigners,'" but rather than melting into an indistinguishable American pot, they became *ethnic Americans* of one kind or another."[41]

A majority of the Greeks who migrated to New Orleans struggled to achieve success in their small enterprises and, in time, melted into the suburbs of New Orleans, where they could afford the affluent houses and enjoy family life in good neighborhoods. By the 1950s and 1960s, a majority of second- and third-generation Greeks in New Orleans did not speak Greek at home. Some of the older, first-generation Greeks were troubled, however, that their offspring did not maintain the language, but did not persist in sending their children to the Greek language school located at the old church on Dorgenois Street. Although not proficient in the ancestral language, Greek Americans maintained the ethnic connection by church attendances, by observing traditional holidays, by gathering with their cohorts at functions of a variety of Hellenic fraternal, philanthropic, and religious associations, and by enjoying selected vestiges of the original regional cultures in music, songs, dances, and cuisine. The New Orleans Greek Americans were certainly no longer strangers; as Kathleen Neils Conzen and others pointed out, they had become ethnic Americans.

In 1969, the Hellenic community, led by its then president Dennis Georges and member George Zissis, organized the first "Greek Night," followed some years later by a Greek Festival.[42] In Orso's opinion, "in an explicit and self-conscious phase," Greek Americans wanted to demonstrate their values by exhibiting selected customs, foods, dances, traditional costumes, and the like, to their American friends and neighbors. These two annual public events were considered successful not by the amount of money that reached the church treasury, but by the satisfaction of the organizers and their "American" guests, as expressed by the level of participation in the music and dancing and the consumption of Greek foods. Although the monetary income to the church was significant, acceptance and approval by the wider society was the main goal. The exhibited Greek-American culture was a hybrid, as were all such similar subcultures in the United States, and no doubt selected to please the New Orleans native populace, who were said to be obsessed with "good" food and drink. New Orleanians pride themselves on their epicureanism. The food and drink chosen by the Greeks was both distinctive and tasty, so there was seldom room for complaint even from the pickiest New Orleans gourmets. The Bouzouki music was unique and sensual, as were the Greek folk dances. The pastries were rich and delicious, and contrasted just enough from the local French or Italian pastries to arouse and stimulate the appetite for something different.

To be sure, Greek Americans of New Orleans were also proud to be heirs to democratic tendencies of Periclean Athens, to the classic Greek art and architecture, to Hellenic philosophers and scientists, and to the rich heritage of Byzantium, but the selective choice of good food, wine, ouzo, singing, dancing, and music in a city said to be "always for pleasure" assured the contemporary approval of their peers and thus the perpetuation of the ethnic difference. However, the ethno-cultural exhibitions on part of the New Orleans Greek community were ridiculed and disdained by the seamen, the *real* Greeks.[43] In the sailors' eyes, the hybrid Hellenic culture, selected and buffed for presentation during a specific period of two or three days a year, simply did not reflect the original, which lacked the "American" elements of organization and commercialization. Real Greeks did not have a good time on cue, at performances scheduled at three, seven, and ten o'clock Saturday afternoon; real Greeks seldom wore folk-costumes. Each group conceived and expressed its own ethnic dimension. It should not come as a surprise that the two disparate Greek communities in New Orleans, the transient seamen and the New Orleans Greek Americans, persisted in having minimal involvement with each other.

Notes

1   The obituary notice in the New Orleans *Times Picayune* of February 9,
      1886, on page 4, stated that Nicholas M. Benachi, 74, a native of the island
      of Chios, arrived in New Orleans "long before the American civil war and
      married into a Creole family." He was "the most prominent member of the
      Greek Church of this city," as well as a "valuable citizen," who "for more
      than a quarter of a century figured prominently in the business circles of
      the city;" the *New Orleans City Guide* (Boston, Houghton, Mifflin Company,
      1938), 305, written under the Federal Writers' Project of the Works Progress
      Administration (WPA), described the "Benachi Mansion," erected by him
      in 1849.

2   "The First Greek Orthodox Church in America," *31st Biennial Clergy-Laity
      Congress, New Orleans 1992* Commemorative Album (New Orleans, Holy
      Trinity Cathedral, 1992); see 1993 manuscript by Seraphim Canoutas,
      Theodore Constant, and Paul Koken, *The Story of the Greeks in America*,
      Chapter 7 "Employment and Business," indicating that several Greek
      merchant houses had branches in New Orleans exporting cotton, cereals,
      and flour to England, such as Peter Rodocanakis & Company; Pavlos
      Galanis; P. Gounaris & Company; Menelaos and Mekas; Emmanuel
      Skaramagas; P. Fakeris & Company; Fragiades & Company; and others. A
      few remained active until the 1870s.

3   Father William G. Gaines, [Souvenir book] *The First Eastern Greek Orthodox
      Church in America: The Holy Trinity of New Orleans* (New Orleans, n.p.,
      1972?), 5, other "early Orthodox Christians in New Orleans" were:
      Alexander Dimitry, James Bratos, Antony Rallis, John Gardas, Panagis
      Drimelis, Michael Pantoleontas, Michael Perovich, Savvas Tripovich; who
      were joined during the decade 1890-1900 by Spyridon Marcus, Ardoulas
      Ferres, Elias Smorait, George Nazar, John Nomikos, Anthony Banas, Ivan
      Padovich, Petros Bengros, Anthony Benias, Adam Malinovich, Elias Bren,
      and Thomas Thomassovich.

4   Father William Gaines, *The First Eastern Greek Orthodox Church in America:
      The Holy Trinity of New Orleans*, 14.

5   Miltiades Efthimiou and George Christopoulos, *History of the Greek
      Orthodox Church in America* (New York, Greek Orthodox Archdiocese of
      North and South America), 2-3, father Agapios, of the Russian Orthodox
      mission in America, served the community for three years, 1864-1867; in
      1866 the congregation moved to its permanent church, and soon retained
      the services of father Stephen Andreades, who had been invited from
      Greece and remained with the Holy Trinity from 1867 to 1875; *31st
      Biennial Clergy - Laity Congress, New Orleans, 1992*, photograph, and page
      "The Evolution of Holy Trinity Cathedral;" also see New Orleans city
      survey of the property prepared by Deputy City Surveyor S. A. Calongne
      of November 26, 1932; *Orthodox Observer*, June 1992, 21.

6   *Centennial of the Greek Eastern Orthodox Church Holy Trinity in New Orleans*
     [Commemorative Book] (New Orleans, n.p., 1965), "History of the first
     Greek Orthodox Church in the Western Hemisphere."

7   Father William Gaines, *The First Eastern Greek Orthodox Church in America:
     The Holy Trinity of New Orleans*, 10; the actual transaction of the sale of
     the property closed on June 29, 1867, at the offices of Notary Public Abel
     Dreyfous, at the price of $1,200, payable in two equal installments, one
     year and two years after the sale; the conveyance was registered under B.
     92 FO 543, New Orleans, on July 2, 1867.

8   *The Times-Picayune*, March 18, 1923, 9, Marco Popovich was born in
     Dalmatia and arrived in New Orleans in 1848, when he was 14. In the
     1860s, he was the proprietor of a grocery store and later became "president
     of the French Market Ice Company." Evidently a Serbian Orthodox, he
     participated actively in the *kinotis* of the Holy Trinity Greek Orthodox
     church until his death in 1923.

9   Father William Gaines, *The First Eastern Greek Orthodox Church in America:
     The Holy Trinity of New Orleans*, 23. At that time, in both Greece and Russia,
     the royal autocrat was head of both state and church.

10   *Orthodox Observer*, June 1992, 21; Slavonic was the language spoken by
     the Slavs in the 9th century, as recorded by Sts. Cyril and Methodius when
     they converted the Slavs to Christianity; over time, Slavic languages such
     as Russian, Serbian, and others developed and changed, and while some
     churches may use the modern vernacular in church services, most tradi-
     tional Eastern Orthodox churches in eastern Europe, such as the Russian
     Orthodox Church, the Serbian Orthodox Church and others, continue to
     conduct the liturgy and other services in the archaic "church"-Slavonic;
     similarly the Greek used in Greek Orthodox church services is the archaic
     Greek used during the golden age of Constantinople, not the modern,
     vernacular Greek.

11   The Historic New Orleans Collection [hereinafter HNOC], R. Christopher
     Goodwin, et al., *New Orleans is Looking Forward to its Past: an Archeological
     Survey and Plan for Sections of New Orleans* (Baton Rouge, Office of Cultural
     Development, 1987) 67; also see John Barry, *Rising Tide: The Great Flood
     of 1927* (New York, Simon and Schuster, 1997).

12   HNOC, Christopher Goodwin, *New Orleans is Looking Forward to its Past*,
     237-238.

13   *Thirteenth Census of the United States, 1910* (Washington, Government
     Printing Office, 1914), Abstract "Population of Cities," 63; "Population -
     Louisiana," Table 12, Country of Birth of the Foreign-born White, page 402,
     shows that the majority of immigrants hailed from Italy, Ireland, France,
     Germany, England, Mexico, and Russia.

14   Joan B. Garvey and Mary Lou Widmer, *Beautiful Crescent: A History of New
     Orleans* (New Orleans, Garmer Press, Inc., 1982), 167-168; there was a
     vendetta against Hennessy ever since he stopped the war between the

Provenzana and the Matranga families over who would control the produce business on the city wharves; after his assassination, 19 Sicilians were arrested and charged; when the jury acquitted most of them, a mob of incensed citizens assembled, battered down the wooden prison gate, shot the prisoners, and hung them for good measure. Unfortunately, New Orleanians felt that *all* co-residents of Italian origin were involved in organized crime.

15 Henry Pratt Fairchild, *Greek Immigration to the United States* (New Haven, Yale University Press, 1911), Table 13, 259; *Thirteenth Census of the United States, 1910*, "Abstract of the Census Population," on page 210, badly undercounted the New Orleans inhabitants from Greece, stating there were 20 in 1910, and 35 in 1900.

16 Babis Malafouris, *Greeks in America 1528-1948* (New York, Isaac Goldman Printers, 1948), 509; Gus Pelias was president of the council of trustees 1942-1943.

17 The Times Picayune *Who's Who in Louisiana and Mississippi: Biographical Sketches of Prominent Men and Women* (New Orleans, Times Picayune, 1918), 22-23; father William Gaines, *The First Eastern Greek Orthodox Church in America, the Holy Trinity of New Orleans*, 14, 23.

18 Joan B. Garvey and Mary Lou Widmer, *Beautiful Crescent: A History of New Orleans* (New Orleans, Garmer Press, Inc., 1982), 155-159; Martin Behrman of the Regular Democratic Organization [RDO] became mayor in 1904 and led the "Behrman Ring;" "Ring politics" grew stronger as Behrman won election after election; anti-Ring reformers formed a "Good Government League," nicknamed the "Goo-Goos;" also see Martin Siegel ed., *New Orleans: A Chronological & Documentary History* (Dobbs Ferry, New York, Oceana Publications Inc., 1975), 111-114.

19 Father William Gaines, *First Eastern Greek Orthodox Church in America, the Holy Trinity of New Orleans*, 23.

20 Joan Garvey and Mary Lou Widmer, *Beautiful Crescent: A History of New Orleans*, 178-179.

21 Father William Gaines, *The First Eastern Greek Orthodox Church in America: the Holy Trinity of New Orleans*, 24; Peter Mantzoros, *AHEPA and I Across the Years* (Glenview, Illinois, Pnyx Publications, 1966), 305-307.

22 George Pappas oral interview with the author, in Gainesville, Florida, October 31, 1996; born in 1918 in Asia Minor, Pappas, along with his parents and siblings, became part of the Greek-Turkish population exchange in the 1920s; his father Vassilios soon emigrated to New Orleans, where he owned and operated his own barbershop. George Pappas became high school valedictorian in 1937, completed Loyola, and after the war, with his brother Michael [Mihalis], started a very successful business selling and servicing electric pumps. Pappas continues to reside in New Orleans and remains active in the Holy Trinity Greek Orthodox church.

23 Paul Kalman, "Bishop to dedicate cornerstone," *Times Picayune*, November

18, 1950, indicated that the "present congregation numbers about 500," however, this count does not include those Orthodox New Orleans residents, who are not formal members of the parish but still attend services periodically. They cannot vote, but they are still considered part of the greater parish, welcome to worship at any church service and attend any liturgy.

24   Father William Gaines, *The First Eastern Greek Orthodox Church in America: the Holy Trinity of New Orleans*, 24.

25   Ibid.

26   George Pappas interview , October 31, 1996.

27   Wesley Jackson, "New Bishop's Consecration: Church status to be advanced," *The Times-Picayune*, October 9, 1960, Secion 2, page 4; at the same time, New Orleans became the seat of a Bishop, an auxiliary to Archbishop Iakovos. The Bishop assisted in the administration and execution of hierarchical duties for churches and parishes in Louisiana, Arkansas, Mississippi, Alabama, the city of Memphis, Tennessee, and the Republic of Mexico.

28   Letter dated November 4, 1960, from Rev. George H. Wilson, executive secretary of the Greater New Orleans Federation of churches to Dean William Gaines, Greek Orthodox Community of Holy Trinity Cathedral, archives of the Holy Trinity Greek Orthodox Cathedral, Robert E. Lee Boulevard at St. Bernard Avenue, New Orleans, Boxes 1960-1965; the same ecumenical spirit pervaded the "100th anniversary of Greek Orthodoxy in New Orleans and the New World," see Wesley Jackson's article in *The Times Picayune* of October 14, 1965.

29   Joan Garvey and Mary Lou Widmer, *Beautiful Crescent: A History of New Orleans*, 167; the Dock Board, really the Board of Commissioners of the Port of New Orleans, created in 1896, had authority never previously delegated to a body by the state legislature. It could expropriate property, demolish and rebuild structures, operate facilities as it chose, and lease them at will. The Dock Board did not hesitate to use all of its authority, since the health of the port was crucial for the life of the city.

30   Andrew Horton, "Odysseus in Louisiana: The Greek Sailors in New Orleans," in John Cooke ed., *Perspectives on Ethnicity in New Orleans* (New Orleans, The Committee on Ethnicity, 1979), 25-26; *The Greek Star* of Chicago, Illinois, April 25, 1996, 2, reported on the Greek shipping magnate Stavros Niarchos, who immigrated to America in 1930, built up his shipping empire under the Panamian flag; in the 1970s his fleet numbered 80 ships, totaling 3.7 million tons.

31   Andrew Horton, "Odysseus in Louisiana: The Greek Sailors in New Orleans," 26.

32   Georgios Anagnostu, "Rituals of Strangers: Greek Merchant Seamen in New Orleans and the Anthropological Rite of Passage," Master's Thesis, Louisiana State University, 1992, 5.

33   Andrew Horton, "Odysseus in Louisiana: The Greek Sailors in New
      Orleans," 26; an able-bodied seaman [AB] earns roughly $500 a month on
      a Greek ship, and a second mate about $1,000; it is not uncommon for a
      Greek worker in Greece to make about $400 or more a month. Financially,
      considering the work performed by an AB and the time away from home,
      the monetary incentive to sail has declined.

34   Ibid., 25.

35   Georgios Anagnostu, "Rituals of Strangers: Greek Merchant Seamen in
      New Orleans," 32; the criteria Greek seamen employ to evaluate a harbor
      revolve around its proximity to an urban center, the "quality" of available
      women, cost of life, and convenience in moving around; New Orleans is
      unique in providing a Greek-based network; also see Andrew Horton,
      "Odysseus in Louisiana: The Greek Sailors in New Orleans," 27; few other
      ports are as convenient: New York is just too large, the clubs spread too far,
      and none really cater to sailors; Houston's amenities are miles away from
      the port; other ports do not have "Greek" nightclubs.

36   Georgios Anagnostu, "Rituals of Strangers: Greek Merchant Seamen in
      New Orleans," 11-12, 71-73, citing Evthymios Papataxiarchis, "Friends of
      Heart: Male Commensal Solidarity, Gender, and Kinship in Aegean Greece,"
      at 170-172, in Peter Loizos and E. Papataxiarchis eds., *Contested Identities,
      Gender and Kinship in Modern Greece* (Princeton University Press, 1991).

37   Georgios Anagnostu, "Rituals of Strangers: Greek Merchant Seamen in
      New Orleans," 34-37; the best known such store, which also serves as a
      landmark on Canal Street near Decatur Street, is the Casa Angelo, owned
      by Mr. Vagellis, a former Greek mariner, who settled, in the 1970s, in New
      Orleans, as a successful businessman.

38   Andrew Horton, "Odysseus in Louisiana: The Greek Sailors in New
      Orleans," 30-32; Georgios Anagnostu, "Rituals of Strangers: Greek
      Merchant Seamen in New Orleans," 37-39; after graduating from the Holy
      Cross Greek Orthodox Seminary in Brookline, Massachusetts, from 1954
      to 1972 father William Gaines was the regular priest at Holy Trinity church;
      he earned Master's degrees in theology, psychology, and classics, taught
      courses at Tulane University, and became the Greek Orthodox Director
      of Campus Ministries; he volunteered a lot of time helping Greek seamen
      complete chores and resolve difficulties while in port.

39   George Pappas oral interview; Mr. Pappas stated that father Gaines had the
      support of a minority of parishioners, so that some tempers flared; in due
      course everyone "mellowed" and re-established good relations.

40   Ethelyn Orso, "The Hellenic Nativistic Revitalization Movement in New
      Orleans, Louisiana," 18, in John Cooke ed., *Perspectives on Ethnicity in New
      Orleans*, 17-23.

41   Kathleen Neils Conzen, David A. Gerber, Ewa Morawska, George E.
      Pozzetta, and Rudolph Vecoli, "The Invention of Ethnicity: A Perspective
      from the U.S.A.," *Journal of American Ethnic History* (Fall 1992), 3-41, at 3.

42   John DeMers, "The Greeks of New Orleans," *New Orleans* magazine, July
      1982, 48-52.
43   Ethelyn Orso, "The Hellenic Nativistic Revitalization Movement in New
      Orleans," 22-23.

CHAPTER 6

PAROCHIAL CONFLICT
IN BIRMINGHAM,
THE IRON CITY

The Hellenic community in Birmingham, Alabama, manifested common patterns as well as notable differences in the way its members melded into the local society and yet retained selected aspects of their ethnic identity.[1] As outlined in chapter two above, in Birmingham, as in other southern urban centers, turn-of-the-century Greek settlers sought and achieved economic independence more swiftly than their counterparts in the industrial regions elsewhere in the United States. Characteristic of their cohorts in the South, they found unexploited commercial niches and engaged in small businesses. These ambitious entrepreneurs also embarked on the process of integration into the native society; they struggled to fit themselves into local social patterns. Also in the area were groups of Greek compatriots, the mine, mill, and smelter workers, who did not conform to Charles Moskos's "southern variant."[2] Within the first decades of the Hellenic community's existence, evident differences emerged between the entrepreneurs, who advanced quickly on the first few rungs of the economic ladder, and the iron-workers, who remained on the bottom rung. The workers lived in company-owned ghetto housing, not unlike other ethnic laborers in manufacturing and smoke-stack centers in the North. They depended on the vagaries of a heavy industry, based on iron ore, furnaces, mills, factories, shift-work, and hard labor by masses of hourly-paid employees.

Both groups, the entrepreneurs and the workers, participated in the *kinotis* centered around the Orthodox church of Holy Trinity. In time, the first generation iron-workers retired, moved, or joined their compatriots in self-employed small businesses. In the early 1930s, the community fractured along several fault-lines, mostly based on old-country regional and parochial prejudices. A large group of parishioners of the Holy Trinity Greek Orthodox church actually split, formed their own independent *kinotis*, and established the Holy Cross Greek Orthodox church. For over twenty years, each faction supported a separate church and priest, until they reunited in the 1950s.[3] One decade later, second- and third-generation Greek Americans again divided on issues concerning race and civil rights, issues rooted entirely in the history, life, and times of the new homeland. Although they clearly demonstrated the nearly total adaptation to the local southern society, at the same time Greek Americans tenaciously held on to aspects of their ethnicity. As Philip Gleason pointed out, assimilation and pluralism were not mutually exclusive, rather, "they overlap and merge into each other."[4] Greek immigrants to Birmingham and its industrial suburbs started that ongoing process about one hundred years ago.

The first Greek to settle in Birmingham was George Cassimus, originally from the Ionian island of Corfu. Just before the turn of the century, the retired sailor spent a few years in Mobile, before trying his fortune in the Pittsburgh of the South.[5] Joined by his brother and fellow Corfiotes, as well as compatriots from the mainland region of Peloponnesos, Cassimus and other Greek newcomers invested their time and money into a variety of food businesses such as restaurants, lunch-rooms, and pushcart vending of fruit and vegetables. Their pluck and success, combined with the growth of the industrial city, attracted more compatriots. By 1900 about one hundred Greeks lived in Birmingham.[6] Over the next decade, as Birmingham prospered, this number tripled to 302 Hellenic immigrants. After the turn of the century, iron industries expanded and established large plants in Ensley and smaller ones in Gadsden, both suburbs of the iron city. Workers came from all over southern and eastern Europe and from other parts of the United States. The Ensley Steel Plant alone employed between 300 and 500 Greeks, who lived mostly in company housing.[7]

Quite a few Hellenic entrepreneurs in Birmingham followed the lead of George Cassimus and opened eateries and sandwich shops.

Established concerns served as a training ground for newcomers, who worked as waiters, bus-boys, dishwashers, and kitchen help, until they could save enough to strike out on their own. The restaurant and short order lunch business filled a nearly vacant niche and provided a way to self-employment. According to one "gastronomically inclined traveling salesman," by 1912, the Greek-owned restaurants "relieved a well nigh intolerable condition" that had confronted Birmingham visitors: the absence of restaurants.[8] Another group of self-employed Greeks operated fruit stands. Just as in Jacksonville, Florida, and other growing cities, this business required a minimal capital investment and could serve as a start for those whose command of English was still shaky. Nick Derzis worked long hours at his Terminal Fruit Stand near the Terminal Station. His daughter Christine Grammas [nee Derzis], remembered the stand stacked with selected fruit, tastefully arranged to attract customers, with an ice box in the back where he would keep the melons cool and sell them by the slice.[9] Charles Pantaze combined fruits with candy and opened a store next to the Bessemer Dummy Line.[10]

In 1902, the Birmingham *Age-Herald* reported that Greeks had a monopoly on fruit stands in the city.[11] Success also had a down-side; some of the city's natives resented the intrusion of foreigners. In the same year, 1902, members of a local business club alleged that the fruit stands were a health nuisance. But speaking for the motion to do away with fruit stands, the speaker disclosed his real sentiments: "These vendors are similar to the Chinamen; they do not build up a town, but send their earnings to the old country. Which should we encourage, our home merchants...or these foreigners?...It is a case of choosing between John Smith, Bill Jones and Harry Williams or Demosthenes, Thucydides and Aristotle."[12] A majority on the city council, however, rewarded the hard work and ambition of the latter; a vote of thirteen to four allowed the Greek fruit vendors to stay on Birmingham's sidewalks.

Typically, the self-employed prospered, especially those who filled unexploited economic niches in the expanding industrial center. Credit, unheard of in Greece, was a major factor here; for example, produce could be purchased on Monday and paid for at the end of the week. [13] With good credit and hard work, one could build up a substantial venture from small beginnings. The Hobson Café on Twentieth Street, opened in 1900 by Tom Balabanos, served fine cuisine in a well-appointed dining room that seated 100. Just four years later, Tom was the proprietor of the Reliance Hotel, which featured "the European plan, steam heated rooms, good service," all for $1.00 a day and up, and offered its patrons a bar, a lunchroom, and a restaurant on the premises.[14] Greeks owned and operated two important food brokerage businesses in Birmingham. Nick Derzis, the former fruit vendor, and Leo Papageorge, a man known in the community for his proficiency in English, teamed up to run the Greek-American Produce Company on Morris Avenue.[15] Alex Kontos also peddled fruit when he first arrived. Then about 1902, he contracted with a Mobile distributor to wholesale bananas in Birmingham; he had a virtual monopoly on this particular fruit and it made him wealthy enough to be known as the "banana king." Since he received all the carloads of bananas, "he [was] the supreme arbiter of their destiny...he [was Birmingham's] miniature Rockefeller."[16]

The Banana King, about 1908 - Photo from Birmingham Public Library.

Whether one-man operations or larger enterprises, all Greek businesses in Birmingham, Montgomery, or other Alabama cities sought to serve the general public; none catered exclusively to Greeks.[17] By 1910 the fruit stands had largely disappeared and given way to elaborate candy shops and fruit stores; their proprietors had spread throughout Birmingham's residential sections. Nick Derzis and his brother Sam were married and had their own homes on North 26th Street; Charles Pantazes, who had gone back to Greece to fetch a bride, lived in a fine house at 1316 Cullom Street; close to fifty Greek families were all well integrated into residences and businesses in the greater Birmingham area. Nearly sixty Hellenic businessmen were members of the Moose, the Elks, the Fraternal Order of Odd Fellows, and the Lions.[18] The local press had praise for the newcomers: "The Greeks...who have come to the Birmingham District with a view of naturalization, have proved to be desirable people. There is room for more of them."[19]

Holy Trinity Greek Orthodox Church established in 1906 in Birmingham. Photo from the 1956 Dedication Album, courtesy of Father Emmanuel Z. Vasilakis, Dean, Holy Trinity – Holy Cross Greek Orthodox Cathedral, Birmingham, Alabama

In fall 1902, leading men of the Greek community formed the Lord Byron Society, whose primary purpose was to raise money for a church.[20] By 1906 the society had $9,500 in the kitty, enough to buy a vacant church building at 19th Street and Avenue C [Third Avenue South] and to re-furbish it for Orthodox needs.[21] Once the future church parishioners established a regular *kinotis*, dedicated to the Holy Trinity, the Lord Byron Society ceased to function, and transferred all remaining funds to an account controlled by the newly elected parish council. The Holy Trinity Greek Orthodox church in Birmingham was the seventh such parish organized in the United States. Dues of $12 per year and voluntary contributions maintained the church building and paid the $100 a month salary to the priest, Father Callinicos Kanellos, who remained until 1912.[22]

The divisions within Birmingham's early Greek populace emerged mainly from the different lifestyles led by the hard-working immigrants. Local histories and community traditions described the divergent lives and times of the Birmingham entrepreneurs on the one hand, and the iron workers, laboring and living in Birmingham's west side suburbs, on the other. Unlike the entrepreneurs in Birmingham, the iron workers tended to crowd into rooming houses, which in turn clustered all within several blocks in the Sherman Heights area of Ensley.[23] 1909 was probably the peak year of Greek employment at the TCI [Tennessee Coal, Iron & Railroad Company] when about 500 Greeks worked and lived in Ensley alone.[24] Over 100 Greek men lived on 17th Street. The laborers worked for relatively good wages, averaging $2.00 to $2.50 a day.[25] Nevertheless, it was not unusual for five or six men to share the same post office box.[26] They began to disperse after World War I. Many moved to Mobile; some joined their more enterprising brethren in Birmingham and started their own businesses.[27]

James M. (Jim) Vakakes was typical of those who switched from working for the TCI to working for himself. He immigrated from the island of Samos, by way of Ellis Island, and as a youngster washed dishes in Hartford Connecticut. His English improved to the extent that he became an interpreter for Greeks working on railroad gangs. In 1910 he arrived in Ensley and worked for the TCI, before he decided to go into business. After making deliveries with his own mules and wagons for a few years, in 1919 he founded the Ensley Building Supply Company.[28] In contrast to the workers who converged into iron-laborers' ghettos in Ensley and several other iron mill locations, most of Birmingham's Hellenic population lived spread out among their American neighbors. Many settled in the city's better sections, in the south side and in north Birmingham's Norwood area. Typically, they formed families, either marrying American women, or more likely, importing brides from back home. In dress and manners they tried to emulate their American neighbors. In 1909, employees of Greek-owned businesses formed the Young Greek Progressive Society, which promoted the learning of English and American citizenship. By 1911 the popular group had upwards of 150 members and over $3,000 in the treasury.[29]

In contrast, the Birmingham chapter of the Panhellenic Union, an organization established to preserve patriotic and emotional ties to the motherland, dissolved in 1912. At the start of the Balkan Wars, in the same year, droves of Greek immigrants returned from America to fight the Turks; while Ensley and other steel and industrial localities produced nearly 200 volunteers, there were eleven from Birmingham. It was not for lack of bravery that the numbers were so lopsided; rather, it had to do with lack of motivation. A majority of the entrepreneurs had their families in Birmingham, and 90 percent had already acquired American citizenship. They offered financial aid to those young iron-workers, predominantly without families, who answered their motherland's call to arms. Several years later, in 1917, a far greater number of young Birmingham entrepreneurs volunteered to join the American army.[30]

As members of Birmingham's Hellenic *kinotis* worked hard to improve their livelihood, they could not completely avoid the great political schism that disturbed most Greek communities during World War I and well into the 1920s, following the disastrous Greek military campaign in Asia Minor. Observers of Greek history noted that most Greeks originating from the islands, and from areas that were part of the Ottoman Empire until 1918, sympathized and supported the leader of the Liberal party, Eleftherios Venizelos, from the island of Crete. Conversely, significant numbers of mainlander Greeks, raised in the independent Kingdom of Greece, professed loyalty to King Constantine, and supported him in his quarrel against Venizelos. Although a number of Hellenic communities in the North and the Midwest separated under the influence of old-country politics, the *kinotis* of the Holy Trinity in Birmingham and suburbs, typical of other southern communities, managed to hang together. Perhaps the nativist pressures forced upon the community by the Klan and its sympathizers, who disdained all foreigners, compelled the Hellenes of Birmingham and Ensley to stick together and to be less intemperate about political struggles back home.

In the early 1920s, throughout the South, Greeks who had achieved some economic progress and who had decided to make their home in the United States, joined the American Hellenic Educational Progressive

Association [AHEPA]. Early endeavors of this fraternal society deflected nativist antagonism against foreigners by showing publicly that Greek Americans espoused "100 percent Americanism," while they adapted and retained selected features of their culture and traditions.[31] In the early 1920s, at the height of Ku Klux Klan activities, the AHEPA had large chapters both in Birmingham and in Montgomery, Alabama. But so did the Greek American Progressive Association [GAPA], which acted to protect its members' ethnic roots by promoting the preservation of Greek culture, the use of Greek at home and at all meetings and get-togethers, and the retention of all ties to the old country.[32] In time, AHEPA earned a most prominent place in the life of Greek America, whereas GAPA suffered an eclipse.[33] Nevertheless, during the 1920s, Birmingham's Greeks were actively engaged in both organizations, and thus presented a divided response to a pressing crisis.

Another division, finally leading to a split in the community, occurred in the early 1930s over the management of the Greek school. By this time, the Hellenic group in the city numbered nearly 1,500 people.[34] About one-half were active in the parish-life of the Holy Trinity, where a number of parents had started an afternoon Greek school. On the surface, factions divided over the choice of one Greek school teacher over another. More than likely the opening of the fissure simply followed the underlying cracks that had existed for years, as "members of the community rallied behind those who originated from the same island or village in Greece."[35] At a general assembly meeting of church parishioners called to decide which teacher to hire, "tempers flared and insults were tossed around the room." Spiro Greenwood, who also happened to be the current president of the AHEPA, rose to speak, but the chairman refused to recognize him.[36] As he left the room, so did other members of the AHEPA. The meeting broke up without completing the agenda.

Within several weeks, a significant group of members of the Holy Trinity, numbering between fifty and seventy-five families, broke away and formed the new parish dedicated to the Holy Cross. Members of the new *kinotis* voted to acquire property and build a new church in the central part of Birmingham, a short eighteen city blocks away from the Holy Trinity, although a contemporary article in the *Birmingham News* stated that the "new church" formed in Birmingham in September 1933, "included many citizens of Fairfield, Ensley and Bessemer."[37]

The *1938 Year Book of the Hellenic Orthodox Church "The Holy Cross"*, published several months before the completion of the new church building, gave this explanation for the split: "a group of progressive Greeks from Birmingham, Alabama, desiring to leave to its younger Greek-American generation a Community fitted for the present day conditions of our life, got together on the night of September 14, 1933, at the Birmingham Elks Home, in order that they might accomplish their desire."[38] Years later, in the 75th anniversary year book of the combined parishes, the division was blamed on "old world prejudices and politics."[39]

The *Birmingham News* article, however, may have unwittingly disclosed the major cause for the rift: Ensley, Bessemer, and Fairfield once abounded with steel mills and people working in them or dependent on them. Although a large proportion of Greek residents in these areas were now in business for themselves, they may have resented the "uptown" Greeks, who might have earlier shown disdain for compatriots of different regional origin. These differences may not have been sharply delineated, but they helped to create the underlying ruptures. Peloponnesians—including Spartans—lived on the north side of Birmingham and owned the majority—but by no means all—enterprises in the city; in contrast, the *nisiotes* [islanders] tended to live on the west side, the steel mills side of town.[40] The mainlanders, who had carved an entry into Birmingham's more conservative business and social circles may have alienated the "progressive Greeks," the islanders, who wanted a community to reflect their own views regarding "present day conditions."[41]

Attempts by religious authorities to reconcile the two sides were not successful. However, rather than force ecclesiastical unity that would likely bring about complete alienation of the protesting group, in September 1935, American hierarch Archbishop Athenagoras appointed another priest to the new Birmingham parish, and subsequently attended the dedication of the new church. The AHEPA, which had experienced some of its own problems with unity, also ended up with two chapters in Birmingham: the organization's headquarters confirmed the formation of a new chapter among those members who remained with the Holy Trinity parish. Despite the organization's claim that it will "educate Greeks in the United States in the matter of democracy," members who belonged to opposite parishes simply could not avoid personal clashes at fraternal meetings.[42] For the next twenty years, Birmingham's Hellenic community divided into competing camps.

After the split, each group exerted very concerted efforts to obtain and keep facilities that would in no way be inferior or smaller than those of the other group. The Hellenic competitive spirit strove to maintain honor and avoid shame, to retain the good opinion of others, especially of the American friends, neighbors, and associates. Both groups laid plans for new buildings. Holy Cross members who had decided to form a new parish in September 1933, contributed monies for a new church building despite the Depression, and celebrated Palm Sunday in the new church in April 1934. Holy Trinity members bought vacant properties next to their church and built an educational building and hall, also in 1934. Holy Cross members then determined the need for a larger church and by 1938 they built the new church next to the 1934 one, "making the old building serve for their educational needs.[43] Both churches soon made grand plans for more building and expansion. Holy Trinity built a stately new Byzantine church, while Holy Cross built an impressive youth center for dances, banquets, and plays. The new Holy Trinity celebrated its completion in October 1950; members of the Holy Cross dedicated their new youth center in February 1951.[44] Fortunately, in the early 1950s, youth groups of both parishes cooperated on a number of projects, and urged by the church hierarchy, by 1953, the two groups decided to re-unite. The Archbishop cooperated in assigning a new priest to the united parish, as delegates from both sides negotiated the reconciliation and with some ingenuity managed to merge the communities under the combined name Holy Trinity - Holy Cross, a name that the amalgamated Birmingham *kinotis* retained to this day.

Reunited in 1953, the parishioners of Holy Trinity – Holy Cross elected a combined Board of Directors, shown in this 1956 photo. [HC] denotes a former President of Holy Cross; [HT] denotes a former president of Holy Trinity. Seated [l-r]: George Louzis, Pete Grammas [HT], Rev. Emmanuel Bouyoucas, Gus Constantine [HC], Cameron Grammas; standing [l-r]: Gus Cocoris [HT], Gregory Derzis, Petro Columbis, Steve Pappas, Sam Nakos [HC], William Roniotis [HC]. Photo from the 1956 Dedication Album, courtesy of Father Emmanuel Z. Vasilakis, Dean, Holy Trinity – Holy Cross Greek Orthodox Cathedral, Birmingham, Alabama.

With this reconciliation, the majority of Birmingham's Greek Americans demonstrated that divisions rooted in regionalism or politics of the old country finally lost their urgency. By the 1960s, Greek Americans in Birmingham had become an integral part of the society in which they lived. They were interested in the same social and political events. The best evidence of their integration into the local American mainstream was that their own conflicts and disunity now centered on the same issues and originated with the same controversies that were experienced by their American neighbors. The ethnic bond that tied the first generation to inherited traditions and culture had substantially changed from what it was at the beginning of the century. Except for the Greek Orthodox religion, which also experienced substantial changes in the American environment, the Hellenic community expressed its ethnic ties on a few special days of the year, at Birmingham's Greek Festival, by way of food, dances, and music.

Holy Trinity – Holy Cross Greek Orthodox Church, Birmingham, Alabama, from the front
page of the 1956 Dedication Album, courtesy of Father Emmanuel Z. Vasilakis, Dean,
Holy Trinity – Holy Cross Greek Orthodox Cathedral, Birmingham, Alabama.

The final disagreement within the Greek community arose in the
1960s, over civil rights issues that resonated especially strongly in
Birmingham. On one side of the conflict were those who had become
part of Birmingham's conservative white society, and thus tacitly agreed
to the status quo, enforced by sheriff Bull Connor and governor George
Wallace. On the opposite side were those who supported Martin Luther
King Jr., desegregation, and equality without undue delay or precon-
ditions. Some informed members of Birmingham's Hellenic community
saw it as a split between liberal and conservative Greek Americans,
which broke along the fault line between conservative and liberal
southern Democrats.[45] The more conservative group had entered the
ranks of the city's white establishment and acquired its views on racial
issues. On the liberal side, only a few brave voices were openly raised
in favor of change.

One of these voices was that of Reverend (Sotirios) Sam Gouvellis,
resident priest at the Holy Trinity - Holy Cross Greek Orthodox Church.

He became active in the civil rights movement and drew publicity in 1963, over a controversial issue of the city's employment of blacks. In an effort to control racial violence and to promote better relations with the black community, Birmingham city officials considered a proposal to hire black policemen. Martin Luther King Jr. said the city must add twenty-five blacks to its force or face more demonstrations.[46] At this time, the *Birmingham Post Herald* reported that a group of clergymen, the Ministry Association of Greater Birmingham, unanimously approved a motion by the Reverend Sam Gouvellis that the city hire black policemen. His activity on behalf of the civil righters shocked and angered many Greek-American professionals and businessmen. They feared that their priest's actions would hurt their own standing in Birmingham's white American community. Within days, some businessmen of Greek origin reported that they had been abused by customers who resented Father Gouvellis's action; others noted that they had steadily lost business since the article appeared.

In a confrontation with Father Gouvellis, angry parishioners condemned his action as a violation of the constitutional provisions that separated church and state. When Father Gouvellis stood his ground, members of the *kinotis*, including a unanimous Board of Trustees of the parish, passed a resolution to remove him from Holy Trinity - Holy Cross.[47] The resolution, along with numerous private letters, made its way to the Archbishop in New York. He could remove the priest, but chose not to do so. Notwithstanding the unrest, Archbishop Iakovos stood firmly on the side of Father Gouvellis and the civil righters. Although the movement to remove the priest subsided, other activities by conservative Greek Americans in Birmingham left no doubt where they stood. In the spring of 1964, just after he had dramatically blocked the doorway of the University of Alabama to deny entry to black students, George Wallace became an honorary member of the Birmingham chapter of the AHEPA.

During the same year, at the seventeenth clergy - laity congress of the Greek Orthodox church in America, Archbishop Iakovos, urged those attending to remove the Greek Orthodox church in the United States "from the sidelines of life," and to involve it in social action, for civil rights and environment, against abortion, discrimination, and drugs.[48] Following the lead of Father Gouvellis, a sizeable part of the community in Birmingham took up the challenge. Although some internal communal discord continued past 1968, when Father Sam Gouvellis transferred to another parish, the *kinotis* avoided an open split. In an effort to be a part of mainstream America, both the population of Birmingham, and the Hellenic community around Holy Trinity - Holy Cross, eventually settled into a truce and sought a more peaceful solution.

The Greek American community in Birmingham demonstrated that members of an ethnic group may select many distinct ways to express their ethnicity These articulations of ethnicity may well depend on local circumstances. They continue even after succeeding generations of the immigrant group and the host society mingled and negotiated a merger.[49] For years, dissonances among the Iron City's early Hellenes were informed by old-country regional and political differences. However, a later discord, in the 1960s, focused on local, American, racial issues. Although involved in this disharmony together with Birmingham's general populace, Americans of Hellenic origin confirmed their ethnic links, adjusted to a different time and conditions, by continued support for the Greek Orthodox Church and the annual Greek festival. Since the rich ethnic background of local Americans of Greek origin encompasses much more than foods and folk-dancing, one should not be surprised if in the future they re-discover other Hellenic cultural and traditional treasures and decide to adapt and share them with their co-residents.

Notes

1   Kathleen Neils Conzen, David A. Gerber, Ewa Morawska, George E. Pozzetta, and Rudolph J. Vecoli, "The Invention of Ethnicity: A Perspective from the U.S.A.," *Journal of American Ethnic History* (Fall 1992) 3, where the authors refute the notion that immigrants moved in a straight-line manner from old-world cultures to becoming Americans, and point to the existence of a process of cultural and social change whereby newcomers ceased to be "foreigners" and yet, over several generations, did not become "One Hundred Per Cent Americans".

2   See discussion respecting the "southern variant" in the first chapter of this work; Charles Moskos asserted that Greek immigrants in the South achieved economic and upward mobility faster and in greater proportion than Greeks elsewhere in the United States. This work tested the Moskos hypothesis and found it generally on target.

3   Jim Golding, "A Progressive Parish That Healed Its Divisions," *Orthodox*

Observer, June 1994.

4   Philip Gleason, "Confusion Compounded: The Melting Pot in the 1960s and the 1970s," *Ethnicity* 6 (1979), 18.

5   James Hantzes, "Greeks in Alabama Before 1912," Master's Thesis, Sanford University, Birmingham, Alabama, 1969, 50-51; Karen Rolen, "The New Patrida: The Story of Birmingham's Greeks," *Birmingfind*, n.d. (a local history project funded by the National Endowment for the Humanities). George Cassimus and his brothers Marcus and Alex were sailors from the British possessed island of Corfu [Kerkyra]; they sailed on a British vessel engaged in running guns to Mobile for the Confederacy, during the Civil War; many years after the war, when they retired from sailing, the Cassimus brothers decided to reside in Mobile. In time, George went to Birmingham and Alex settled in Montgomery, Alabama.

6   *Thirteenth Census of the United States, 1910* (Washington, D.C., Government Printing Office, 1914), Abstract page 63; Birmingham had a population in 1890 = 26,178; in 1900 = 38,415; and in 1910 = 132,685; a phenomenal 345% growth in one decade. According to the 1910 Census, however, there were only 5,730 white foreign-born people in the city, among them 1,343 English and Scotsmen, 1,360 Italians, 592 Russians and Finns, 706 Germans, 243 Greeks and 233 born in "Turkey", but probably also Greeks from Asia Minor.

7   Karen Rolen, "The New Patrida: the Story of Birmingham's Greeks," *Birmingfind*.

8   Ibid.

9   Christine Grammas [nee Derzis], Christine Sepsis, and Frances Vakakes oral interview by the writer, June 29, 1992, at the Holy Trinity - Holy Cross Greek Orthodox Cathedral meeting room, downtown Birmingham. Nick Derzis was formerly Nicholaos Deriziotis.

10   Dio [Dionysis] Adallis, *Greek-American Reference Book and Business Guide* (Birmingham, n. p., ca. 1917), Birmingham Section, 3-98, at 4, cited in James Hantzes, "Greeks in Alabama Before 1912," 53.

11   Karen Rolen, "The New Patrida: The Story of Birmingham's Greeks," *Birmingfind*.

12   Ibid.

13   James Hantzes, "Greeks in Alabama Before 1912," 56.

14   Karen Rolen, "The New Patrida: The Story of Birmingham's Greeks," *Birmingfind*.

15   Ibid.; Leo Papageorge was formerly Leonidas Papageorgiou.

16   Ibid.; also see article "Son Succeeds Banana King," *Birmingham Post*, December 3, 1934; the article indicated that Alex Kontos, Birmingham's first wholesale banana dealer, died and his son Chris would carry on the large enterprise; Alex Kontos "was 63. Forty-five years of his life were spent in Birmingham building himself up from the status of a penniless immigrant from Sparta, Greece, to that of a millionaire recognized as one of the

largest banana importers in the South."

17   Burgess, *Greeks in America*, 173.

18   Dio Adallis, *Greek-American Reference Book and Business Guide 1912-17*, Birmingham Section, 14-68.

19   *Birmingham Age-Herald*, January 18, 1910, 4; also see Sofia Lafakis Petrou, "A History of the Greeks in Birmingham, Alabama," unpublished manuscript, 10-15: Birmingham Greeks also tended to shorten their names to make them easier to pronounce: Lorantzatos became Lorant, Derziotis changed to Derzis, etc.; others underwent a complete transformation, for example, Margounis became Morgan, Papathanesiou turned into Stevens, and Thoumopoulos into Thomas.

20   "The Cosmopolitan Aspect of a Great and Growing City," *Birmingham News*, October 31, 1903, 24; the society included 150 members of the community, had a constitution and by-laws, elected officers and a board of governors.

21   Karen Rolen, "The New Patrida: The Story of Birmingham's Greeks," *Birmingfind*; Constantine Macris, a painter living in Wylam, Georgia, designed the traditional iconostasis, a partition with doors and rows of icons that separates the sanctuary and altar from the nave - the main part of the church where the faithful stood, usually men on the right and women on the left. See chapter 4 of this work dealing with the Greek Orthodox church in the United States, where in time churches are furnished with pews and the strict gender separation ceases. According to Seraphim Canoutas, *The Greek-American Guide* (New York, Helmis Press, 1912), 368, other Greek pioneer families in the city included Balabanos, Colias, Contoroupis, Derzis, Jebeles, Costellos, Papageorge, Likis, Gulas, Kontos, Petras, Sarris, Lorant [Lorentzatos], Kakoliris, Mitsinikos, Grammas, Harduvel, Giannoudas, and Greenwood; most of them from the island of Corfu or from mainland Peloponnesos.

22   Thomas Burgess, *Greeks in America* (Boston, Sherman French and Co., 1913), 171-174 described father Germanos Smirnakis, the second priest at Birmingham's Holy Trinity. The Patriarchate in Constantinople had appointed both, rather than the Greek Orthodox church in Athens; see chapter 4 of this work.

23   James Hantzes, "Greeks in Alabama Before 1912," 25.

24   "Laborers Being Rushed to Ensley," *Birmingham Age-Herald*, December 16, 1909, 2; also see *Thirteenth Census of the United States, 1910* (Washington, D.C., Government Printing Office, 1914), Abstract Schedules for Jefferson County, Alabama, showing 54 Greeks residing in the house at 554 17th Street in Ensley; other houses full of Greeks were 412 17th Street, 1708 Avenue East, and 1610 First Avenue.

25   James Hantzes, "Greeks in Alabama Before 1912," 65; at the same time, textile mills in Lowell paid $6.00 to $8.00 a week; railroad workers got $1.75 to $2.00 a day, while dangerous mining work in Colorado brought

$3.00 a day; see Theodore Saloutos, *Greeks in the United States* (Cambridge, Harvard University Press, 1964), 57, and Henry Pratt Fairchild, *Greek Immigration to the United States* (New Haven, Yale University Press, 1911), 139.

26   James Hantzes, "Greeks in Alabama Before 1912," 31.

27   Ibid., 62.

28   *Birmingham News*, June 19, 1950, in this newspaper interview Vakakes, who married Ensley native Frances Rouss in 1916, stated, "I lost everything in the Depression;" however he must have retained his spirit and vigor, because in 1931 he teamed up with Bedford Seale to start the Seale Lumber Company, and nearly twenty years later, in 1950, Vakakes and Seale were still partners in this successful enterprise in Ensley.

29   Thomas Burgess, *Greeks in America*, 174; Young Greek Progressive Society seemed to be a local forerunner of the American Hellenic Educational and Progressive Association (AHEPA); see chapter 3 of this work.

30   Sofia Lafakis Petrou, "A History of the Greeks in Birmingham, Alabama," 10, citing Dio Adallis, *Greek American Reference Book and Business Guide*.

31   See chapter 3 of this work. To deflect nativist anger and prevent anti-foreign reprisals, the AHEPA charter called for promotion "of pure and undefiled Americanism" among people of Greek origin in the United States; members of this fraternal organization spoke and conducted all their formal meetings in English and urged compatriots to become American citizens.

32   Sofia Lafakis Petrou, "A History of the Greeks in Birmingham, Alabama," 29; in 1923 GAPA claimed over 150 members in Birmingham.

33   See chapter 3 of this work, "Fraternal Bonding and Conservatism: Jimmy Joined AHEPA."

34   *Birmingham News*, April 5, 1932, cited in Sofia Lafakis Petrou, "A History of the Greeks in Birmingham, Alabama," 29.

35   Sofia Lafakis Petrou, "A History of the Greeks in Birmingham, Alabama," 30; evidently, one teacher, Mr. Georgopoulos, was a Greek mainlander, whereas the other teacher, Mr. Anagnostou, was an islander; author Petrou based her account of the events on interviews of participants.

36   Ibid., 31; descendant of a British merchant who had once settled on the island of Corfu, Spiro Greenwood was one Greek immigrant who never had to "Americanize" his surname; as an islander and an influential member of the community, he would have spoken in favor of Mr. A.; therefore the chair, evidently favoring Mr. G., and supported by a good number of those present, did not allow Greenwood to have the floor.

37   *Birmingham News*, March 4, 1934, article indicated that the "Hellenic Orthodox Community of the Holy Cross has completed plans for a new church to be located on 25th Street near 7th Avenue North... Construction will begin at once." James Vakakes of Ensley was vice-president of the new *kinotis*. The church building stood completed by the end of 1938; the formal dedication took place April 16, 1939, see *Birmingham Post*, April 15, 1939.

38   *1938 Year Book of the Hellenic Orthodox Church "The Holy Cross"* (Birmingham, n.p., 1938); in the lead article, "The Birth of Our Community," organizers stated that 75 families became members of the new church.

39   *Commemorating the 75th Anniversary of Holy Trinity - Holy Cross Greek Orthodox Cathedral, Birmingham, Alabama 1906-1981* (Birmingham, n.p., 1981), first page of text following pictorial section.

40   Irene Lafakis oral interview with the writer in Birmingham, Alabama, June 30, 1992.

41   *1938 Year Book of the Hellenic Orthodox Church "The Holy Cross"* demonstrated that the new community also included many entrepreneurs; the year book contained ads of Greek-owned businesses, 76 of these located in Birmingham, 4 in Ensley, 3 in Bessemer, 4 in Fairfield, and 4 in Gadsden.

42   See chapter 3 of this work, where the Charter of AHEPA catalogues intended activities.

43   See "Brief History of the Greek Parish of Birmingham" in *Dedication: Holy Trinity Greek Orthodox Church 1906-1956* (Birmingham, n. p., 1956), printed 3 years after re-unification, the brochure contains photographs of the 1956 Church Board of Directors, including leading members of the Holy Trinity, such as Pete Grammas, Gus Cocoris, Cameron Grammas, and Gregory Derzis; as well as members of the Holy Cross, viz. Gus Constantine, Sam Nakos, William Roniotis, and George Louzis.

44   *Birmingham News*, February 18, 1951; Birmingham mayor Cooper Green cut the ribbon.

45   Irene Lafakis oral interview.

46   *Birmingham Post Herald*, October 9, 1963; in a write-up on October 10, *Birmingham News* supported the employment policy: "Is Birmingham that different from other cities that it cannot adopt a common sense policy which has proven highly successful elsewhere?...It is past time that we faced up to reality," cited in Sofia Lafakis Petrou, "A History of the Greeks in Birmingham, Alabama," 41.

47   Sofia Lafakis Petrou, "A History of the Greeks in Birmingham, Alabama," 41.

48   *Newsweek*, July 13, 1964, 52; the seventeenth clergy - laity congress took place in Denver, Colorado; where delegates, consisting of both the church clergy and representatives of every *kinotis*, partook in a long and sometimes provocative discussion on the use of the English language in liturgy; the Archbishop had allowed the use of English, as 60 percent of the then membership of church parishes consisted of third-generation Greek Americans, children of US-born parents.

49   Kathleen N. Conzen et al., "The Invention of Ethnicity: A Perspective from the U. S. A.," 12; ethnic expressions also varied over time, as both the newcomers and the host society changed.

CHAPTER 7

GREEKS ON THE GULF:

AEGEAN DIVERS MODERNIZE FLORIDA'S SPONGE INDUSTRY

A sailboat from Tarpon
Sets off for sponge fishing
And a young sailor aboard
Sighs and looks back at the shore.[1]

During the first half of the 1900s, Greek immigrants in Tarpon Springs formed a greater proportion of the town's population than in any other urban area in the United States. For several climactic decades they played a controlling role in the public and commercial life of the larger community.[2] They developed and dominated Florida's sponge industry and the wealthier strata of the Greek community achieved rapid integration into the economic and civic activities of Tarpon Springs' larger society. At the same time, a more substantial segment of the first generation Greek immigrant population, whose life revolved around the seafaring sponge boats, showed little desire for social and cultural adaptation to American ways. In that respect, parts of Tarpon Springs mirrored the large "Greektown" communities, formed by Greek newcomers in their thousands in New York City and Chicago, where an almost smug self-sufficiency characterized their day-to-day lives.[3]

The influx of so many new residents into Tarpon Springs, to the point where Greeks almost outnumbered local American whites and the small black community, permanently changed the commercial, political, and social structure of the town.[4] For two generations, most Tarpon Springs Greeks continued to speak the Greek vernacular—*dimotiki*—in their homes.[5] Until well into the 1950s, marriages with non-Greek spouses were very much an exception. As early as 1907, the newcomers hired a Greek-Orthodox priest, formed a parish, and developed a religious life around the local Greek Orthodox church.[6] Some of the Greek community's social and religious life transpired only within the *kinotis*. On the other end of the spectrum, a number of Tarpon Springs Greeks achieved high levels of integration with the local American business community. Although such conformance and rapid adaptation were evident in a number of cities throughout the South, nowhere other than in Tarpon Springs were the Greeks so dominant in both economic and civic life and yet so well accepted and respected. Usually, the larger an immigrant group was in relation to the general population in an area, the greater was its exposure to pointed discrimination.[7] In direct contrast, the Greeks of Tarpon Springs never knew the stigma of restrictive covenants, never experienced exclusion from social organizations or veterans' groups, and never endured denial of their petitions for naturalization. As producers of natural sponges, a most marketable commodity, as businessmen, and as voters, the Tarpon Springs Greeks both adapted to and influenced the commercial and political habits and behavior of their Anglo neighbors. Moreover, businessmen of Greek origin who managed to enter the economic and civic levels populated by the native leadership became a benign mediating force between the American and the Greek segments of Tarpon Springs.

Aegean sponge gathering methods significantly changed pre-industrial sponging practices in the area. Since the 1850s, years before the Greeks arrived, migrant Bahamian wreckers and turtlers, concentrated at Key West, provided the beginning of the American sponge industry. They searched for sponges growing on the shallow ocean floor in the waters off Florida's Gulf coast.[8] Early spongers used two-man dinghies to find sponge-beds in water from ten to twenty-five feet deep. One man rowed and the other used a long-handled hook to pry sponges from their moorings on the ocean floor. Men and boat thus earned the epithet "hooker." To focus better on the ocean floor, a glass-bottom bucket called the water-glass sometimes completed the spongers' primitive implements. Most hookers took the catch to Key West's "Conchtown," where Bahamian immigrants—"Conchs"—lived. There they removed the hard skin and the organic matter called "gurry," until only the skeleton—the sponge—remained. Sponges sold by the pound on Key West's sponge market. The 1870 United States Census recorded six hundred spongers with one-hundred fifty hooker boats, and sales of 155,120 pounds of sponge for $141,011, averaging ninety cents per pound. By the mid-1870s the sponge market brought $230,000 yearly to Key West.[9]

To increase production, schooners towing four or five dinghies worked their way along the shore of the shallow keys. Dinghies dumped their catch on the deck of the mother ship for cleaning.[10] Hooker seamen then stored sponges in "crawls," square stake-fenced pens by the water's edge, where the harvest cured, alternately sun-dried and washed by the tide. On market days, packers then purchased the sponges, clipped them into shape and profited by resales to large sponge dealers in New York or New Orleans. Although most of the sponge boats operated out of Key West, where the sponge market thrived, by 1890 boats out of Tarpon Springs, Cedar Key, St. Marks, and Apalachicola added their sponges to the harvest of Key West Conchs.

About 1892, John Cheyney, a Philadelphia businessman and associate of Florida's financier, visionary, manufacturer, robber baron, and fellow Philadelphian Hamilton Disston, moved to establish a competing sponge-market. Cheyney leased property at Baillie's Bluff, just north of Tarpon Springs and the mouth of the Anclote River. There he bought sponges from local hookers, and resold them to dealers in New York. Moreover, some Florida "crackers" and local blacks also learned to handle the water-glass and the hook. However, Key West spongers had long claimed the sponge beds in the whole Gulf of Mexico, and soon after the first dinghies from Baillie's Bluff put out to sea, the Conchs attacked them. The local men soon learned to stick together and fight back. In 1898, the Spanish-American War caused the whole sponge trade to move from Key West to Cheyney's new market at Tarpon Springs. Although part of the market and most boats returned to Key West after the war, Tarpon Springs remained a busy marketplace.[11] In 1901 alone, Cheyney's market reputedly shipped sponges worth over $1,000,000.[12] Evidently, demand in the United States was great enough to absorb all the sponges harvested in Florida, and to still require more imports from the Mediterranean.[13]

Expanding its sponge trade to include purchases from Florida, the

Lembesis Company, a Greek-owned New York firm exporting and importing sponges, employed a regular buyer in Florida. In 1896 that buyer was John Cocoris, a recently hired, young Greek immigrant. His job was to watch the prices in Key West and Tarpon Springs and to buy and process sponges for shipment to New York.[14] Cocoris took up permanent living quarters at Baillie's Bluff, near the sponge market. Born and raised in Leonidion, a Greek seaside town on the Aegean, Cocoris knew how sponges were collected off the islands of Aegina and Hydra. There, as well as off the Dodecanese islands on the eastern side of the Aegean, where the ocean floor was deeper and more treacherous than beneath the tame Gulf waters, Greek spongers had learned to dive for sponges.[15] Since the mid-1860s, they had used diving suits made of layers of rubber and cotton, with a copper breastplate, to which they attached a large rounded helmet fitted with round glass lookout windows in front and sides. From the top of the helmet extended a long hose, like an umbilical cord, to the diver's boat, providing surface air hand-pumped by a deck-hand. Cocoris knew that divers could easily work at depths of up to 150 feet, in contrast to hookers, whose long-handled hook could hardly reach depths of thirty-five feet. He decided to enlist the help of his brothers in an effort to organize profitable sponge diving in the Gulf.

In 1901 John Cocoris returned to Leonidion to marry and bring his bride Anna to Tarpon Springs; in addition, he arranged for his three brothers, George, Constantine, and Elias to join him in the New World. The brothers soon made extensive trips into the Gulf to locate and survey sponge beds. Finding what looked like limitless growth of excellent sponges at accessible depths, they made plans to import the Greek diving equipment and a diving crew. Since they had no start-up capital, during the next two years they stayed with John and Anna, and gathered, prepared, trimmed, and packed enough sponges to bring them $4,000 on the New York market. This money paid passage from Aegina to America for a five man crew, consisting of a captain, two divers and two deckhands, and the diving equipment for one boat. At Tarpon Springs, the Cocoris brothers also bought an old sailboat, refurbished it for sponge diving, and renamed it *Elpis* - Hope.[16]

Sponge diver, in diving suit [scafander] with weighted boots, holding the air hose [life-line] secured to the helmet, which was in turn attached to the breastplate. As long as the life-line tender hand-pumped air through the hose, the diver could gather sponges off the ocean floor at depths up to 140 feet. Photo from the State Archives of Florida; the State Library and Archives Florida Memory Project.

On June 18, 1905, the first sponge boat equipped for diving sailed out of the mouth of the Anclote River into the waters of the Gulf of Mexico. A few miles into the Gulf, the *Elpis* lowered sail and the first diver descended. The lifeline tender hand-pumped air and watched for signals the diver sent by tugging at the rope loosely attached to the hose. The first trip succeeded beyond expectation. George Frantzis, who lived in Tarpon Springs and knew the Cocoris brothers well, learned that "every ten minutes Kavasilas, the diver, sent up a basket filled with large wool-sponges which were the best and sturdiest."[17] After about two hours, the diver came up and the second team went into action. They removed from the first diver the round helmet with the air hose, attached it to the breastplate of the already suited second diver, and sent him into the deep. By evening, in alternate dives, the two divers had loaded the boat with good sponges. The spongers then returned to the Anclote Keys, two islets in the Gulf near the river, to deposit their daily catch into crawls. Every few days they took loads of sponges to Cheyney's warehouses, and to the market at Baillie's Bluff. Within weeks, the operation had expanded to include a schooner, which made daily trips between the Anclote Keys where it deposited the catch and the *Elpis*, which stayed in place, thus allowing for extra diving hours.[18]

Diving in depths up to 140 feet opened vast new virgin sponge fields in the Gulf. Agents at the Tarpon Springs market continued buying the ever greater yield. The Cocoris brothers' operation expanded quickly. They built a house and a warehouse on the Anclote Keys to store sponges. They bought additional boats and converted them to sponge diving vessels with equipment and crews imported from the islands where sponge was gathered for centuries. Years later, Cocoris remembered how "every six months I bought a new boat and got some good divers from Greece."[19] Within the year, sponge diving in America attracted other Greek divers, sailors, and entrepreneurs. The first spongers here wrote to friends and relatives back home about the wealth of the Mexican Gulf. They emphasized that the work was not as dangerous as diving in the Mediterranean. The greater depths to which divers over there descended caused "the bends" or even paralysis; in contrast, the shallower waters of the Gulf appeared placid, with a much lower frequency of accidents. News spread over the Greek Aegean, and a chain migration began, especially from the Dodecanese islands of Symi, Kalymnos, and Halki, as well as from Spetse, Hydra and Aegina in the western Aegean. By 1906 over five-hundred spongers had immigrated to Tarpon Springs and hired on either as divers and crews.

In the early days of mechanized sponge-harvesting, Tarpon Springs had no cleared harbor and no established port. The banks of the Anclote River provided anchorage, about two or three miles inland from the Gulf, and the route to deposit points led through dangerously shallow waters. Lining the river banks one saw a forest of masts of diving boats, schooners, and even hook-boats, as some Greeks adapted to the old Conch method of sponge-gathering. A sandy road connected the dirt wharves with the village of Tarpon Springs. Some warehouses lined the road, as well as shacks and huts that provided residences for the spongers. Here men slept in bunks, and sometimes even in nets on the boats. Many cooked meals outside, in their backyards, where they also washed their clothing. Greeks populated the north-western part of Tarpon Springs, closest to the Anclote River and the docks, and in time spread into other white parts of the town of Tarpon Springs, around Spring Bayou.[20]

The system of shared earnings developed about the same time. Several competing traditions exist respecting this method of payment to the sponge boat crews, however, there is no doubt that the method was developed by captains and diving boat crews and that it was unique to the sponge industry in Florida. One writer explained the economics of a sponge boat in cultural terms. Individualistic, highly competitive Greeks, she wrote, found the idea of working for hourly or daily wages "not merely dull but downright degrading."[21] Payment in shares, however, knit the crew into a team, and each man did his best, thereby assuring success for all. Asked whether the share system was traditional to the Aegean, Stephen Katzaras, owner of one of the packing houses and long-time member and director of the Sponge Exchange, asserted that it was not. According to Katzaras, the system developed in Tarpon Springs, so as to lessen the risk for captains and boat-owners.[22]

The first divers and crews worked for wages. There were constantly more boats available than crews, especially divers, so that in 1906 the wages they commanded rose to as much as $300 monthly.[23] Initially, the prices for sponges were also high. The virgin sponge-beds yielded large, firm specimen, rarely harvested at hooking depths. In the early months, this crop sold for $8 to $10 per bunch. Between January 1 and February 15, 1906, sponges brought over $60,000. By mid-April forty diving boats were at work, and fifty by mid-May.[24] The January to mid-May yield soared to $250,000, with $20,000 worth sold weekly. Diving boats now gathered 500 to 600 bunches monthly. By the end of May 1906, however, prices had broken because of the heavy supply. Buyers now offered between $2.75 and $3.00 a bunch, and lacking other choices, the captains accepted the bids. Such low-priced sales, however, could not support the high wages. Under pressure by the captains, who usually also owned the boats, divers and other crew members agreed to partially share the risk of the enterprise, to accept the share system, and to ride the volatile market together with the captains and owners.

The share system soon became an established practice.[25] With small variations over the years, a typical diving boat crew divided the proceeds of their trip so that the owner-captain took five shares, each diver got three shares, and the other crew members, deck-hands and life-line tenders, the cook, and later the engineer received two shares each. After selling the catch at the sponge market, captain and crew tallied all costs, deducted them from the proceeds, and split the remainder according to the shares. The expenses to be deducted from the net proceeds came to include the complete cost of operating the boat. These costs encompassed the diving suits, as well as food, gas and oil, interest, insurance, and repairs.[26] As outlined in table 12A, an owner-captain received five shares out of the nineteen.[27] A non-owner captain, however, received three to four shares, while the investor-owner retained one to two shares, generally still insuring an excellent return on an investment of about $2,500, the contemporary value of an equipped diving boat.

Greek presence in the Gulf waters, easily detected by the appearance of their colorful boats, and especially their new, mechanized method of harvesting the ocean for sponges, created resentment in the ranks of Conch hookers. Fights between hookers and divers were frequent in the few ports in the great arc of the Gulf from Apalachicola through St. Marks, Cedar Key, and all the way down to Key West. At times, conflict even broke out when boats met on the Gulf waters. Several Greek sponge boats docked to re-supply in Key West caught fire and burned.[28] During the first two decades of the 1900s, the "Sponge War" alternately simmered and flared up. At times the Coast Guard had to be called in to keep the two sides apart, even though the hookers stayed in water up to four fathoms deep, and the diving boats worked in waters from six to twenty five fathoms in depth.[29]

The deep dislike harbored by the Key West spongers and sponge merchants for their Greek competition was best exemplified by a *Tampa Morning Tribune* headline of April 24, 1915: "Key West Officers go for Illegal Spongers." The following column outlined that on receiving reports from sources not identified in the column, Sheriff P. L. Jaycocks and a force of "special deputies" left Key West to sail to Rocky Channel "for the purpose of arresting Greek sponge fishers," who were "violating the law with regard to taking sponge in certain waters and below certain sizes."[30] The reporter did not say whether the special deputies were chosen for their skill in measuring raw sponges and determining at what depth the sponges were gathered, or for their physical prowess.

"The law" mentioned in the newspaper column referred to the attempts by Key Westers to use state or federal legislation to curtail or eliminate diving for sponges. In 1906, Key Westers presented a bill to the US Senate, labeled "An Act to prohibit aliens from taking or gathering sponges in waters of the United States." A preamble indicated that the necessity for the proposed legislation arose because within the past year and one-half "foreigners and aliens, mostly Greeks," have been fishing for and gathering sponges in American waters off the coast of Florida "to the great injury of the industry and to American citizens engaged in the same business."[31] John Cheyney, accompanied by George Meindanis, originally from the island of Hydra, who had finished law school in Greece and immigrated to Tarpon Springs, traveled to Washington to lobby against the Bill. The final compromise effectively banned diving for sponges in waters shallower than fifty feet; in addition, the legislation prohibited sale of sponges smaller than five inches in diameter.[32]

By 1908, sponge prices stabilized; however, the share system of compensation for diving boat crews remained in permanent use. Those directly involved in sponge gathering lived well with the share system; work in Tarpon Springs provided a decent living, with a definite chance for betterment. Working on a profit-sharing system in America was better than eking out a more dangerous and much poorer living back in the Mediterranean.[33]

In Tarpon Springs the diving boat captain's authority and responsibility also extended to contracting compatible divers and crew. Before the trip, while the captain was still making his selection, it was customary for each member of the crew to receive an advance against his future share, to lock in the agreement and to provide a minimal sum for the crews' families while the breadwinners were absent at sea. To get better hands and good divers, the captain arranged for the advances even if he had to borrow the money from financiers and bankers at high rates of interest. This created some friction, because all was well if the trip made money, but if it was a "broke trip," the captain suffered the loss, since advances were traditionally never returned. To lower his risk, every captain haggled to reduce the advance. Despite the claim that the share system assured an equal opportunity to everyone performing the same job, there was room for individual rivalry. Some captains earned a reputation of being able to find good sponging places on every trip, thus they had a first pick of the potential crew members. Certain divers also built a good reputation; perhaps they had a perfect safety record combined with the agility and ability to quickly fill their sponge nets and to stay in the water longer. Such divers could count on higher advances and a berth with any captain. Since the proportion or number of shares allotted to the different crew members did not change, some divers and crews expressed their competitive spirit by going with a "good" captain, but for less advance money. In contrast, "good" divers and experienced crews shopped around for ever greater advances. And some captains may have hoped for an increased total sponge harvest and hired the better divers even though they had to pay a high advance.

As the duration of trips settled at six months, the whole sponge-fleet was in port around Christmas and in mid-summer. During these weeks tension and holiday mood mingled until the close of negotiations. Katzaras pointed out that improvements in engines in the late 1940s brought boats into port every three to four weeks. The average trip still lasted six months, but the convenience of being in port frequently meant that the sponge catch could be sold earlier. As a result, captains negotiated reduced advances. For example, Katzaras related, even the best diver might get $200, just to tide him over for a few weeks until the next sponge catch sold at the Sponge Exchange. A similar method of payment existed in the American whaling industry.[34]

The United States Bureau of Fisheries recorded the much increased sponge output by the then Hillsborough County Greek diving boats for the years 1905 to 1908. Larger than ever sponge harvests clearly reflected the arrival of the divers, and the development of a notable sponge industry.[35] The fact that some of the men were the best sponge fishermen of the world automatically granted them and the town itself a certain degree of prestige. Most immigrant spongers and those attracted to related industries such as boat builders, sponge buyers and packers decided to stay permanently. Soon they began bringing over their wives and families.

By 1907, together with women and children, modest new houses appeared. The new community also built the first Greek Orthodox Church, a small wooden structure dedicated to St. Nicholas, the Patron Saint of all Greek seamen.[36] Within the following decade the Greek residential area grew into a pattern of red brick streets and white wooden houses, with palms and goats in the front yards.[37] The one-story cottages featured broad, southern front porches. Their residents, however, painted them in typical Mediterranean pastel colors of orange, blue, brick red, and coral green. The picturesque ambience, with its resonant lifestyle and music, the language and culture, the sponge docks and the Greek Orthodox church, gave one larger section of Tarpon Springs the appearance of an island in the Aegean Sea.

To serve the working boat owners and seamen laborers in the new industry, migrants from other Greek communities in the United States and new immigrants opened restaurants, candy stores, coffee houses, grocery and fruit stores, taverns, and other enterprises. These newcomers joined the established boat-building and repair facilities, and chandleries. In addition to these working people, another group of Greek businessmen, basic to the industry, operated permanently in Tarpon Springs. They were primarily investors who came to finance boat building and boat trips, and brokers who extended loans to those who bought boats or who needed money now, with future earnings serving as security for repayment. Still others were independent dealers in sponges, or agents for the big sponge merchants in New York, New Orleans, St. Louis, Philadelphia, and Cincinnati.[38]

In 1911, the *Tarpon Springs Leader* boosted and advertised the desirable qualities of the city "noted for being the sponge market of the world; for its equitable climate the year round, and for its many advantages as a winter resort." A logo consisting of a metal diving helmet and breastplate, sitting on an anchor, stood in a very conspicuous position on the newspaper's masthead. A column headed "A Correct List of Things of Which Our City Can Now Boast" enumerated the largest sponge market on earth, 250 sponging vessels, two railroads, one Greek club, twenty-one coffee parlors, five real estate agencies, six fruit stands, and one cigarette factory.[39] Not surprisingly, the sponge business was a very prominent subject, and made almost every issue. For example, the November 11, 1911, issue carried on its front page a picture of the interior of the sponge packing house owned by D. Davis & Sons of New York. The accompanying story named Christy Catsaros as the local general manager, and John Cocoras (sic) as the head buyer.[40] A high proportion of Greek immigrants achieved prominent places in the commercial life of Tarpon Springs. Moreover, a number of Greeks took part in the civic life of the town. Pioneer John Cocoris, for example, won election to the sheriff's office and successfully contested a seat on Tarpon's five-person council..[41] Others again entered the Rotary and other American organizations.[42]

By 1910, Tarpon Springs had changed from a small fishing and resort village of some five hundred people, into a busy commercial center with several thousand residents, bursting with new people, noise, and activity.[43] The complexion of the town radically changed in another way, as the Greek group competed in size with its American counterpart. Most of the town's "blue-bloods," and winter-vacation residents had left for good. Local inhabitants, together with newcomers from other parts of Florida and the American South, formed part of the town's non-Greek population. These were mostly people from modest social and economic ranks, looking for better opportunities in a growing town. A small African-American population, which had earlier provided services for vacationing whites, found no rejection on part of the Greeks; on the contrary, their working relationship improved and increased as jobs became open in the sponge industry.[44] With the arrival of more laborers who found work in the sponge packing houses and other shore services, and also among the diving boat crews, the African-American population experienced notable growth. Where formerly blacks had only served wealthy whites, they now worked with Greeks at a more equal level. Coming from the Mediterranean basin where many people are dark-skinned, the Greeks, themselves often swarthy, had none of the southern whites' ethnocratic attitude. As the sponge industry expanded and the need for labor developed, blacks filled many openings in the sponge boat crews as well as ashore. They were often cooks, life-line tenders, and even divers. During the long weeks and months when the boats were at sea, and when Greeks and African Americans ate and slept together in the sponge boats, many blacks learned to speak passable Greek. As one writer noted, however, friendliness at work did not extend to social interaction at family level.[45]

Boat building was one of the crafts imported into Tarpon Springs as a direct result of the expansion of sponging. The makeshift sloops and schooners were not really satisfactory for the Greek spongers. Late in 1905, a complete authentic sponge boat from Greece, the *Areta*, arrived aboard a cargo vessel. Skilled boat builders also arrived with adzes in their hands, and boat designs in their heads. Within two years, fifty new diving boats were on the sea. In the 1920s and 1930s, with the sponge industry robust, and the constant need for maintenance of many boats, both the diving and hooking kind, three shipyards stayed busy. In the Kimilis yard, the largest and named after its owner, Mr.

Kimilis and a crew of African Americans undertook to scrape and paint any boat, and tune and tidy it for the owner. Passers by usually saw black men perched on a plank alongside the hull of the boat, or in a bosun's chair halfway up the mast, working away. No sooner did one boat slide into the river, than another churned its way into line to be hauled up.[46]

Except for details and colors, any two boats might have been twins, as they were all patterned from the same Mediterranean model. Originally the boat was a double ender, propelled by sails. Centuries of use resulted in extra wide beams and deep round hulls, to keep the boat from rolling in heavy seas. When gasoline engines were introduced after 1915, the captains replaced one prow with a square back, and the sails became auxiliary power. After several accidents, when divers' lifelines were tangled in the propeller, the seamen designed and installed mesh-wire protective baskets around the propellers. Ship colors were similar to colors of Greek houses. The hull above the waterline was usually painted white, with the deck and cabins blue. Below the waterline brick red seemed best to take the punishment of dock scrapings and sea water. Bulwarks were orange, blue, black, or again brick red.[47]

The foremost difference between the Greeks on the one hand and the native American white and black communities on the other were the Greeks' unique religion and language. One could easily identify the Greek crews and even some of the business-people in town, especially those who catered to fellow Greeks, by the preponderant use of their mother-tongue. They were certainly the only congregants of the Greek Orthodox Church of St. Nicholas, the only ones to celebrate Christmas two weeks late, and the only ones to stage such extensive ceremonial celebrations at Epiphany and Easter.[48] Moreover, they had a different and more pungent cuisine. Most Greeks also lived in a separate part of town, where a good number owned their colorful homes. However, the Greek merchant elite, those involved in the commercial life of Tarpon Springs centered around the sponge industry and those catering to non-Greeks, ignored all ethnic boundaries. With the affluence of the spongers, the commercial interaction between Greeks and non-Greeks increased. New stores opened in town; banks were established; Greeks and local Americans learned to know each other better and to benefit from integrated commercial activities. However, depending on their work, which seemed related to their origins in the Mediterranean, not all newcomers partook equally in this interaction.

Members of the sponge boat crews were largely from the island of Halki, whereas the packing house people were usually *Symiaki*—from the island of Symi, typified by Stephan Katzaras, the aforementioned packing house owner. The financiers of the trips and lenders of advances to captains seem to originate from various islands of the Aegean as well as on the mainland of Greece and Asia Minor. Of course, there were notable exceptions. Kalymnos was the third Dodecanese island which yielded a large number of immigrants to Tarpon Springs, and there were Kalymnians among the sponge crews and also among the packers.[49]

The Greek community itself created certain differences and formed social strata along the lines of geographic origin and ascribed attitudes and ethos. The Halkite crews of the sponge boats were generally known to be cheerful, careless of money, great spenders, not worried too much about the future. People from Symi were almost all traders, shrewd at business, saving their money, unostentatious, and by this nature became the packers and middlemen of the sponge business. Financiers seem to be from neither of these two islands, but can trace their origins from other places in the Mediterranean; their arrival in Tarpon was usually preceded by a stay in one or more of the bigger cities in the northeastern or mid-western United States, where they made their stake and then came to Tarpon to try their hand at business in the sponge industry.

The pioneer himself, John Cocoris, had his roots in Leonidion, the Spartan region of the Greek mainland; he first worked in New York. However, he acted more like a carefree captain of a diving boat than like his fellow investors. During the most lucrative years, John had a box that sat on a side table in his living room, and it was said he placed into the box all the money he made from sales of sponge on the sponge exchange, and whenever he, his wife, or any friend who was in his house needed money, they helped themselves out of the box. By the late 1920s, John was almost broke; he gave up the sponge business and moved with his family to Jacksonville, Florida.[50]

The investors, sailors, shore-services providers, and merchants all lived off sponging, but formed different strata within the Greek group, and had dissimilar contacts with the wider community of Tarpon Springs. Those who adapted least to the American ways were the ones who had to make the least change in their lifestyle, the sailors, divers, and sponge producers. The crew members, sailors, divers, engineers, as well as the captains remained uninterested in social upward mobility or in getting close to their fellow Americans. They spent time with each other and of all immigrants had the least interaction with local non-Greeks. The closest relations with other than fellow Greeks occurred when locals, to a greater extent local blacks, went to work as crews on the boats. Often crews and captains poked fun at the packers' interest in profits and money. Contact and friendship with his fellow crew members, both at sea and in the coffee house were for any true seaman of more value than monetary gains made from the sale of sponges. These seagoing immigrants participated least in civic affairs, barely took an interest in elections, hardly ever joined in any American sphere of interaction, and learned English only for the most rudimentary needs.

The packers presented a very different attitude from the seagoing men. The packing house owners as well as their employees interacted on a variety of levels with local Americans. The packers represented the middling level of immigrants who adapted and interacted to a considerable degree with their American fellow citizens. The interaction took place mostly at the commercial plane, but also overflowed into the social, civic, and political areas wherein the packers adopted many American ways of thinking and action and even joined as members in clubs and sodalities of all sorts. Most of the packers were well off, if not wealthy. They accumulated property, lived usually in their own houses, and sometimes even showed evidence of conspicuous consumption in their travel, entertainment, or education of their children. Although the shrewdness of the Greek trader had not been lost on these businessmen, it was confined within the limits of American business ethics. For these people money was a means of upward mobility in the community of Tarpon Springs. They were accepted in clubs and groups associated with the American segment of the city. Their children invariably attended colleges and universities away from home, and were the future Greek American professionals, whose own children became third generation Americans who just happened to be of Greek origin.

The greatest degree of adaptation took place among the small group of financiers. With profits made in the sponge industry and wisely invested, they built up small fortunes, which in turn enabled them to expand into real estate, banking, and investments into businesses of all sorts. The nature of their businesses, in turn, brought them into contact with the elite group of Americans who were in the same businesses. They attended American cocktail parties, they were friendly with other wealthy Americans, and interacted in all areas with American society, while not losing their membership in the Greek group. Significantly, although there were certainly enough wealthy Greeks to support a Greek newspaper, no such paper or publication ever appeared. The financiers and bankers, the Greek economic elite formed the smallest segment of the Greek community in Tarpon Springs and achieved the greatest degree of Americanization and upward mobility.

For example, seven Greek American Tarponites, all prominent in the Greek community, were the chief shareholders and officers of the United Divers Supply Company, a most successful Florida corporation headquartered, of course, in Tarpon Springs.[51] Among them were Nikolas Arfaras, a well-to-do merchant, who financed boat-building, advanced loans for sponge fishing trips, and became the owner of several sponge-boats; as well as George Meindanis and Emmanuel Macrinaris, who were both involved in Tarpon Springs' civic life and stood as candidates for City Council.[52] Tarpon Springs' newspaper the *Evening Leader* identified Macrinaris "with the largest business interests in this city." The E. Macrinaris Shipbuilding Corporation was only one of these interests.[53] Another prominent businessman involved in United Divers Supply was Demosthenes Alissandratos, whose clothing store did very well financially and took much advertising space in the *Evening Leader*.[54]

As in other cities in the South, a number of name changes occurred, mostly within the Greek middle and upper strata. Again, these were not just changes that made polysyllabic Greek names and surnames easier to pronounce on part of their American counterparts—who found many such names to be tongue-twisters—but changes which completely obscured the Greek origins. George Emmanuel served as the president of the Greek *kinotis*; Father Arsenio Davis was the priest at St. Nicholas church and tended the needs of the Greek Orthodox faithful; J. K. (John Kaninas) Douglass was a prominent Tarponite businessman and a World War I, US Army veteran; his relative John E. Douglass was mayor of Tarpon Springs for at least one term 1915 - 1917; Harry Bell was a popular Greek actor from Tampa and founder of the Spongers Mutual Benefit Association of Tarpon Springs.[55]

Contemporary local newspapers constantly exhibited evidence of the high and friendly regard shown by fellow Tarponites for the town's Greek citizens. Perhaps no major paper in any city in the South carried news of the Greek community's doings as did the *Tarpon Springs Leader*, later renamed the *Evening Leader*. Front page headlines reported that "Greeks gave a Play at Orpheum Theater - For the Benefit of the Patriarch of Constantinople" as readily and on the same front page as they posted the news that the "Social Season Has A Brilliant Opening - Mr. and Mrs. Bert Nash Gave Pretty Breakfast Dance."[56] Even other regional newspapers, for example the *Tampa Daily Times*, reported news of larger community activities, such as the Epiphany ceremony and the diving for the cross.[57] America's entry into the war, in April 1917, prompted *The Evening Leader* to declare, "Tarpon Greeks Loyal." Commenting on a visitor's remarks that he was surprised to find so many American flags in a place composed almost entirely of Greeks, the editor explained that Tarpon's population was only one-third Greek, since "a very large number of Tarpon's Greek citizens are Americans in fact," and the editor confidently proclaimed, "there is not one of them among the 1,500 who are credited with a residence in this city who would not fight to the death in support of the stars and stripes."[58] Indeed, the "First Call of 95 Men to Appear at Clearwater" did contain Greek surnames.[59]

More Greek citizens' names appeared on the "Honor Rolls" of the paper's record of Liberty Bond sales. The roll for the "4th Liberty Loan," indicating that the buyers have paid the first installment of at least ten percent or more, contained 106 surnames such as Albaugh, O'Cramer, Henderson, and Green and 36 clearly Greek surnames such as Arvanitis, Bitros, Castrounis, and Emmanuel.[60] In 1919, John Kaninas Douglass, "a Greek and the only one in the American army to hold the high rank of ordnance sargeant" was just one of the boys who came home from the war in Europe covered with glory; other Greek Americans took part both in organizing the drive for the "Fifth or Victory Loan" and in heavily contributing to the purchase of these government bonds. Of the thirty-two committeemen appointed to promote the Victory Loan, six were Greek: John Diamandis, Charles Themelis, Emmanuel Macrenaris, Nikolas Arfaras, Demosthenes Alissandratos, and Dr. John E. Douglass.[61]

The Greek Orthodox Church, easily the most conservative Greek entity until the 1930s, managed to elicit a favorable press and to move towards adapting a more conciliatory stand on adapting to American ways. An *Evening Leader* issue of spring, 1919, carried on its front page a photograph of "Rev. Seraphim Stelides, Rector of St. Nicholas Greek Orthodox Church," with a statement that Father Seraphim was "cosmopolitan in his ideas and believes in the union of all disciples of Christ, regardless of creed." The photograph depicted Father Seraphim clad in a black suit and clerical collar, with a nicely trimmed beard and mustache, and a large cross hanging on his chest.[62] Evidently both sides in Tarpon Springs, the native press and the Greek Orthodox clergyman attempted to show Byzantine Christendom in the best light. In January and again in June 1919, the *Evening Leader* prominently spread the news of visits to Tarpon's Greek Orthodox parish by Reverend Thomas J. Lacey, rector of the Episcopal Church of the Redeemer, in Brooklyn, New York. That year, local newspapers wrote about Epiphany as "The Greek Cross Day." The president of the Greek community, John Diamandis, said that the day "has been settled as a wholly local feast day of the town, not only for the Hellenes but also for the Americans." For the first time Father Seraphim held prayer services at the bayou in both Greek and English, before he tossed the cross into the water and the young divers retrieved it.[63] Years later, in an article in the St. Nicholas Parish 1937 yearbook, Reverend Lacey noted his early and extensive ties with the church at Tarpon Springs, explained the significance of Epiphany to Christians and specifically to Greeks, and remarked how the religious ritual "became an impressive patriotic and civic demonstration."[64] As George Creel's Americanism during the war turned into the 100 percent Americanism of the 1920s, as Americans throughout the nation joined the Ku Klux Klan, and as Floridians elected nativist Sidney Johnston Catts to be their governor, the Greeks of Tarpon Springs continued to enjoy the favorable opinion and even esteem of their fellow citizens.

Well into the 1940s the spongers' fleet varied between one hundred and two hundred boats. In the later years, diving boats habitually made two to three trips a year, staying out four to five months on each trip. The first trip of the year usually started in January, just after Epiphany and the blessing of the boats. The second started after Easter, and the last one ended by Christmas. Owners and crews continued to use the share system, with workers and owners sharing the risks as well as profits, right through the depression of the 1930s and the booming World War II and post-war years. The system even survived the rough days of the sponge blights, after 1947.[65] The economic impact of the increasing value of the sponge catch had a considerable effect on Tarpon Springs, and by extension, on Florida's economy. After 1910, the income from sponges alone ran between half a million and a million dollars yearly. The week of January 3, 1919 posted $28,700 in sponge sales, projecting about $1,500,000 for the year.[66] During World War II, the annual income rose to almost three million dollars, a large sum for a small town of 5,000 people. The ripple effect of sponge industry money multiplied its benefits throughout the state.[67] In this period of abundance, available excess money saved by the spongers went mainly into real estate. The aim of many a Greek family was first, to own a home, however small, and secondly, to own a property that would produce income. In this way, the shrewder members of the community acquired property after property, including lots for future building. Gradually, the proportion of real estate in Greek hands matched their numbers in the city.

In 1934 the Civil Works Administration commissioned a study of the sponge industry. Statistician Fred K. Sage found that in 1933, sponging employed only 516 men on eighty boats, and 114 men in the 16 packing houses. There were 50 diving boats, and 30 hookers. Sage compiled the figures of expenses and receipts of the Tarpon Springs fleet for 1932 and 1933 for both diving boats and hookers. He concluded that on the average one half of the total income was expended for equipment and supplies for the boat, and the other half was divided among the crew in shares. He concluded that "the men working in the production of sponges [were] making only the barest of livings for themselves and their families."[68] Sage calculated that on the average divers made about $660 for one year's work; and some crew members made only $330 yearly. But Sage examined only the lowest two years of the sponge production, 1932 and 1933. Other years up to 1947 yielded more money in sales, and presumably more money to be shared between captain-owners and crews. One authoritative source calculated that in a "good" year, with a big sponge harvest and high prices coinciding, a situation that prevailed between 1941 and 1946, a diver could earn "almost nine thousand dollars."[69]

Whether or not crews obtained a higher or lesser amount in the share distribution, of course, depended on the expenses as well as on the higher catch. This was best illustrated in Sage's work, which reported that the total received for sponge sales in 1933 was just marginally higher than the amount received in 1932. Yet because the food, supplies, and fuel were between fifteen and twenty-five percent lower in 1933, the crews shared a far greater amount.[70] There was no clarification why the food costs for practically the same number of crews differed by as much as 20 percent from one year to the next.[71] Since expenses came "off the top," in the idiom of sponge workers, there was opportunity for a dishonest captain to cheat his men and thus increase his own profit. Usually, however, the men knew precisely which captains cheated in this manner. Often, however, if a captain was known for finding the sponge-fields and making good profits, the men went with him in spite of his dishonesty.[72]

Another group in the sponge industry that protected its own interests first were the buyers and packers. Even before 1910, to end the chaos and disorganization of transactions at Baillie's Bluff, local buyers and dealers in sponges founded the Tarpon Springs Sponge Exchange. About fifty buyers organized a non-profit corporation, which then bought land in town, close to the rail connections with the Anclote River docking facilities, and erected a building with office facilities and large, open-air sponge storage units. Appropriately, John Cheyney became one of the founders and the first president of the Tarpon Springs Sponge Exchange.[73] Within a few years, Greeks controlled the capitalist ranks of buyers and dealers. Men such as Nicholas Arfaras, George Emmanuel, and John Diamandis gradually displaced the older, native American traders.[74] The Sponge Exchange stored the catch that individual boats brought in from time to time. Usually tied in garlands on 54"-long string by size and quality, sponges were placed in locked iron bar compartments surrounding the large courtyard. Sales took place, by auction, every Tuesday and Friday.[75] Sponges were sold by quality and weight, and at times by the piece. The auction was silent, in that each buyer wrote his bid on paper and handed it to the exchange manager. He took all bids on any particular lot, selected the highest one and called it out loudly. The captain called out "sold" if the bid was acceptable, or refused the bid, in which case the lot was withdrawn for the next auction.[76] If the bids were unacceptable on the next auction day as well, the captain and his crew were obliged to take that lot away, and sell it outside the exchange.[77]

The Sponge Exchange. Sponge boat captains stored their sponges in compartments and offered them for sale at weekly auctions. Photo from the State Archives of Florida; the State Library and Archives Florida Memory Project.

In practice, captain and crew accepted lower bids simply because all local buyers were members of the Exchange, and it was inconvenient to find other buyers, and costly to take time away from work at sea and look for buyers in New Orleans or New York. At times captains accused the buyers of conspiring underhandedly to buy low. Just after the Great Depression gripped the country, in 1931 and 1932, despite a steady demand for sponges, buyers paid reduced prices for the catch.[78] By 1932 boat owners and crews banded together to protect themselves from price-fixing buyers and formed the Sponge Producers Association. This group organized its own bonded warehouse and acted as a unit to get better prices from the buyers. Values paid by the buyers to producers returned to their pre-depression levels.

In 1933, the National Industrial Recovery Act required representatives of industries, who were granted immunity from antitrust prosecution, to draft codes of "fair competition" for their industries. The codes set production limits, wages and working conditions, and forbade price cutting and other unfair practices. Then, to administer the codes, the federal government established the National Recovery Administration. The lively and many-sided sponge industry struggled to work out standard codes of hours and wages for the producers—the seagoing fishermen and laborers on the one hand, and competitive prices for the packers and distributors on the other hand. Industry representatives from Key West and Tarpon Springs met to resolve problems inherent in their complex trade, but they failed to reach any agreement. They could not standardize values of sponges, and the traditional share system on the boats did not lend itself to an hourly pay scale.

Throughout the 1930s and the boom years of World War II, division continued among the various interest groups in the industry. Sponge gatherers, including owners-captains, divers, and crews desired the highest prices for sponges. Buyers of the Sponge Exchange, in contrast, looked to pay the lowest prices possible when buying sponges and, after packing the product, to receive the highest prices available from large dealers. Demand remained high, and so did the prices paid to gatherers, especially during the war when sponge imports ceased. For example, large "sheepswool" sponges valued at just over $4.00 a pound in 1940, brought over $12.00 in 1941, and over $20.00 from 1944 to 1946.[79] In 1947, when buyers attempted to lower the prices to pre-war levels, boat owners and captains resolved to maintain prices by forming their own Sponge Producers' Exchange, and trading directly with the dealers in New York.[80] Buyers of the traditional Sponge Exchange countered with a broadside against the boat owners, alleging that in their greed they not only kept 25 percent of the price paid for every load of sponges sold as their personal share, while charging the crews with inflated expenses, but they now created chaos in a perfectly well run industry, by attempting to take over buyers' customers. The Greek community in Tarpon Springs was split down the middle. Arguments raged, people stopped speaking to each other, endless strife engulfed the town. The mayor of Tarpon Springs, Fred Howard, called a meeting of all factions to try to smooth things out, but most spongers boycotted the meeting.[81]

The sponge boat owners and captains refused to sell their catch at the Sponge Exchange and looked for independent buyers and wholesalers outside of Tarpon Springs. The resulting delay in receiving their share of the money alienated the seamen crews. With just the right timing, the CIO-backed United Steel Workers now organized about 400 divers and crews.[82] But before the first contract could be negotiated, the 1947 blight punished all sides. The "red tide" appeared about the same time as the Du Pont Company introduced synthetic sponges.[83] The disease of the sponges, as well as other forms of marine life, first occurred in the Bahamas Islands, then seemed to move westward. It destroyed the gelatinous membrane that covered the sponges on the seabed. When the diver hooked the sponge to dislodge it from the rock or coral it grew on, the sponge fell apart. If such a sponge were brought up on deck, it exuded a very foul odor and rapidly decomposed. For the next few years, sponge production fell drastically. The disaster affected the whole population involved in the industry. Special church services were conducted in St. Nicholas Greek Orthodox Church, as congregants prayed for the end of the blight. In time, some of the divers and other workers left the industry. Younger men moved north to the steel mills of Youngstown, Ohio, and Gary, Indiana. Others retired, or picked up new work, and opened small gift shops, selling, not surprisingly, sponges and shells. The Greek population of the city shrunk by the exodus of younger men and women, who found jobs elsewhere and sent part of their earnings home.

During the 1950s and 1960s, as divers and other crews retired, no one took their place. Even when the blight receded and the sponge were again plentiful, the children and grandchildren, the second and third generations brought up and educated in America, chose not to follow their fathers and grandfathers to a life at sea. A few younger people went into vocations and became electricians and auto mechanics, many joined the family businesses on shore. Others continued in school and entered the professions as lawyers, engineers, dentists, and doctors. When the sponge beds recovered over a three-year period from 1954 to 1957, the crews to man the sponge boats failed to reassemble. About a dozen deep-diving boats and perhaps as many hooker boats engaged in full-time sponge fishing, but the glory days of this venerable and important industry never returned. An attempt to import more divers from Greece was marginally successful, and yielded only twenty special visas. The sponge industry in the Greek Aegean was doing well, and the push to emigrate no longer existed. After the blight ended, in 1954, the Sponge Exchange had its building repainted and the murals retouched, anticipating a revival of the sponge trade. The great revival never took place. In 1972, the exchange took its place on the National Register of Historic Places. Some years later, in 1982, the city commissioners had the building bulldozed and replaced with a plaque.

Despite the demise of the great sponge industry, Tarpon Springs retained a large proportion of its population of Greek origin. Along with natives and newcomers to other prime areas along Florida's Gulf coast, Tarponites switched to real estate development and tourism. The town never lost its Greek flavor; on the contrary, the only "Greektown" in the South became a tourist attraction. St. Nicholas Cathedral, Pappas' Restaurant, and the whole area in the vicinity of the old sponge docks attract thousands of visitors every year. Third generation Greek Tarponites are for the most part professionals, actively at work in businesses and commercial institutions, rather than on the docks. A few maintain their heritage, and their economic well-being, with highly developed tourist attractions revolving around the sponge industry. Greek bakeries, restaurants, souvenir emporiums, and specialty shops crowd the area around the docks and down Dodecanese Avenue. Elderly Greeks from all over the United States come to Tarpon Springs to retire. Using HUD money, the AHEPA intends to build a sixty-unit retirement home there. Epiphany ceremonies still take place every January 6th. Church services at St. Nicholas Cathedral precede a well-rehearsed walk down Tarpon Avenue to the bayou, where several thousand spectators gather to see one of the young divers retrieve the white cross tossed into the calm shallow waters. The historic heritage of Tarpon Springs' sponging days can be glimpsed among the hustle contrived to attract multitudes of colorfully clad tourists. Several docked sponge boats seem to be part of the well-advertised "Sponge Museum" a simulated part of the once glorious sponge diving fleet. Visitors, who often outnumber Tarponites, are by no means a homogeneous group; some are looking for a Disney world on the Gulf Coast, as others seek the history that characterized the heyday years of the sponge industry.

Turning to the beginning of the century, early Greek immigrants to Tarpon by no means presented a homogeneous group either. First generation Greek Tarponites were divided by a combination of regional origin, dialect, class, and politics. Internal debates were inevitable between people from different islands and the mainland, between crews and divers going to sea and those who stayed to develop their businesses on shore, between those who mixed with and adapted to the local English-speaking population, when others kept to their own section of town. The group, however, adopted the symbolic umbrella of Greek ethnicity to provide the basis for solidarity to combine votes in favor of their own candidates within the local power structure. Even as they laid claim to American election practices and adopted American ways of commerce and finance, the Greek immigrant population in Tarpon was also numerous enough to maintain its language and religion, situated in a distinct Greek seaside ambience, made more comfortable by New World amenities such as electricity and plumbing.

At the same time as they pursued their diverse claims to power, status, and resources, along the way Greek newcomers defused the hostility of the mainstream ethnoculture by depicting themselves as completely compatible with American principles and ideals. As pointed out by the authors of "Invention of Ethnicity" and by John Higham, particular moments of societal crisis, such as wars and economic depressions have been periods of intensified invention of ethnicity. As demands for loyalty and conformity to "American" norms increased, immigrant groups responded by asserting and demonstrating the compatibility of their ethnocultures with national ideals. This compatibility, carefully worked out by selective adaptation, was amplified by the generational transition that also affected the Tarpon Springs Greeks. A critical moment arrived when the second generation came of age and challenged Greek-born parents for positions of leadership within the community. Maintenance of language, gender roles, and endogamy, painstakingly created by the immigrant parents, were questioned and challenged by the American-born. The second and third generation of Tarponite Greek Americans displayed some commitment to the perpetuation of ethnic organizations and institutions, but on their own terms, and in changing conditions, not the least being a choice of easier ways to make a living.

TABLE 12A

A Table showing the typical division of shares by the crew of sponge diving boat, as related by different sources:

Sources	1	2	3	4	5
Boat-owner + captain	2 + 3	5	5	3 to 4 + 1	4
each diver	3	3	3	4 to 4½	4
lifeline man	2	1½	1½	2 to 2½	2
deckhand	2	1½	1½	1½ to 2	1
cook	2	1½	1½	2	2
engineer*	2	2	2	3 to 3½	2

Source 1 = Stephen Katzaras, oral interview by the writer, February 27, 1993, at Tarpon Springs. Tape deposited at the University of Florida Oral History Department.

Source 2 = Fred K. Sage, "Report of Sponge Industry of Tarpon Springs, Florida," 1933, at the P. K. Yonge Library of Florida History, University of Florida.

Source 3 = E. P. Macrenaris, address before the Tarpon Springs Rotary Club, "The Sponge Industry of Tarpon Springs," 1930, at the P.K. Yonge Library of Florida History, University of Florida.

Source 4 = Gertrude Stoughton, Tarpon Springs, Florida: The Early Years, 1975.

Source 5 = George Th. Frantzis, Strangers at Ithaca: the Story of the Spongers of Tarpon Springs, 1962.

* engineers became members of sponge boat crews only after gasoline engines replaced sails, sometime after World War I.

TABLE 12B
A Table showing the number of divers usually hired to work different depths and the average length of time a diver stayed at each depth.

number of divers in crew	depth worked	average length of dive
2	30 to 50 feet	120 min. (2 hrs.)
3	50 to 75 feet	75 min. (1:15 hrs)
4	75 to 100 feet	45 min.
5 +	100 to 130 feet	20 min.

Sources:

Stephen Katzaras, oral interview by writer, February 27, 1993, at Tarpon Springs. Tape Deposited at the University of Florida Oral History Department.

Fred K. Sage, "Report of Sponge Industry of Tarpon Springs, Florida," 1933, at the P. K. Yonge Library of Florida History, University of Florida.

E. P. Macrenaris, address before Tarpon Springs Rotary Club, "The Sponge Industry of Tarpon Springs," 1930, at the P. K. Yonge Library of Florida History, University of Florida.

George Th. Frantzis, Strangers at Ithaca: the Story of the Spongers of Tarpon Springs, 1962.

Notes

1   Steve Frangos, "Greek Island Songs," *The Greek American* [weekly publi-
     cation in Long Island, New York] March 16, 1996: In the early 1930s
     Skevos [Steve] Zembellas arived from the island of Kalymnos to Tarpon
     Springs, wrote Kalymnian songs and music, and recorded them with local
     Tarpon Springs Greek musicians such as George Katsaros and Kosta Kalivas;
     these are the opening lines of a popular Tarpon Springs Greek love song
     composed by Zembellas and heard in the coffee shops, tavernas, and little
     restaurants on the Tarpon Springs fishing docks.

2   *Thirteenth Census of the United States, 1910* (Population Bureau of the
     Census, Washington, D.C., 1910), Volume II, 297-333; particularly Table
     2, Population of Incorporated places: the town of Tarpon Springs grew
     from 541 people in 1900 to 2,212 people in 1910, mostly due to immi-
     gration of Greeks; Also see Edwin Clarence Buxbaum, "The Greek-American
     Group of Tarpon Springs, Florida: A Study of Ethnic Identification and
     Acculturation," Ph. D. dissertation, (University of Pennsylvania,
     Philadelphia, 1967), 350-352, where Buxbaum asserted that from 1920 to
     1947 the Greeks formed a majority of the Tarpon Springs population.

3   State and federal census figures for Tarpon Springs, including the *Seventh
     Census of the State of Florida, 1945*:

1895 (state)	562	1925 (state)	2,685
1900 (federal)	541	1930 (federal)	3,414
1905 (state)	740	1935 (state)	3,520
1910 (federal)	2,212*	1940 (federal)	3,402
1915 (state)	1,938	1945 (state)	4,727
1920 (federal)	2,105		

     * this drastic increase and other large fluctuations are related to the sponge
     industry.

4   *Thirteenth Census of the United States* - Population, shows the total Tarpon
     Springs 14th Precinct head-count broken down as follows:

     1,050 Greeks born either in Greece or Turkey
     1,192 white Americans and other foreign-born whites
     207 black or mulatto Americans and West Indians
     2,449 [Total shown on p. 305 of Census = 2,445]

5   *Dimotiki* language of the common people, as opposed to *katharevusa* the
     puristic, literary language used by those with higher education.

6   According to records compiled by Bishop John of Amorion, the retired
     Bishop of the Greek Orthodox Diocese of Atlanta, Greek immigrants formed
     the Tarpon Springs Greek Orthodox parish and in 1907 built the first
     Church of St. Nicholas; but also see the yearbook *Thirty-second Anniversary
     of the Greek Community of Tarpon Springs, Florida* (Tarpon Springs, St. Nicholas
     Parish, July 1937), at the P. K. Yonge Library, University of Florida, which
     indicates that the *kinotis* (community) was *organized* in 1905.

7   Roger Daniels, *Coming to America: A History of Immigration and Ethnicity in American Life* (Harper Collins Publishers, Princeton, N. J., 1990), 211; Daniels enumerated several examples of such cases of discrimination, which occurred when an immigrant group took on a "certain critical mass;" Daniels showed such prejudice directed against Armenians in Fresno, Jews and Italians in parts of New York, and others.

8   Caroline Johnson Comnenos, "Florida's Sponge Industry: A Cultural and Economic History" (Ph.D. dissertation, University of Florida, Gainesville, Florida, 1982), 4-6.

9   *Ninth Census of the United States, 1870*: Census of Florida, 1870, original Census schedules, Schedule 4: Products of Industry Monroe County (Microfilm 87-AA, reel 3, P. K. Yonge Library of Florida History, University of Florida); also see Comnenos, "Florida's Sponge Industry," 10.

10   The schooner was a large, slow transport vessel, a boat with single sail, about 35 to 45 feet long.

11   John N. Cobb, "The Sponge Fishery of Florida in 1900," United States Commission of Fish and Fisheries, *United States Fish Commission Report for 1902* (Washington, D.C., 1904), 170, 177, 273, cited in Comnenos, "Florida's Sponge Industry," Chapter II.

12   Gertrude Stoughton, *Tarpon Springs, Florida: The Early Years* (New Port Richey, Florida: Tri-Arts Studio, 1975), 43.

13   A variety of sponges filled needs in many industries, including medical, cosmetic, millinery, clothing, industrial padding, janitorial, ceramic and pottery, tile setting, and curio shops. Also see Fred K. Sage, "Report of Sponge Industry of Tarpon Springs, Florida," Civil Works Administration (CWA), (Pinellas County Project #52-89) 1933, and Federal Emergency Relief Act (FERA) project 52-7-31, reporting that four kinds of commercial sponges grow in the Gulf waters: wool (the most valuable), yellow, wire, and grass.

14   Works Progress Administration (WPA), Writers' Program, Florida, "Biographical Sketches of Greeks in Jacksonville" (The P.K Yonge Library of Florida History, University of Florida, Gainesville): John Cocoris oral interview, 1939.

15   Ernle Bradford, *The Greek Islands* (London: Collins Press, 2nd ed., 1970), 228; four of the twelve Dodecanese islands on the eastern side of the Aegean that had a tradition of sponge-fishing since Homeric times were Halki, Symi, Kalymnos, and Astypalia; the name "Dodecanese" came from the Greek words *dodeka* = twelve and *nesos* = island.

16   George Th. Frantzis, *Strangers at Ithaca: the Story of the Spongers of Tarpon Springs* (St.Petersburg, Florida: Great Outdoors Publishing, 1962), Chapter 2. Frantzis was a member of the Greek community in Tarpon Springs and based his writing on personal knowledge. George Cocoris bought the sailboat from one William Low for $180, and fitted it with the air-pump equipment and a diver's ladder.

17   Ibid., 48, 52; the two divers were Demosthenes Kavasilas and Stelios Bessis; captain Paulos Moutsatsos and life-line-tenders + deckhands Eleftherios

Moutsatsos and Miltiades Stathis formed the remaining crew of the *Elpis;* all the men were "imported" from Aegina.

18   Ibid., 54; the Cocoris brothers named their schooner *Pelican.*

19   WPA, "Biographical Sketches," J. Cocoris interview, 1939.

20   Hillsborough County, an area of 1,062 square miles surrounding Tampa and along the Gulf coast in existence since 1834, lost about 309 square miles with the creation of Pinellas County in 1911; included in Pinellas County were Clearwater, Tarpon Springs, St. Petersburg, and Gulfport: see the *Florida Handbook 1949-1950* (Tallahassee: Peninsular Publishing Company, 1949), 130.

21   Stoughton, *Tarpon Springs,* 48.

22   Stephen B. Katzaras oral interview by the writer, February 27, 1993, at Tarpon Springs. Tape deposited at the University of Florida Oral History Department. "Stephen Katzaras Sponge Co." was listed among the buyers and members of the Tarpon Springs Sponge Exchange in Frantzis, *Strangers in Ithaca,* 70.

23   Comnenos, "Florida's Sponge Industry," 81.

24   Henry Frank Moore, "The commercial sponges and the sponge fisheries," *Bulletin of the Bureau of Fisheries* XXVIII (1908), 443, (Washington, Gov't. Print'g. Office, 1910), at the P.K.Yonge Library of Florida History, University of Florida.

25   See Table 12A; Fred K. Sage, "Report of Sponge Industry of Tarpon Springs, Florida," Civil Works Administration (CWA), (Pinellas County Project #52-89) 1933, and Federal Emergency Relief Act (FERA) Project 52-7-31 (at the P.K.Yonge Library of Florida History, University of Florida); Katzaras interview; also see Stoughton, *Tarpon Springs,* 73.

26   Emmanuel P. Macrenaris (aka Macrinaris or Makrinaris), address before the Tarpon Springs Rotary Club, "The Sponge Industry of Tarpon Springs," ca. 1930, at the P. K. Yonge Library of Florida History, University of Florida.

27   This provision was calculated with two divers. Diving at greater depths required 4 or 5 divers; the captain's proportion then would be 5 out of 21 or 22 shares. See Table 12B.

28   For similar conflicts between people working in traditional ways and others using industrial or proto-industrial practices see Herbert G. Gutman, *Work, Culture, and Society in Industrializing America* (New York, Vintage Books, 1977), 55-61.

29   Frantzis, *Strangers in Ithaca,* 59.

30   *The Tampa Morning Tribune,* Saturday, April 24, 1915.

31   Senate Bill 4805, House of Representatives Report No. 4443, 1906; also see Helen Halley, "A Historical Functional Approach to the Study of the Greek Community of of Tarpon Springs" (Ph.D. dissertation, New York, Columbia University, 1952), 111-114.

32   House of Representatives, Report No. 4444, 1906, contained the following passages: "...Greeks, having had years of practice in the deep waters of the Mediterranean and becoming experts in the art of diving, can in a diving suit, called 'skafander,' made for that purpose, go into much greater depths

than can be reached by the hookers..." and "So vigorously have these Greeks pushed their operations that within a year and a half the boats in Florida waters, with diving attachments, have increased to at least 75 or 80..."

33   Katzaras interview. Back home, Aegean captains retained their crews for trips that lasted from twelve to eighteen months and paid the amount agreed upon to each diver and crewman in advance. Monies were usually left with the man's family, to keep whether he returned or not. Although the ship stopped at ports to unload and pick up fresh supplies, the crew was obliged to stay for the duration. The ship-owner, usually also the captain, took a larger risk and the commensurate larger share of the profit. Moore, "The commercial sponges and the sponge fisheries," *Bulletin of the Bureau of Fisheries*, XXVIII (1908), 440, described the bounty system that operated among the hookers of Key West, in contrast to the Aegean practice, and similar to the share system in Tarpon Springs. Like the share system, its adoption reflected the profit-conscious environment of the New World and not some notion of selfless communal endeavor. With slight variations, arrangements usually required the owner to provide the hooker boats with simple equipment and food in return for one half of the catch. The bounty was divided into 1-1/4 share for each hooker and one share for the captain, the rowers, and the cook. The captain conducted the negotiation of shares and advanced monies against the bounty.

34   Elmo P. Hohman, *The American Whaleman: A Study of Life and Labor in the Whaling Industry* (New York: Longmans, Green & Co., 1928), 217; the seamen on whalers were not paid by day or by month, nor by the whale caught. Although crews on whaling ships were more numerous, they too were selected by the captain and their earnings consisted of a specified fractional share known as the lay, calculated as a part of the total net proceeds of a voyage. Also see Hohman, p. 266: The able and ordinary seamen, stewards, cooks, and blacksmiths were entitled to shares that varied from 1/100 to 1/160 of the net proceeds. Green hands and boys had to be content with "long lays" which fluctuated from 1/160 to 1/200. Significantly, within each rank, the intense individualism of the wage bargain brought about variations caused by a man's experience, skill, courage, and the length and number of other voyages he may have had. The lay averaged out to $180 for each 937 days, over and above expenses for food, clothing, and some personal items like tobacco. Also see Richard Ellis, *Men and Whales* (New York: Alfred Knopf, 1991), 171-173.

35   Moore, "The commercial sponges and the sponge fisheries," *Bulletin of the Bureau of Fisheries* XXVIII (1908), tables.

36   *Thirty-second Anniversary of the Greek Community of Tarpon Springs*, 44.

37   Harry Remde, *The Thirteenth Island*, (Boston: Peripatetic Press, 1946), 7.

38   Frantzis, *Strangers at Ithaca*, 55; Stoughton, *Tarpon Springs*, 46.

39   *Tarpon Springs Leader*, Saturday, October 28, 1911.

40   *Tarpon Springs Leader*, November 11, 1911; the head buyer was John Cocoris, who brought the first scafander (diving suit) to Tarpon Springs.

41   WPA, "Biographical Sketches," J. Cocoris interview, 1939; the Tarpon Springs newspaper *The Evening Leader* of September 8, 1916, showed John Cocoris as one of five Councilmen, involved in the Sanitation and Ordinances Committees.

42   Remde, *The Thirteenth Island*, 8; the title alludes to the fact that most of the Tarpon Springs Greek immigrants came from the "twelve islands," the Dodecanese Islands in the eastern Aegean.

43   Frantzis, *Strangers at Ithaca*, 67; Edwin C. Buxbaum, "The Greek-American Group at Tarpon Springs, Florida: A Study of Ethnic Identification and Acculturation" (Ph.D. dissertation, University of Pennsylvania, 1967), 38-44.

44   Examining the population schedules of 13th Census, 1910, especially the columns headed "address" and "occupation" one could note some ethnically and racially mixed jobs and residential areas. For example, 111 Grand Boulevarde Street was occupied by Bertram Knowles, a white baker and his wife Alice, both from the West Indies; 113 was the residence of Robert Ivy, a white sponge packer born in Florida; in 114 lived W. Cadwallader, a white baker from Ohio, and his two sons, both sponge clippers and born in Florida; next to them, in 117 resided Robert Russell, a black sponge hooker from the West Indies, with his daughter Elonorah and son-in-law Zachariah Munroe; 118, 119, and 120 served as residences for three more black families—Hanna, Storr, and Smith—involved in sponging and other work; a white Greek machinist resided in 121; and two white Florida families, the McCrearys and the Aldermans occupied 122 and 123 Grande Boulevarde.

45   Buxbaum, "Greek-American Group at Tarpon Springs," 46-47.

46   Remde, *The Thirteenth Island*, 41.

47   Ibid., 41.

48   Before 1923, all Eastern Orthodox Churches followed the "old" Julian calendar, which ran about thirteen days late as compared to the "new" or "western" and more accurate Gregorian calendar. In 1923 the Greek-, Romanian-, and Antiochian Orthodox Churches adopted the Gregorian calendar; other Eastern Orthodox churches continued to use the Julian calendar. Easter, the holiday of Christ's resurrection, is probably the most celebrated religious holiday, with ceremonies taking place inside and outside the church building and over the span of several weeks. Just after Christmas, on the 6th of January—Epiphany day—the fleet is blessed and the cross is thrown into the sea and recovered by young divers.

49   Buxbaum, "The Greek-American Group of Tarpon Springs," 135-141; evidently Kalymnos is the modern center of European sponge industry; however, in the early days of this century, Symi was the center of the industry followed by Halki.

50   Oral interview with Jerry Felos, February 1994; notes in possession of the author; John Cocoris was known as a great spender, careless of money, but a wonderful friend, husband, and parent. In a WPA interview in 1939, conducted in his apartment in Jacksonville, Florida, John Cocoris related

that before his health deteriorated, he had made plenty of money in
sponge diving, and even bought a yacht for some pleasure cruising.

51   A legal notice of the partners' intention to obtain corporate letters patent
appeared in the *Tarpon Springs Leader* of October 28, 1911; the signatories
asking for the corporate charter were Demosthenes Alissandratos,
Emmanuel Makrinaris (sic), George Meindanis, George Cretekos, Peter
Economos, Antonios Kalimeris, and Nikolas Arfaras.

52   *Tarpon Springs Leader* of October 28, 1911; *The Evening Leader* of March
12, 1915. City elections were held at the beginning of April every 2 years
and on odd-numbered years. For E. Macrinaris Shipbuilding Corporation
see the *Evening Leader*, January 16, 1919, and the front-page headline
"Launching At The Yards Of E. Macrinaris Ship Building Corporation
Tomorrow 3:00 P.M."

53   News of the Greek elites' social life also received attention; an article in the
Evening Leader of April 18, 1917 described the marriage of Anthoula
Makrinaris, daughter of Emmanuel's brother Nicholas to Argirios Leussis;
the headline read "Prominent Greek Families United in Holy Wedlock."

54   See, for example, the *Evening Leader*, August 3, 1917.

55   The *Tarpon Springs Leader* of December 30, 1911, carried a front page write-
up about a Greek play and Harry Bell's performance at the Orpheum
Theater, "which was filled with a large audience of our Greek citizens and
a limited number of Americans;" for J. E. Douglass and other city officers
of Tarpon Springs see the *Evening Leader*, September 8, 1916; Father Davis
was mentioned in the *Evening Leader*, April 7, 1917; a notice of incorporation and application for the charter of the Spongers Mutual Benefit
Association of Tarpon Springs, Florida appeared in the *Evening Leader*,
March 24, 1919,

56   *Tarpon Springs Leader*, December 30th, 1911

57   *Tampa Daily Times*, January 22, 1912, "Greeks Celebrated 'Digging (sic)
the Cross'."

58   *The Evening Leader*, April 16, 1917.

59   *The Evening Leader*, August 11, 1917. Another list headed "Aliens Exempted"
contained about 50 Greek surnames of men who had escaped the draft
until "the consent of the various governments for conscription of aliens is
obtained." - see *The Evening Leader* of August 27, 1917.

60   *The Evening Leader*, October 10, 1918.

61   *The Evening Leader*, January 17, 1919 on J. K. Douglass and April 12, April
16, May 1,1919 on bonds.

62   *The Evening Leader*, March 11, 1919, front page.

63   *The Evening Leader*, January 10 and 15, June 6, 1919.

64   *Thirty-second Anniversary of the Greek Community of Tarpon Springs*, 22; full
and half-page photographs of Reverend Thomas Lacey appear on pp. 16
and 17 of this publication.

65   In fact, the system remains in use to the present day on the few sponge

boats based in Tarpon Springs.

66   *The Evening Leader*, January 3, 1919, page 2.

67   *Florida Times-Union* of Jacksonville, January 27, 1946, reporting that production began on a sponge fishing movie, "showing the complete workings of Florida's $3,000,000 sponge fishing industry...with the entire fleet of 175 sponge boats taking part."

68   Sage, "Report of Sponge Industry," 1933.

69   Buxbaum, "Greek-American Group at Tarpon Springs," 111.

70   Sage, "Report of Sponge Industry," 1933.

year	received from buyers	expenses food, fuel	other expenses	shared by crews
1932	$587,373	235,500	120.024	231,849
1933	597,458	185,000	117,724	294,234

71   Sage, "Report of Sponge Industry," 1933.

72   Buxbaum, "Greek-American Group at Tarpon Springs," 110.

73   Stoughton, *Tarpon Springs*, 41.

74   Ibid., 41. Cheyney remained a member and extended his interests into banking, lumber, turpentine, citrus, real estate, and everything that went on in town, including politics. For 40 years he was the most powerful citizen in the community he had created. Cheyney died in 1939, at 81. Louis Adamic interviewed him in the last year of his life, and wrote a chapter on Cheyney and the Tarpon Springs Greeks in his book *From Many Lands*.

75   Macrenaris, address to Rotary, "The Sponge Industry."

76   Katzaras interview. Stoughton, *Tarpon Springs*, 51; perhaps mistakenly, Stoughton described the auction as "the immemorial Greek sponge sale," however, this writer found no sources establishing this method of sponge sales in Greece.

77   Macrenaris, address to Rotary, "The Sponge Industry."

78   R. H. Fiedler, "Fishery Industries of the United States, 1931," United States Bureau of Fisheries, *Report of the Commissioner* (Washington, D.C., 1932), appendix II, 330, and reports for 1933, 1936, 1937, 1938, 1940, 1941, and 1942, cited in Comnenos, "Florida's Sponge Industry," Tables on 239-251.

79   A. W. Anderson and E. A. Power, "Fishery Statistics of the United States, 1945," United States Fish and Wildlife Service (USFWS), *Statistical Digest*, No. 18 (Washington, D.C., 1949), 236, 238, 242; A. W. Anderson and C. E. Peterson, "Fishery Statistics of the United States, 1949," USFWS, *Statistical Digest*, No. 25 (Washington, D.C., 1952), 167, cited in Comnenos, "Florida's Sponge Industry," 305-306.

80   Comnenos, "Florida's Sponge Industry," 280.

81   Ibid., 280-281.

82   Ibid., 282.

83   Buxbaum, "The Greek-American Group of Tarpon Springs," 58.

CONCLUSION

Previous chapters examine the steady settlement of Greek immigrants in the southern states and the ways they chose to adapt to the distinct southern society, which in turn imposed some of its codes of behavior on the newcomers. Turn-of-the-century growth of commerce and transportation, and the attendant urban development of the New South cities attracted Hellenic migrants, who were able to supply the needs of a growing population for restaurants and sandwich shops, confectionery and fruit stores, shoeshine and hat cleaning parlors, and sundry other services. As outlined primarily in chapter two, as well as in the chapters on AHEPA, New Orleans, and Birmingham, economic gain and social acceptance rewarded the hard work and compliance to the mores of southern communities.

To explore and scrutinize the process of immigrants' selective adaptation to their new homeland, individual chapters chronicled continued changes in their lives, and the lives of the families and institutions they created, from the early 1900s until the 1960s. Thus the complete work deals with both, the first generation immigrants who chose to stay in America, as well as with their offspring, the second and third generations, who were born in America but still maintained that ethnic tie to the cultural baggage their parents and grandparents had judiciously retained. Clearly, the proportion of first generation Greek immigrants who attained economic and social upward mobility was vastly greater in the South than in the industrialized, urbanized, northern and midwestern areas, where Greek communities were numerically large, but where their embourgeoisment lagged by more than one generation.

In the South, the Greeks responded to pressures to conform. Their conformity was evidenced by their ability to avoid immigrant ghettos and to generally blend into the white segment of the segregated society, by the ubiquitous anglicization of names and surnames, by some intermarriages with local Anglo women, and by invitations to join local American fraternal organizations. Simultaneously, however, they also resisted the pressures of assimilation. Their resistance was best exemplified by their communal activities; they formed their own fraternal and social organizations, established church communities, built churches, hired priests, and participated in the establishment of a Greek Orthodox Archdiocese in the United States. But by no means did the Greeks all behave in the same manner, just as "the South" was full of contrasts and exerted a variety of influences, so Greek individuals and sub-groups demonstrated their ethnicity—their Hellenic cultural, and traditional ties—in different ways.

The differences are particularly exemplified in the three chapters dealing with Greek communities in New Orleans, Birmingham, and Tarpon Springs. Especially in Tarpon Springs, where Greeks comprised nearly one-half of the population, one can detect a whole range of adaptation systems on both sides, by native Anglos and by immigrant Hellenes. Florida's sponge capital was the only town in the South where Greek immigrants were so numerous and yet accepted and respected, probably because they were so instrumental to the town's prosperity.

Chapter four, discusses significant changes that evolved in the expression of the traditional culture represented by the continued practice of Greek Orthodox religion. Although the first generation organized the incipient communities, formed a *kinotis* in many a city in the South, and built or bought and maintained the first churches, it was the second and third generation which exerted pressures to bring English into the liturgical services, to have the families sit together, and to have Orthodoxy recognized not as a Greek church in the United States, but as an American religious denomination which happens to be called Greek Orthodox. As with every living and vibrant entity, so with the church, changes continue to take place. Perhaps a future historian will be able to answer the question whether adherence to Greek Orthodoxy signifies a reassertion of ethnicity or a continued adaptation to a complex and diverse host society.

A similar query remains unanswered with respect to fraternal organizations. With the revival of ethnic consciousness over the past generation, several *topika somateia* have improved their image and increased their membership. They have become serious political pressure groups, effectively lobbying both Washington and Athens on behalf of their regions. And the foremost American organization formed by Greek Americans, the AHEPA, no longer sees its primary goals to be the Americanization of Hellenes, and their acquisition of American citizenship. Since the membership now consists of Americans, with a special interest in Hellenism, the organization has engaged in philanthropy and political lobbying. At the same time it is battling a lack of enthusiasm, not to say apathy, in its ranks, and is looking for a cause that will again fire up a burgeoning membership as in the days when Ahepans sold millions of dollars worth of War Bonds or when they took up the American banner of the Truman Doctrine. AHEPA's most recent mission is to promote education, philanthropy, civic responsibility, family and individual excellence. It remains to be seen whether a re-invigorated promotion of Hellenic values provides the winning purpose and mission to be passed on to the next generation of AHEPA members.

Finally, how will Greek Americans resolve the question of ethnic identity? At least one group of historians suggests the ethnics re-invent selected ethnic expressions from one generation to the next, and offer these expressions as proof of that group's worth and evidence of its viable, continued existence. Will the re-inventions continue, or will there be other ways to resolve diversity and assure coexistence among Americans? A large number of Greek Americans have adapted and adopted all the worries and conflicts, all the victories and successes of America as their own. They have seen their compatriots, both Republicans and Democrats, elected to Congress; they even had a presidential candidate, but one who was by no means supported by all Greek Americans. They participate in all facets of public, private, social, and political life of the country.

A good proportion of Americans, who happen to be of sufficiently distant Greek origin, may not find it necessary to assert their worth in terms of invented ethnicity, no matter how much the ethnicity is rooted in real traditions and actual cultural mores. Will they be lost to the Greek American ethnic group, or will there always remain a cultural thread, a connection to their Hellenic heritage? Finally, one cannot ignore the discussion comparing and contrasting the experiences of immigrants who arrived in the early 1900s and those who came to America recently, within the last two decades. This elaborate subject, complex and involved, is best left for another book.

Bibliography

Primary Sources

Public Documents and Histories

Adallis, Dio. *Adallis' Greek Merchants' Reference Book and Business Guide.* N.p.: ca. 1912.

Efthimiou, Miltiades and George Christopoulos. *History of the Greek Orthodox Church in America.* New York: The Greek Orthodox Archdiocese of North and South America, 1986.

Garvey, Joan B. and Mary Lou Widmer. *Beautiful Crescent: A History of New Orleans.* New Orleans: Garmer Press, Inc., 1982.

Jacksonville City Directory 1910. Jacksonville: R. L. Polk, 1910

Moore, Henry Frank. "The Commercial Sponges and the Sponge Fisheries." In *Bulletin of the Bureau of Fisheries XXVIII (1908).* Washington: Government Printing Office, 1910.

Moskos, Charles. "*Ethnic Life - The Greeks.*" In *Encyclopedia of Southern Culture,* edited by Charles R. Wilson and William Ferris. Chapel Hill: University of North Carolina Press, 1989.

Pensacola City Directory. Jacksonville, Florida: R. L. Polk and Co., 1910.

Sage, Fred K. "Report of Sponge Industry of Tarpon Springs, Florida." Civil Works Administration, Pinellas County Project 52-89, 1933

Senate Bill 4805, House of Representatives Report No. 4443, 1906

Sholes' Directory of the City of Savannah, 1900. Savannah: Morning News Print, 1900.

Siegel, Martin, ed. *New Orleans: A Chronological and Documentary History.* Dobbs Ferry, New York: Oceana Publications Inc., 1975.

The Times Picayune. *Who's Who in Louisiana and Mississippi: Biographical Sketches of Prominent Men and Women.* New Orleans:

Times Picayune, 1918.

U. S. Bureau of the Census. *Twelfth Census of the United States, 1900.* Washington: Government Printing Office, 1911.

U. S. Bureau of the Census. *Thirteenth Census of the United States, 1910.* Washington: Government Printing Office, 1914.

Works Progress Administration, Writers' Program, Florida, "Biographical Sketches of Greeks in Jacksonville." 1939. [unpublished]

Works Progress Administration, Writers' Program, Georgia. *Atlanta, A City of the Modern South.* Atlanta: Atlanta Board of Education, 1942.

Works Progress Administration, Writers' Program, Louisiana. *New Orleans City Guide.* Boston: Houghton, Mifflin Company, 1938.

Newspapers and Periodicals

AHEPA magazine, [official organ of the American Hellenic Educational and Progressive Association—AHEPA] 1923-1928.

Atlanta Constitution, 1913.

Birmingham Age-Herald, 1910.

Birmingham, *Birmingfind,* ca. 1978.

Birmingham News, 1903, 1932, 1934,1950, 1951.

Birmingham Post, 1934.

Birmingham Post-Herald, 1963

Charleston, S.C., *News and Courier,* 1914, 1968, 1974, 1981.

Charlotte Observer, 1986.

Chicago, *Greek Star,* 1996.

Chicago Pnyx, 1968-1986.

Jacksonville, *Florida Times - Union,* 1946, 1988-1998.

Jacksonville Journal, 1925.

Life, 1965.

Long Island, New York, *Greek American,* 1996, 1997

Mobile, Alabama, *Mobile Register,* 1912.

New Orleans, *Times Picayune,* 1886, 1923, 1950, 1960.

New Orleans, 1982.

New York, *Hellenic Pilgrimage,* 1988-1990.

New York, *Loghia,* 1994.

New York Times, 1916, 1970.

Orthodox Observer, 1956-1997.

Tampa Daily Times, 1912
Tampa Morning Tribune, 1915.
Tarpon Springs, Florida, *The Evening Leader,* 1915 - 1919.
Tarpon Springs Leader, 1911.

Institutional Records

Annunciation Greek Orthodox Church Consecration Album. Pensacola,
    Florida: n. p., 1973.
*Centennial of the Greek Eastern Orthodox Church Holy Trinity in New
    Orleans.* New Orleans: n. p., 1965.
*Commemorating the Seventy-Fifth Anniversary of Holy Trinity - Holy Cross
    Greek Orthodox Cathedral, Birmingham, Alabama, 1906-1981.*
    Birmingham: n. p., 1981.
Dedication: Holy Trinity Greek Orthodox Church 1906-1956.
    Birmingham: n. p., 1956.
*Greek Orthodox Church of the Annunciation, Atlanta, Fiftieth Anniversary
    Album, 1905-1955.* Atlanta: n. p., 1955.
Greek Orthodox Church of the Annunciation, Dedication. Atlanta: n. p.,
    December 20, 1970.
Greek Orthodox Theological School "Holy Cross." Pomfret, Connecticut:
    n. p., ca. 1952.
Holy Trinity Greek Orthodox Church: A Fifty-Year History. Raleigh, North
    Carolina: n. p., 1987.
*Nineteen-Thirty-Eight Yearbook of the Hellenic Orthodox Church "The Holy
    Cross."* Birmingham: n. p., 1938
*Official Journal of the 12th Biennial Ecclesiastical Congress of the Greek
    Orthodox Church of North and South America.* Savannah: n. p.,
    1954.
*Seventy-Fifth Anniversary Album of the Annunciation Greek Orthodox
    Church in Mobile, Alabama.* Mobile: n. p., 1987.
*Seventy-Fifth Anniversary of Holy Trinity Greek Orthodox Church of
    Charleston, S. C.* Charleston: n. p., 1984.
*Seventy-Fifth Anniversary of St. Paul's Greek Orthodox Church - Savannah,
    Georgia, 1907-1982.* Savannah: n. p., 1982.
*Sixtieth Anniversary Album of St. Paul's Greek Orthodox Church in
    Savannah.* Savannah: n. p., 1967.
Thirty-First Biennial Clergy-Laity Congress, New Orleans, 1992. New

Orleans: Holy Trinity Cathedral, 1992.

*Thirty-Second Anniversary of the Greek Community of Tarpon Springs,
Florida.* Tarpon Springs: St. Nicholas Parish, 1937.

Thirty-Second Biennial Clergy-Laity Congress, July 3-7, 1994,Chicago.
Chicago: Album Committee of the Congress, 1994.

*Twenty-Fifth Biennial Clergy-Laity Congress of the Greek Orthodox
Archdiocese of North and South America* [commemorative album].
Atlanta: n. p., 1980.

Family and Personal Papers

Bishop John of Amorion. Papers relating to the Greek Orthodox
Church in America and the Diocese of Atlanta. St. Photios Greek
Orthodox Shrine, St. Augustine, Florida.

Bokas, George. Papers.

Carantzas, Constantine (Costa). Carantzas family papers.

Chronaki, Bessie. Papers, including "A History of the Greek
Community in Charlotte, North Carolina 1908-1988."

Felos, Sam and Jerry (Gerasimos) Felos. Papers.

Kokenes, Constantine (Gus). Papers, including "History of the Greek
Orthodox Community of Charlotte, N.C."

Lafakis, Sofia Petrou and Irene Vodantis Lafakis. Papers.

Nixon, Xenophon. Papers.

Saloutos, Theodore. Papers. Immigration History Research Center,
University of Minnesota, Minneapolis.

Stamatelos, John Demetrius. Papers, including "History of the Greek
Orthodox Church of Pensacola, Florida, 1909 to 1959."

Stathis Tina (Stamatina), Elizabeth Stathis, and Jennie Haramis (nee
Stathis). Stathis family papers.

Secondary Sources

Alastos, Doros. *Venizelos.* London: n. p., 1942.

Anagnostu, Georgios. "Rituals of Strangers: Greek Merchant Seamen
in New Orleans and the Anthropological Rite of Passage." Master's
thesis. Louisiana State University, 1992.

Asselanis, Fanny. "The Greek Community in Savannah." Paper
prepared for the Friends of the Library presentation, April 19,

1977. [unpublished]

Bailyn, Bernard. *The Peopling of British North America: An Introduction.* New York: Vintage Books, 1988.

Bayor, Ronald. "Ethnic Residential Patterns in Atlanta, 1880-1940." Paper presented at the Georgia Institute of Technology, Atlanta, Georgia. [unpublished]

Bernard, Richard M. *The Melting Pot and the Altar.* Minneapolis: University of Minnesota Press, 1980.

Bodnar, John. *The Transplanted: A History of Immigrants in Urban America.* Bloomington, Indiana: Indiana University Press, 1985.

Boyd, Rosamonde Ramsay. *The Social Adjustment of the Greeks in Spartanburg, South Carolina.* Spartanburg: Williams Printing Co., ca. 1950.

Bradford, Ernie. *The Greek Islands.* 2nd. ed. London: Collins Press, 1970.

Brandes, Stanley. "Reflections on Honor and Shame in the Mediterranean." In *Honor and Shame and Unity in the Mediterranean,* edited by David D. Gilmore. Washington: American Anthropological Association, 1987.

Burgess, Thomas. *Greeks in America.* Boston: Sherman French and Co., 1913.

Buxbaum, Edwin Clarence. "The Greek-American Group of Tarpon Springs, Florida: A Study of Ethnic Identification and Acculturation." Ph.D. diss. University of Pennsylvania, 1967.

Canoutas, Seraphim. *Hellenism in America.* New York: Kosmos Printers, 1918.

Canoutas, Seraphim, Theodore Constant, and Paul Koken. *The Story of Greeks in America.* Manuscript, 1993

Carageorge, Theodore. "The Greeks of Pensacola." In *Ethnic Minorities in Gulf Coast Society,* edited by Jerrell H. Shofner and Linda V. Ellsworth. Pensacola, Florida: Proceedings of the Gulf Coast History and Humanities Conference, 1979.

Carnes, Mark Christopher. *Secret Rituals and manhood in Victorian America.* New Haven: Yale University Press, 1989.

Chalmers, David M. *Hooded Americanism: the History of the Ku Klux Klan.* 3rd. ed. New York: Franklin Watts, 1981.

Comnenos, Caroline Johnson. "Florida's Sponge Industry: A Cultural and Economic History." Ph.D. diss. University of Florida, 1982.

Conzen, Kathleen Neils. "Immigrants, Immigrant Neighborhoods, and Ethnic Identity: Historical Issues." *Journal of American History* 66 (December 1979): 603-615.

Conzen, Kathleen Neils, David A. Gerber, Ewa Morawska, George E. Pozzetta, and Rudolph J. Vecoli. "The Invention of Ethnicity: A Perspective From The U. S. A." *Journal of American Ethnic History* 12 (Fall 1992): 3-41.

Cooper, William J. And Thomas E. Terrill. *The American South*. 2nd ed. New York: McGraw Hill, 1996)

Counelis, James Steve. "Greek Orthodox Church Statistics of the United States, 1949-1989: Some Ecclesial and Social Patterns." *Journal of the Hellenic Diaspora* 16 (Spring-Summer-Fall-Winter 1989): 129-159.

Crooks, James B. *Jacksonville After the Fire, 1901-1919: A New South City*. Jacksonville, Florida: University of North Florida Press, 1991.

Daniels, Roger. *Coming to America: A History of Immigration and Ethnicity in American Life*. Princeton, New Jersey: Harper Collins, 1990.

Davis, T. Frederick. *History of Jacksonville and Vicinity*. Gainesville: University of Florida Press, 1964.

Demos, Vasilikie. "Maintenance and Loss of Traditional Gender Boundaries in Two Greek Orthodox Communities." *Journal of the Hellenic Diaspora* 16 (Spring-Summer-Fall-Winter 1989): 77-93.

DeSantis, Vincent P. *The Shaping of Modern America: 1877-1920*. 2nd. ed. Arlington Heights, Illinois: Forum Press, 1989.

Dickson, Peter W. "The Greek Pilgrims: Tsakonas and Tsintzinians." In *New Directions In Greek American Studies*, edited by Dan Georgakas and Charles Moskos. New York: Pella Publishing, 1991.

Fairchild, Henry Pratt. *Greek Immigration to the United States*. New Haven: Yale University Press, 1911.

Fogelson, Robert M. And Richard E. Rubenstein, eds. *Hearings on the Ku Klux Klan 1921*. New York: Arno Press & The New York Times, 1969.

Frantzis, George Theodore. *Strangers at Ithaca: the Story of the Spongers of Tarpon Springs*. St. Petersburg, Florida: Great Outdoors Publishing, 1962.

Frangouli-Argyris, Justine. *The Lonely Path Of Integrity: Spyridon, Archbishop of America (1996-1999)*. Athens, Greece: Exandas

Publishers, 2002.

Gaines, Father William. *The First Eastern Greek Orthodox Church in America: The Holy Trinity of New Orleans.* New Orleans: n. p., ca. 1972.

Gilmore, David. "The Shame of Dishonor." In *Honor and Shame and Unity in the Mediterranean,* edited by David Gilmore. Washington: American Anthropological Association, 1987.

Glazer, Nathan and Daniel Patrick Moynihan. *Beyond the Melting Pot: the Negroes, Puerto Ricans, Jews, Italians, and Irish of New York City.* Cambridge: the MIT Press, 1963.

Gleason, Philip. "Confusion Compounded: the Melting Pot in the 1960s and 1970s." *Ethnicity* 6 (1979): 10-20.

Goldfield, David. *Cottonfields and Skyscrapers.* Baton Rouge, Louisiana: State University Press, 1982.

Goodwin, R. Christopher. *New Orleans is Looking Forward to its Past.* Baton Rouge: Office of Cultural development, 1987.

Gordon, Milton. *Assimilation in American Life: the Role of Race, Religion and National Origins.* New York: Oxford University Press, 1964.

Gutman, Herbert G. *Work, Culture, and Society in Industrializing America.* New York: Vintage Books, 1977.

Halley, Helen. "A Historical Functional Approach to the Study of the Greek Community of Tarpon Springs." Ph.D. diss. Columbia University, 1952

Handlin, Oscar. *The Uprooted.* New York: Grosset & Dunlap, 1951.
_____ . "Immigration in American Life: A Reappraisal." In *Immigration and American History,* edited by Henry Steel Commager. Minneapolis: University of Minnesota Press, 1961.

Hantzes, James. "Greeks in Alabama Before 1912." Master's thesis. Sanford University, 1969.

Harney, Robert F. "Religion and Ethnocultural Communities." *Polyphony* 1 (Summer 1978): 3.

Herzberg, Steven. *Strangers Within the Gate City.* Philadelphia: Jewish Publication Society of America, 1978.

Higham, John. "Integrating America: The Problems of Assimilation in the Nineteenth Century." *Journal of American Ethnic History* 1 (Fall 1981): 7-25.
_____ . *Send These to Me: Immigrants in Urban America.* rev. ed. Baltimore: Johns Hopkins University Press, 1984.

_____ . *Strangers in the Land: Patterns of American Nativism, 1860-1920.* 2nd. ed. New Brunswick: Rutgers University Press, 1988.

Hirschman, Charles. "What Happened to the White Ethnics?" *Contemporary Sociology* 20 (March 1991): 183.

Hobsbawm, Eric and Terence Rangers, eds. *The Invention of Tradition.* Cambridge: Cambridge University Press, 1983.

_____ . "America's Melting Pot Reconsidered." *Annual Review of Sociology* 9 (1983): 397-423.

Hohman, Elmo P. *The American Whaleman: A Study of Life and Labor in the Whaling Industry.* New York: Longmans, Green & Co., 1928.

Horton, Andrew. "Odysseus in Louisiana: The Greek Sailors in New Orleans." In *Perspectives on Ethnicity in New Orleans,* edited by John Cooke. New Orleans: The Committee on Ethnicity, 1979.

Jaret, Charles. "The Greek, Italian, and Jewish American Ethnic Press." *Journal of American Ethnic Studies* 7 (Summer 1979): 47-70.

Jackson, Kenneth T. *The Ku Klux Klan in the City 1915-1930.* New York: Oxford University Press, 1967.

Kivisto, Peter. "The transplanted then and now: the reorientation of immigration studies from the Chicago School to the new social history." *Ethnic and Racial Studies* 13 (October 1990): 455-481.

Leber, George J. *The History of the Order of AHEPA.* Washington: AHEPA, 1972.

Lord Kinross. *The Ottoman Centuries: The Rise and Fall of the Turkish Empire.* New York: Morrow Quill Paperbacks, 1977.

MacLean, Nancy. *Behind the Mask of Chivalry: The Making of the Second Ku Klux Klan.* New York, Oxford University Press, 1994.

Malafouris, Babis. *Greeks in America.* [In Greek] New York: Isaac Goldman Company, 1948.

Mantzoros, Peter N. *AHEPA and I Across the Years.* Glenview, Illinois: Pnyx Publications, 1966.

Monos, Dimitrios Ioannis. "Upward Mobility, Assimilation, and the Achievements of Greeks in the United States, With Special Emphasis on Boston and Philadelphia." Ph.D. diss., University of Pennsylvania, 1976.

Moore, Leonard J. *Citizen Klansmen: The Ku Klux Klan in Indiana, 1921-1928.* Chapel Hill: University of North Carolina Press, 1991.

Morawska, Ewa. *For Bread with Butter: the Life-Worlds of East Central Europeans in Johnstown, Pennsylvania, 1890-1940.* Cambridge:

Cambridge University Press, 1985.

Moskos, Charles. *Greek Americans: Struggle and Success.* New
Brunswick, New Jersey: Transaction Publishers, 1980.

_____. "Greek American Studies." In *The Greek American Community
in Transition,* edited by Alice Scourby and Harry Psomiades. New
York: Pella Publishing Co., 1982.

Novak, Michael. *The Rise of the Unmeltable Ethnics.* New York: the
Macmillan Company, 1971-1972.

Orso, Ethelyn. "The Hellenic Nativistic Revitalization Movement in
New Orleans, Louisiana." In *Perspectives on Ethnicity in New
Orleans.* New Orleans: The Committee on Ethnicity, 1979.

Panagopoulos, Epaminondas P. *New Smyrna: An Eighteenth Century
Greek Odyssey.* Gainesville, Florida: University of Florida Press,
1966.

Papas, John. *The Greek Church in Courts.* Sanford, Maine: author, ca.
1944.

Peristiany, J. G., ed. *Contributions to Mediterranean Sociology.* The
Hague: Mouton, 1968.

Peristiany, J. G., and Julian Pitt-Rivers, eds. *Honor and Grace in
Anthropology.* Cambridge: Cambridge University Press, 1989.

Phillips, Steven. "Paths in the Greek Orthodoxy in America." *Odyssey*
(July-August 1996): 29.

Pozzetta, George E. and Gary R. Mormino. *The Immigrant World of Ybor
City: Italians and their Latin Neighbors in Tampa, Florida, 1885-1985.*
Chicago: University of Illinois Press, 1987.

Pozzetta, George E., ed. *American Immigration and Ethnicity.* Vol. 5,
Immigrant Institutions: the Organization of Immigrant Life. New York:
Garland Publishing, Inc., 1991

_____., ed. *American Immigration and Ethnicity.* Vol. 13, *Assimilation,
Acculturation, and Social Mobility.* New York: Garland Publishing,
Inc., 1991.

_____. "Foreigners in Florida: A Study of Immigration Promotion,
1865-1910." *Florida Historical Quarterly* 53 (2), (October 1974):
164-180.

_____. "From Rustbelt to Sunbelt: Patterns of Ethnic Migration and
Integration in America 1940-1989." In *Shades of the Sunbelt: Essays
on Race, Ethnicity, and the Urban South,* edited by George E. Pozzetta
and Randall Miller. Westport, Connecticut: Greenwood Press,

1988.

Rabinowitz, Howard N. *The First New South 1865-1920.* Arlington Heights, Illinois: Harlan Davidson, 1992.

Remde, Harry. *The Thirteenth Island.* Boston: Peripatetic Press, 1946.

Robinson, Genevieve. "The Acropolis of Hellenism in America: First Generation Greeks in Lowell, Massachusetts 1895-1922." Ph.D. diss. Boston College, Massachusetts, 1986.

Saloutos, Theodore. "Cultural Persistence and Change: Greeks in the Great Plains and Rocky Mountains West, 1890-1970." *Pacific Historical Review* 49 (February 1980): 85.

_____. "The Greek Orthodox Church in the United States and Assimilation." *The International Migration Review* 7 (Winter 1973): 395-407.

_____. *The Greeks in the United States.* Cambridge: Harvard University Press, 1964.

_____. *They Remember America: the Story of the Repatriated Greek-Americans.* Berkeley: University of California Press, 1956.

Scourby, Alice. *The Greek Americans.* Boston: Twayne Publishers, 1984.

Scourby, Alice and Harry Psomiades, eds., *The Greek-American Community in Transition.* New York: Pella Publishing Co., 1982.

Sfekos, Stephen J. And George E. Matsoukas, eds. *Project for Orthodox Renewal: Key Issues Facing Orthodox Christians in America.* Chicago: Orthodox Christian Laity, 1993.

Shevill, Ferdinand. *A History of the Balkans.* New York: Dorset Press, 1991.

Social Science Research Seminar on Acculturation, *American Anthropologist* 57 (1955): 1240-1252.

Sollors, Werner, ed. *The Invention of Ethnicity.* New York: Oxford University Press, 1989.

Stoughton, Gertrude. *Tarpon Springs, Florida: The Early Years.* New Port Richey, Florida: Tri-Arts Studio, 1975.

Thistlethwaite, Frank. "Migration from Europe Overseas in the 19th and 20th Centuries." In *Population Movements in Modern European History*, edited by Herbert Moller. New York: Macmillan, 1964.

Vecoli, Rudolph J. "The Contadini in Chicago: A Critique of the Uprooted." *Journal of American Ethnic History* 51 (1964-1965): 404-417.

_____. "European Americans: From Immigrants to Ethnics." In *The Reinterpretation of American History and Culture*, edited by William H. Cartwright and Richard L. Watson. Washington: National Council for the Social Studies, 1973.

_____. "The Formation of Chicago's 'Little Italies.'" *Journal of American Ethnic History* 2 (Spring 1983): 5-20.

_____. "Prelates and Peasants: Italian Immigrants and the Catholic Church." *Journal of Social History* 2 (Spring 1969): 217-268.

_____. "Return to the Melting Pot: Ethnicity in the United States in the Eighties." *Journal of American Ethnic History* 5 (Fall 1985): 17.

_____. "From The Uprooted to The Transplanted: the Writing of American Immigration History 1951-1989." In *From 'Melting Pot' to Multiculturalism*, edited by Valeria Lerda, Rome: Bulzoni Editore, 1991.

Vlachos, Evangelos. *The Assimilation of Greeks in the United States.* Athens, Greece: National Centre of Social researches, 1968.

Wheeler, Thomas, ed. *The Immigrant Experience: The Anguish of Becoming American.* New York: Dial Press, 1971.

Wood, Wayne W. *Jacksonville's Architectural Heritage.* Gainesville: n. p., 1989.

Woodward, C. Vann. *The Origins of the New South, 1877-1913.* Baton Rouge: Louisiana State University Press, 1952.

Wyatt-Brown, Bertram. *Southern Honor: Ethics and Behavior in the Old South.* New York: Oxford University Press, 1982.

Wynar, Lubomyr R. *Encyclopedic Directory of Ethnic Organizations in the United States.* Littleton, Colorado: Libraries Unlimited, Inc., 1975.

Yans-McLaughlin, Virginia. *Family and Community: Italian Immigrants in Buffalo, 1880-1930.* Ithaca: Cornell University Press, 1977.

Young, Kimball. *Sociology: A Study of Society and Culture.* New York: American Book Company, 1949.

Zotos, Stephanos. *Hellenic Presence in America.* Wheaton, Illinois: Pilgrimage Press, 1976.

Zunz, Olivier. *The Changing Face of Inequality: Urbanization, Induatrial development, and Immigrants in Detroit, 1880-1920.* Chicago: University of Chicago Press, 1982.

Index